TENANT DEFAU
COMMERCIAL

TENANT DEFAULT UNDER COMMERCIAL LEASES

Fourth edition

Andrew E Parsons LLB

*Solicitor, Litigation and Dispute
Resolution Partner, Radcliffes le Brasseur*

© Andrew E Parsons 2006

Published by
xpl law
Stonehills House
Howards Cute
Welwyn Garden City
Herts AL8 6PU

ISBN I 85811 334 2

Typeset by DPSL

Printed in Great Britain by Lightning Source

For Caroline and Alice Parsons and for my
For my daughter Alice, Eve and Ernie

CONTENTS

PREFACE TO THE FOURTH EDITION

The third edition was prompted by the implementation of the Civil Procedure Rules ("the CPR"). Those Rules were intended to simplify the litigation process and make this cheaper.

Since the last Edition changes to the CPR have continued (for example CPR Part 55 which deals specifically with possession actions). It is doubtful whether the litigation process is any simpler or cheaper, and certainly many published editions of the Civil Procedure Rules are as extensive as the old *White Book* containing the Rules of the Supreme Court.

Amendments to the CPR continue to appear regularly – and will no doubt continue to do so. That is an occupational hazard that any litigator expects!

There have also been several significant changes in substantive landlord and tenant law since the last Edition, particularly the insolvency legislation (including the Insolvency Act 2000 and the Enterprise Act 2002). They have served to restrict further the remedies open to a landlord when a tenant becomes insolvent.

At the time of writing there is much debate regarding the law of forfeiture and the need for reform. However, until there is parliamentary time available to implement any change I have sought to provide summary practical assistance in what is often an esoteric area of law.

Finally, my thanks to my wife Caroline and daughter Alice for their support, and Alice for her help which has enabled me to produce yet another edition of what I hope readers will find to be a useful reference book.

I have tried to state the law as at October 2005.

AEP
London
October 2005

PREFACE TO THIRD EDITION

Since the last Edition, the system of civil justice has seen the greatest change that any of us will have experienced as a result of the implementation of Lord Woolf's Civil Justice Reforms.

I have included the changes effected by the Civil Procedure Rules which came into force on 26 April, 1999 so far as they relate to tenant default in the relevant chapters. At the time of writing, however, the Rules are very new and there is no case law explaining their method of interpretation yet available. The application of the Rules is dependant upon accompanying practice directions and these are still being produced by the Lord Chancellor's Department. As new practice directions are issued these will clearly have to be taken account of. The book does not however seek to be a full guide to all the intricacies of the Civil Procedure Reforms, but simply to outline the main provisions as they affect tenant default.

I wish to record my thanks to my colleagues Robert Highmore, and Jill Cheater at Radcliffes for their help and advice on a number of aspects in this book, and to my secretary, Debbie Phillips, for her much appreciated help. I also wish to pay tribute to David Andrews, my co-author of the First and Second Editions, for the invaluable work which I have sought to build on in the Third Edition. I must however take full responsibility for this Edition.

Finally, my thanks to my wife Caroline and daughter Alice for their understanding of the time it takes to produce even a modest book such as this.

I have tried to state the law as at June 1999.

AEP
London
June 1999

PREFACE TO SECOND EDITION

The Landlord and Tenant (Covenants) Act 1995 came into force on 1 January 1996.

We have given a full account of the changes effected by the Act, so far as they relate to tenant default, in Chapter 7. We have also noted various parts of the book dealing with topics upon which the Act will have an impact.

We wish to record our thanks to Michael Higginson and Roger Jackson, partners in the property department at Radcliffes Grossman Block, for their help and advice on a number of aspects of their specialist field.

Work on the second edition was, for the most part, completed in October 1995 but matters were then delayed because it was thought necessary to await verification that the 1995 Act had, indeed, become law on I January 1996 as had been anticipated.

DWA
AEP
London
January 1996

PREFACE TO FIRST EDITION

There is no shortage of textbooks on the law of landlord and tenant, and there are numerous guides to debt-collecting. Our principal aim has been to bring together "under one roof" the various matters that are of concern to landlords of commercial premises, and their advisers, when considering how to cope with tenant default. We have not sought to prepare a detailed treatise on the more esoteric points of landlord & tenant law, but have tried to provide assistance on a practical approach to default for those who do not specialise in this field of law.

In a subject of this kind there is, inevitably, a certain amount of overlapping and this tends to lead to a corresponding element of repetition. To those who will read this book from cover to cover we apologise unreservedly. Our reason is that we are writing in the main for those who will "dip into" the book and so have preferred, on balance, to include all matters of possible relevance in relation to each topic rather than indulge in wholesale cross-referencing which can be even more tedious.

We are indebted to a number of colleagues who have given valuable assistance in different ways. Specifically we thank Mr Paul McAndrews, solicitor, and our secretaries, Linda Wainwright and Nikki Jones, for their much appreciated help and support.

We have tried to state the law in accordance with the materials available to us at the end of July 1993, although it has been possible to incorporate one or two additional matters at proof stage.

DWA
AEP
London
November 1993

TABLE OF STATUTES

TABLE OF CASES

CHAPTER 1
TENANT DEFAULT

CHAPTER 1
TENANT DEFAULT

Default can arise in any number of different ways. Typically it will be non-payment of rent/service charge, failure to repair, breach of the alienation or user covenants, unauthorised alterations or an act of insolvency.

The first indication that there is a problem will often be when the rent/service charge is not paid or following a routine attendance at the premises.

Once the landlord is on notice of something untoward, those advising him (be they solicitor, surveyor or manager) must act quickly to take stock of the situation and consider all possible courses of action. The alternatives are dealt with in the following chapters. The landlord must consider (a) what attitude to adopt and (b) what his aims are.

LANDLORD'S ATTITUDE

The important thing is to try to ascertain the cause of the default. Is there a temporary problem arising from, say, cash-flow difficulties, or is it more basic, such that the landlord may have to consider ending the tenancy? For example, the landlord may be worried about the possibility of serious damage to his reversion. Urgent action may be required (such as an injunction) to ensure that none of the available remedies are put at risk, e.g. an immediate stop on rent may have to be imposed if it is not a continuing breach of covenant.

LANDLORD'S AIMS

Most landlords want to preserve the income from their investments but, conceivably, the landlord might think he has a chance of re-letting the premises more profitably if he can get possession (particularly in a rising market) or he may have plans to re-develop. Moreover, he will always have at the back of his mind the question of liability for rates if he gets back possession of the property. Finally, of course, he may wish to sell his interest – with or without the sitting tenant. Different considerations may apply if he has a former tenant who is a first-class covenant (and has entered into an authorised guarantee agreement under the Landlord and Tenant (Covenants) Act 1995, section 16 if the lease was granted after 1 January, 1996) – see Chapter 7.

LANDLORD'S ALTERNATIVE ACTIONS

1. LETTING THE LEASE CONTINUE

1. Instalment arrangement: This may give the tenant a breathing space which will enable him to overcome his temporary problems. It could be coupled with a rent concession – either permanent or temporary. Payment by a series of post-dated cheques or by standing order should be considered.

Table of actions available to the Landlord

Action	Commentary
Demand from 3rd Party	e.g. former tenants, guarantors. Compliance with L&T (Covenants) Act 1995 required
Demand from Sub-tenant	Serve notice pursuant to S.6 Law of Distress (Amendment) Act
Distress	Action against current tenant and goods on demised premises only. Will constitute waiver of any breach of covenant. Restrictions apply if tenant in administration.
Peaceable re-entry	S.146 Notice needed if non-rent claim. Restrictions apply if tenant in administration.
Forfeiture by Court Action	S.146 Notice needed if non-rent claim. Restrictions apply if tenant in administration. or liquidation. Sub tenancy ends (subject to any application for relief).
Statutory Demand	Arrears over £750 only
Sue for rent	May be restrictions if tenant facing insolvency proceedings
Bankruptcy	Statutory demand needed
Liquidation	Statutory demand needed
Disclaimer	Only if bankruptcy/liquidation. Guarantor obliged to take new Lease? May be application by sub-tenant or mortgagee for vesting order
Surrender	Sub tenancy remains
Call on Rent deposit	May waive any breach of covenant. Restrictions apply if tenant in administration.

2. Suing for arrears/service charge only: i.e. not going for possession.
3. Distraining for the rent: This is a cheap, speedy and often very effective remedy, but there are pitfalls.
4. Getting rent from a sub-tenant: Serving the appropriate notice(s) can be arranged without difficulty but the possibility of waiver and the overall occupancy situation must be considered.
5. Entering and carrying out the repairs that should have been done by the tenant: provided the lease allows for this.
6. Rent deposit: If the landlord can get the tenant to put up a rent deposit, the added security may provide sufficient short-term comfort. Although undoubtedly an advantage, such a deposit may give rise to certain problems. The position between landlord and tenant will probably turn on the language used in the documentation and on how the deposit is structured, but a number of difficult, and possibly unresolved, questions as to the landlord's entitlement arise if the tenant becomes insolvent or the lease is assigned. On what basis is the deposit held? Are the monies held on trust for the landlord or the tenant and, if so, on what terms? Does the landlord need the permission of court to enforce the deposit if the tenant becomes insolvent? In the case of a company tenant, is the deposit void if it is not registered as a charge under the Companies Act 1985, sections 395 and 396? Is there provision whereby, following assignment of the leasehold interest, the landlord can still avail himself of the deposit? Can the landlord transfer the deposit, or the benefit of it, to a purchaser of the reversion?
7. Seeking an injunction: if the tenant is in breach or threatens a breach of, say, the user covenant or some other covenant in respect of which the court would give injunctive relief.
8. Action against previous tenants or sureties.

2.   TERMINATING THE LEASE

- Forfeiture by action through the court – although an application for relief may follow.
- Peaceable re-entry – again relief may be sought.
- Negotiating a surrender.
- Making an individual tenant bankrupt or petitioning for the winding-up of the tenant company. As often as not the threat is sufficient to get the tenant to pay but, if this line is pursued, it will probably result in the trustee/liquidator disclaiming the lease. Those with derivative interests may seek vesting orders.

NOMENCLATURE

Numerous references are made in this book to tenant insolvency. Although a tenant is often, colloquially, described as being insolvent, there are, in fact, several different types of legal status encompassed within that one expression. Each is subject to different rules. The different types of "insolvency" are:

1.   MEMBERS' VOLUNTARY LIQUIDATION

A company may be solvent but the members may want to wind it up. This will involve a members' voluntary liquidation. The directors swear and then file a declaration of solvency. The assets of the company are sold to meet its liabilities.

If it turns out that the company is, in fact, unable to meet its debts, the creditors will be told and there will then be a creditors' voluntary liquidation.

2.   CREDITORS' VOLUNTARY LIQUIDATION

If the company is insolvent and unable to meet its debts, the members of the company hold a meeting to pass the winding-up resolution and appoint a liquidator. There is then a meeting of the creditors at which the appointment of the liquidator is approved or somebody else is appointed.

3.   ADMINISTRATION ORDER

It often happens that the directors and creditors of a company in financial difficulties do not want to see the company put down. In such cases the directors or creditors can present a petition to the court to obtain an administration order. The court appoints an insolvency practitioner as administrator. He runs the company whilst trying to decide what he can do to enable it to be rehabilitated. During the period of the administration a moratorium is imposed which effectively prevents any action being taken against the company by its landlord or other creditors. The restrictions on the landlord's rights were recently extended by the Enterprise Act 2002.

4.   ADMINISTRATIVE RECEIVER

Somebody who holds a floating charge (created prior to 15 September 2003, when the Enterprise Act 2002 came into force) over the assets of the company – usually known as a debenture holder – may find that the interest and/or capital on the loan(s) secured on the assets are not being paid and decide to appoint an administrative receiver. The receiver's powers are set out in the

Insolvency Act 1986 (as amended) but his aim will be to sell the assets over which the charge is held to pay off the loan(s) and interest. However, since the Enterprise Act 2002 came into force, subject to certain limited exceptions, holders of floating charges created after 15 September 2003 can no longer appoint administrative receivers – instead they can appoint administrators without going to court.

5. LPA RECEIVER

A person holding a fixed charge over a specific asset, e.g. a mortgagee of a lease the company holds, may appoint what is known as an LPA receiver. His powers are as set out in the charge and the Law of Property Act 1925. An LPA receiver is unaffected by the Enterprise Act 2002.

Except that a landlord cannot execute a judgment against goods which are the subject of a floating charge that has crystallised, the appointment of a receiver does not significantly affect the landlord's remedies against the tenant.

6. VOLUNTARY ARRANGEMENTS

Pursuant to the Insolvency Act 1986, a debtor who is in financial difficulties may enter into a composition with some or all of his creditors or may make a scheme of arrangement in relation to his affairs. Such arrangements can be made in relation to both corporate insolvencies (rarely) and individual insolvencies (frequently), and they effectively give the debtor a statutory "breathing space".

The effect of a voluntary arrangement on the landlord's right to recover rent and service charges was considered by Judge Cooke QC in *Burford Midland Properties Ltd* v *Marley Extrusions Ltd* [1995] 30 EG 89. He held that the arrangement covered only the rent and service charges which had accrued at the date the scheme was made. It did not cover future rents which, as and when they fell due, the landlord could claim from the tenant and the original tenant. However, there is a greater weight of authority the other way to suggest that future rent could be included in a voluntary arrangement (*Doorbar* v *Alltime Securities Limited* [1994] BCC 994 and see also *Cazaly Irving Holding Ltd* v *Cancol Ltd* [1995] EGCS 146).

7. BANKRUPTCY

Bankruptcy occurs in the case of an individual debtor, i.e. not a company, against whom a bankruptcy order is made by the court. The order can be made at the instigation of the debtor himself but is ordinarily taken out by the creditor(s) on the basis that the individual is unable to pay his debts.

8. COMPULSORY LIQUIDATION

This is the liquidation of a company by an order of the court following the presentation of a petition for the winding-up of the company. It arises most frequently because the company is unable to pay its debts and is being forced into liquidation as a result of action by one or more of its creditors.

9. DISSOLUTION

Voluntary and compulsory liquidation are the most usual methods by which the existence of a company comes to an end. A further method of termination is dissolution. This is not an action taken by the court, creditors or members of a company but is rather a termination of the company by the Registrar of Companies. It most usually occurs where there has been a breach of the Companies Act requirements for the company to file documentation, often accounts or the annual return. The company is struck off the Register of Companies and dissolved by the Registrar. A dissolution also occurs at the end of a liquidation when the winding-up procedure has been completed.

CHAPTER 2
ACTION FOR RENT/SERVICE CHARGE ARREARS

CHAPTER 2
ACTION FOR RENT/SERVICE CHARGE ARREARS

The most common example of tenant default is non-payment of rent or service charges. This will create a debt and constitute a breach of the lease. The most obvious response by the landlord is to commence court proceedings to obtain payment of the sums due. This may be either by action simply to obtain payment or may be coupled with a claim for possession based upon the proviso for forfeiture in the lease. This chapter deals with action for rent and service charges alone: the following chapter deals with the situation where there is also a claim for possession.

IS THE RENT DUE?

It is self-evident that action cannot be taken until the rent is due. This should be carefully checked in the lease. The due dates will normally be specified and as often as not will be the usual quarter days (namely 25 March, 24 June, 29 September and 25 December). If no payment dates are specified but the amount of the rent has been agreed, it will be payable at the end of each year in the case of a fixed-term lease, or at the end of each period of a periodic tenancy.

The tenant has until midnight to pay the rent on the day on which it is due. Thereafter it will be in arrear.

Rent paid before the due date is considered to be an advance to the landlord with an agreement that on the due day it will be treated as fulfilment of the tenant's obligation to pay: *De Nicholls v Saunders* (1870) LR5 CP589.

Rent due on a specific day or within a number of specified days thereafter will not be in arrear until after that day or the specified number of days has expired.

The commencement date of the lease may be important to ascertain if rent is due as payments are often referable to this. Where a lease is granted for a term expressed in the lease to commence on a date prior to its execution, the term does not commence until the date the lease is actually granted (executed): *Roberts* v *Church Commissioners for England* [1972] 1 QB 278. However, the parties may create obligations under the lease prior to the date of grant even if the term of the lease is defined by reference to a date before its grant: *Bradshaw* v *Pawley* [1980] 1 WLR 10. In that case the obligation to pay rent in respect of a new lease under the Landlord and Tenant Act 1954, Part II was held to arise before the date of execution of the renewal lease.

MANNER AND PLACE OF PAYMENT

The lease may contain an express provision requiring rent to be paid at a certain place. If there is an express covenant to pay rent but no place is appointed for payment, the tenant's obligation is to seek out the landlord and pay him on the due day: *Haldane* v *Johnson* (1853) 8 Exch 689. Despite this common law rule, rent is now usually paid by cheque, standing order or direct debit from the tenant's bank to the landlord's. The rent is payable to the landlord or to his agent authorised to receive it. Payment is due in cash unless it is stipulated, or the parties agree, to the contrary.

Rent can be paid by cheque either where the landlord has accepted this in the past, or he accepts the specific payment. Provided the cheque is met on first presentation, the rent is treated as being paid on the date the cheque is delivered: *Coltrane* v *Day* [2003] 17 EG 146.

Payment by cheque is conditional payment. The landlord could refuse it. If it is accepted but the cheque is not honoured when presented, the landlord's remedies remain intact: the debt is not satisfied until the cheque is paid.

Rent paid by post is at the risk of the tenant unless the landlord has expressly or impliedly authorised payment in this manner: *Pennington* v *Crossley and Son Ltd* (1897) 13 TLR 513.

Where the sending of a cheque by post is the accepted mode of payment the cheque must be posted by the due date to constitute prompt payment. Payment occurs on the date of posting: *Commercial Union Life Assurance Co Ltd* v *Label Ink Ltd* Unreported 24 July 2000. However, this is conditional on the cheque being honoured: *Beevers* v *Mason* (1978) 248 EG 781. If the landlord subsequently re-presents a dishonoured cheque this will not constitute a waiver of the fact that payment was not made by the relevant due date: *Hannaford* v *Smallacombe* [1994] 15 EG 155.

If the tenant pays rent to the wrong person, he remains liable to pay to the correct landlord. But the landlord may be estopped from claiming payment if it was he who represented to whom the rent should be paid: *Williams* v *Bartholomew* (1798) 1 Bos & P 326.

A landlord is not obliged to give a receipt for rent, nor to accept rent that is tendered (e.g. if he believes there is a subsisting breach): *Preston* v *Linlands Ltd* (1979) 239 EG 653. In such circumstances, the tenant's only remedy is to apply for a declaration that the lease is not liable to forfeiture.

Landlords should be aware that regular acceptance of late payment may prejudice their ability to object to the grant of a new tenancy under the Landlord and Tenant Act 1954 Part II based upon persistent delay in paying rent (section 30(1))

RENT DEMAND

Although there are important rules in relation to the demand for rent if forfeiture is contemplated, there is no common law requirement for the landlord to demand payment before commencing proceedings if those proceedings merely claim payment of the sums due: *Van Haarlam* v *Kasner* [1992] 36 EG 135. The provisions of the Landlord and Tenant Act 1987, sections 47 and 48, requiring the landlord's name and address on all rent demands and notice to be given to the tenant of an address at which notices may be served before rent or service charges can he recovered, do not apply generally to commercial premises: tenancies protected by the Landlord and Tenant Act 1954, Part II are expressly excluded from those provisions of the 1987 Act. If a tenancy does not come within this exclusion a Section 47 and 48 Notice will be required. The prudent landlord will, nevertheless, demand payment of rent before it falls due and where the landlord has elected to charge VAT will, of course, render a VAT invoice.

Prior to commencing proceedings the landlord's solicitors must also send the tenant a formal letter before action requiring payment of the outstanding arrears. This is to protect the landlord's position on costs and to comply with the pre-action requirements of the Civil Procedure Rules. See Precedent 7 for a specimen.

If the landlord is also intending to pursue former tenants or guarantors for payment of the rent, a notice under the Landlord and Tenant (Covenants) Act 1995, Section 17 must be served – sec Chapter 7.

AMOUNT OF RENT

The common law requires the amount of rent to be certain. This is invariably stated in the lease and in the case of commercial premises is usually subject to regular rent review. Following review, and to ensure that there is certainty that the new rent is agreed and recoverable as such, it should be recorded in a rent review memorandum signed by the parties. If the rent has merely been agreed, for example between surveyors, it may not be enforceable if there is uncertainty caused by a lack of documentary evidence.

The lease will normally provide when the new rent is to take effect. If the rent has been agreed by the review date then it will become due from that date. If it has not been agreed by the review date:

1. The lease will usually specify what is to happen. For example, it may provide that the tenant must continue to pay rent at the old rate, with any excess that becomes due once the rent has been agreed to be paid on the quarter day following completion of the review. The lease may also provide for interest on that excess, but if the lease is silent there is no automatic right to interest.

2. If the lease does not make provision, it may be arguable that no rent need be paid until the new rent has been ascertained. This may, however, be a somewhat risky position for the tenant to take, and in the absence of direct authority it would be prudent to continue to pay the rent at the existing rate. Where the lease is silent, the tenant's obligation to pay the new rent will take effect from the quarter day following completion of the review: *South Tottenham Land Securities Ltd v R. & A. Millett (Shops) Ltd* [1984] 1 WLR 710. Where the rent review is decided at arbitration the review is completed when the award is made and published to the parties, i.e. when the arbitrator informs the parties that his award is available: *The Archipelagon* [1979] 2 Lloyd's Rep 289.

An agreement by an assignee with the landlord to pay the reviewed rent by stepped increases will bind the original tenant. Thus, if the assignee defaults, the landlord may pursue the original tenant for payment: *GUS Property Management Ltd v Texas Homecare Ltd* [1993] 27 EG 130.

Where the lease is assigned by the tenant between quarter days, the Apportionment Act will apply. The assignor will be liable to pay rent up to the date of the assignment, and the assignee thereafter. However, the landlord can seek to forfeit for all the rent due following the assignment, notwithstanding that the assignee is only personally responsible for the post-assignment rent. *Parry v Robinson-Wylie Ltd* (1987) 54 P+CR 187.

Overpayment of the rent due by mistake is recoverable by the tenant: *Nordin & Peacock plc* v *D. B. Ramsden & Co Ltd* (No 2) Butterworths case reports 5.2.99 (applying *Kleinworth Benson* v *Lincoln City Council* [1998] 4 All ER 513). The tenant's time to reclaim the overpayment only begins to run when he becomes aware of the mistake-see Limitation Act 1980 section 32 (1) (c). However, if there is underpayment of rent because the landlord has miscalculated this, the underpayment is recoverable by the landlord: *University Superannuation Scheme Ltd* v *Marks & Spencer plc* [1999] 4 EG 158.

If a tenant gives notice to terminate the tenancy and then fails to vacate, the landlord will be entitled to twice the rent that would otherwise be due: Distress for Rent Act 1737, section 18.

The proposed limit of £350 payable for over three years under the Commonhold and Leasehold Reform Act 2002 will not apply to commercial leases.

IN ADVANCE OR IN ARREAR?

Most leases provide for payment to be made in advance, but if the lease is silent the rent is due in arrear.

WHO IS RESPONSIBLE FOR THE RENT?

The primary liability to pay the rent falls on the current tenant. Where there is a surety he will have concurrent liability. There may also be liability on the original or previous tenants (and their sureties). It will usually be appropriate to join them as parties to the proceedings: see generally chapter 7.

DEDUCTIONS FROM RENT

The landlord should consider whether the tenant has made, or seeks to make, deductions from rent which may explain his failure to make payment in part or at all: see *Televantos* v *McCulloch* [1991] 1 EGLR 123 (p 40 below). In summary, deductions may be made only if:

- they are authorised by the lease; or
- they are authorised by statute; or
- the tenant has paid sums that the landlord has a duty to pay which enables the tenant to treat them as a counterclaim and set-off against the rent due.

If failure by the landlord to pay such sums would affect the tenant's peaceable enjoyment of the demised premises then he will have implied authority from the landlord to pay the sums and set them off against rent.

Originally, any deduction from rent by way of set-off could only be in respect of a liquidated sum. Now it would seem that an unliquidated claim for damages for breach of covenant by the landlord can also be set off – for example, if the landlord has failed to fulfil his repairing obligations and the tenant has expended money on doing the necessary works. But the landlord's obligation to repair normally only arises on notice and so he should have been given notice of the disrepair. It would also seem that (unless the tenant relies on the equitable doctrine of set-off below) the tenant must have actually paid out the sums he seeks to set off: *Lee-Parker* v *Izzet* [1971] 3 All ER 1099.

A right of set-off by a tenant will usually be enforceable against an assignee landlord due to the Law of Property Act 1925, section 142: *Lottery King Ltd* v *Amec Properties Ltd* [1995] 2 EGLR 17. However, the Landlord & Tenant (Covenants) Act 1995 means section 142 does not apply to leases granted after January 1, 1996. As a result, and because of section 23(1) of the 1995 Act which absolves an assignee from liability in respect of covenants prior to the date of the assignment, does this mean a tenant will lose his right of set-off if the landlord commits a breach and then assigns the reversion? Of course the breach may be continued but otherwise the court has held that where pre-assignment arrears are claimed by an assignee landlord, this claim will be subject to a right of set-off arising prior to that assignment: *Smith* v *Muscat* [2003] EWCA 30 EG 144.

Under the Landlord and Tenant (Covenants) Act 1995 a landlord is not able to recover any fixed charge from a former tenant or his guarantor unless, within six months of the charge becoming due, he serves on that person a notice informing him that the charge is now due and that the landlord intends to recover that amount and any interest payable – see page 105 below.

EQUITABLE SET-OFF

There is no right of set-off if the tenant has not carried out and paid for the repairs but, in some circumstances, he may be entitled to rely on the doctrine of equitable set-off if he has a cross-claim for damages against the landlord. In *British Anzani (Felixstowe) Ltd* v *International Marine Management (UK) Ltd* [1980] QB 137, the tenant was able to set off £1 million following the landlord's failure to repair two warehouses, against £540,000 rent arrears, even though the landlord's obligation was contained not in the lease but in the prior agreement to construct the warehouses and lease them to the tenant.

To rely on this doctrine, the tenant must show that the counterclaim is so closely connected to the landlord's claim for rent as to go to the root of it. The tenant's equitable set-off cross claim must relate to the quality of occupation or physical state of the premises: *Inntrepreneur* v *Star Rider* [1998] 16 EG 140.

The tenant is not entitled to deduct rent simply because the premises have been damaged or are partially unusable, e.g. as a result of flood or fire. Unless the lease provides for suspension of rent in such circumstances (as leases often do), the rent will continue to be payable.

There may be an exception to this rule if, on the facts, it could be held that the lease has been frustrated. In *National Carriers Lt* v *Panalpina (Northern) Ltd* [1981] AC 675, the House of Lords ruled that the doctrine of frustration was capable of applying to leases. In the later case of *Nynehead Developments Ltd* v *R. H. Fibreboard Containers Ltd* [1999] 2 EG 139, the court also held that a lease may be terminated by frustration where the landlord fails to control other tenants on his site as this constituted a breach of the implied obligation not to denegrate from the grant. In that case the landlord had failed to take action to prevent other tenants parking their vehicles and skips on the tenant's forecourt. The court has also held that frustration has occurred where the landlord of a shopping mall fails to control a nuisance caused by another tenant: *Chartered Trust plc* v *Davies* [1997] 49 EG 135. However, frustration will in practice be rare.

A further exception may arise if the landlord's failure to comply with the covenants in the lease is so serious as to constitute a repudiation of the lease. In those circumstances, rent will no longer accrue due: *Hussein* v *Mehlman* [1992] 32 EG 59 (in that case a failure by the landlord to comply with the implied repairing covenants allowed the tenant to vacate the property and return the keys, bringing the lease to an end by acceptance of the landlord's breach). This is only likely to arise in exceptional cases.

A clause in the lease may expressly prohibit any set-off. This will prevent the tenant lawfully relying on a set off (although he may still have a counterclaim). Such a clause does not fall foul of the provisions of the Unfair Contract Terms Act 1977 as it is within the exclusion for contracts relating to land in Schedule 1, para l(b) of the Act: *Electricity Supply Nominees Ltd* v *IAF Group Ltd* [1993] 1 WLR 1059. But in *Connaught Restaurants Ltd* v *Indoor Leisure Ltd* [1994] 1 WLR 501, the Court of Appeal held that a provision in a lease that the rent should be paid "without any deduction" was, of itself, not sufficient, in the absence of any context suggesting the contrary, to exclude by implication a tenant's equitable right of set-off. Clear words were needed to exclude the tenant's remedy. The word "deduction" was said to be too imprecise. It would seem, therefore, that to exclude the tenant's equitable right of set-off the draftsman will have to do so explicitly.

The decision in *Connaught* casts doubt on the earlier case of *Famous Army Stores* v *Meehan* [1993] 09 EG 111 where, on similar wording, Steyn J held that on the true construction of a lease which provided that the rent should be paid "without any deductions" the effect was to exclude, by agreement, any right of set-off.

If the lease excludes set-off, this will also prevent the tenant setting off a damages claim against the unpaid rent: *Altonwood Ltd* v *Crystal Palace FC* [2005] EWHC 292 Ch.

Where money is held by way of a rent deposit, this may not be the subject of set-off where the deed expressly provides so: *Walker Cain Ltd* v *McCaughey* [1999] All ER 358.

SERVICE CHARGES AND OTHER MONIES PAYABLE

Default in the payment of rent will often be accompanied by failure to pay service charges. There is no precise, universal definition of a service charge, but it represents payment for the provision of services by the landlord. These may include the landlord's expenditure on repair, maintenance, porterage, or the common parts, but will depend entirely on the provisions in the lease defining the tenant's liability. In the absence of express provision there is no liability.

Service charges, inevitably, tend to be of variable amounts. The statutory rules relating to service charges payable in respect of dwellings (e.g. Housing Act 1996) do not apply to commercial property, which is governed by the common law and the wording of the lease. Questions often arise on the construction of the wording in the lease and whether the service charges levied are correct. There is an implied term in all leases that the service charges are to be fair and reasonable: *Finchbourne Ltd* v *Rodrigues* [1976] 3 All ER 581. This does not apply to a covenant to reimburse the landlords for the cost of purchasing insurance cover. There is no implied term that the sum paid must be fair and reasonable. The tenant's obligation is simply to reimburse the landlord for the sums expended: *Havenridge Ltd* v *Boston Dyers Ltd* [1994] NPC 39. But where a dispute arises, each case will turn on its own facts.

Any requisite certification, consultation procedure or supplying of estimates relating to service charges required by the lease must be carried out before the liability to pay arises: *Northways Flats Management Co (Camden) Ltd* v *Wimpey Pension Trustees Ltd* [1992] 31 EG 65.

A provision making a landlord's obligations "subject to the lessee paying the maintenance contribution" does not create a condition precedent to the performance of the landlord's obligations: *Yorkbrook Investments* v *Batten* [1985] 2 EGLR 100.

Most leases provide that service charges are reserved as rent, in which case they will be recoverable and will fall due in the same manner. If not so expressly reserved, action for payment of them may be maintained only as a simple debt, unless a claim for possession is also made which is based on the failure to pay as a breach of covenant other than the covenant to pay rent. A claim for possession in such circumstances will require service of a notice under the Law of Property Act 1925, section 146 (which is not otherwise required where the service charges are reserved as rents).

Other monies payable to the landlord which are stated in the lease to be recoverable "as if rent" may also be the subject of forfeiture proceedings: *Escalus Properties* v *Robinson* [1995] 31 EG 71.

INTEREST

The lease may also include a covenant to pay interest at a specified rate if the rent (or other monies due to the landlord) are not paid on time. If such a provision is included in the lease, the amount due should be added to the landlord's claim against the tenant. If there is no provision for payment of interest, the landlord will be entitled to interest only after proceedings are issued pursuant to either the Supreme Court Act 1981, section 35A (for High Court proceedings), or the County Courts Act 1984, section 69 (for county court proceedings) – currently at the rate of 8% p.a.

Where there is a contractual rate of interest, since judgment has been entered the judgment debt will then attract interest from the date of the judgment at the judgment rate rather than contractual rate: section 2(3)(b)(ii) County Courts (Interest on Judgment Debts) Order 1991.

PENALTIES

The lease may provide for interest to be payable at a higher specific rate in the case of default. This is recoverable as such and is not unenforceable as a penalty: *Lordsvale Finance plc* v *Bank of Zambia*, The Times, 8 April, 1999.

A provision requiring rent that would otherwise be calculated by reference to the tenant's receipts to be calculated by reference to an open market rent is also not unenforceable as a penalty: *Crown Estate Commissioners* v *Possfund Custodian Trustee Ltd* [1996] EGGS 172.

RENT DEPOSITS

In order to give a landlord increased security, rent deposits are often taken. Where the rent remains unpaid the landlord may draw down from the rent deposit in respect of the sums due. Careful regard to the terms of the rent deposit deed will be required for the terms under which the draw down may be effected and the tenant's obligation to "top up" the rent deposit once drawn down has been made. In many cases, if the tenant fails to "top up" the rent deposit, this is expressly stated to be a breach of covenant in respect of which the landlord may forfeit.

Tenant insolvency may affect the landlord's ability to rely on the rent deposit. This will depend on the nature of the deposit which may be:

- A charge-the rent is held in a separate account and is charged by the tenant to the landlord. This must be registered as a charge at Companies House.
- A trust-the landlord holds the money on trust for the tenant.
- The landlord's property – the money is paid over to the landlord and becomes his property to draw down in default or repay in specified circumstances.

As a result of the Enterprise Act 2002, a landlord cannot enforce security over a tenant in administration without the consent of the administrator or the leave of the court. Where a rent deposit is held by the landlord on terms that the account funds belong to the landlord, the landlord may still draw on this if the tenant goes into administration. However, where (as is commonly the case) the rent deposit is held in an account in the tenant's name with the funds charged to the landlord, if the tenant goes into administration the landlord may not enforce the security over the deposit without the consent of the administrator or the leave of the court. Whilst it is difficult in practice to see what objection could be raised to the exercise of this security, a landlord will still face delay and cost in enforcing his rights over the rent deposit in such circumstances.

There are, however, a number of alternatives to rent deposits:

- Directors' parent company guarantees.
- Bank guarantees.
- Insurance policies specifically to provide security for rent.

Where the landlord has elected to charge VAT, the landlord should be careful to ensure that the amount of any rent deposit is equal to the rent plus the VAT. Otherwise, when the landlord makes a claim on the deposit, it will only be left with 82.5% of the deposit monies as the landlord will be required to account to Customs and Excise for the VAT element.

COURT PROCEDURE

If rent and/or service charges are due, the landlord can sue the tenant on the covenant to pay, merely for the amount due. This is often combined with a claim for possession (see Chapter 3) in order to put pressure on the tenant, but it is not necessary to include such a claim. There may be reasons why the landlord does not wish to rely on the right of forfeiture, thereby terminating the lease; for example, if there is a surety who can be relied upon to make payment, or if it would be difficult to re-let the premises.

Having ascertained the amount to be claimed and that it is due from the tenant, consideration should be given to the parties to be sued. The current tenant will obviously be a party, and it will usually be appropriate to join any surety and/or previous tenant(s) or their sureties. In cases to which the Landlord and Tenant (Covenants) Act 1995 applies notice will have to have been served on a former tenant or his guarantor in accordance with section 17 of the Act – see page 105 below.

1.   LIMITATION

No action for arrears of rent may be maintained six years after the date the arrears fell due: Limitation Act 1980, section 19. Rent is defined in section 38(1) and includes a rent charge and a rent service. This limitation period also applies to a claim against a surety: *Romain v Scuba TV Ltd* [1999] EG 126. However, the six years only begins to run from the time the cause of action arises. If the surety's liability only arises on service of a demand on him which is expressly required by the lease, the commencement of the six year period will be delayed until that demand is served.

The Landlord and Tenant (Covenants) Act 1995 (s 17) prevents a landlord from recovering any fixed charge from a former tenant or his guarantor unless, within six months of the charge becoming due, he serves on that person a notice informing him that the charge is now due and that the landlord intends to recover that amount with interest – see page 105 below.

2.   JURISDICTION

The Civil Procedure Rules which came into force on 26 April 1999 establish the jurisdictional limits for commencing court proceedings. Any claim may be started in the county court. However, proceedings may only be started in the High Court where the value of the claim is £15,000 or more: CPR Part 7, Practice Direction paragraph 2. The claim may however be started in the High Court if it is particularly complex or important to the public in general.

If the landlord is using either the High Court or the county court, proceedings seeking simply payment of arrears may be issued in any court no matter where the tenant resides or where the cause of action arose. However, the action may be transferred:

1. The action will automatically be transferred to the defendant's home court if a defence is filed by an individual. The home court will be determined by reference to the address for service of the defendant. It will, however, remain open to the claimant to apply for the case to be dealt with at a court other than the defendant's home court.
2. If the landlord obtains judgment in default against an individual, any application to set this aside will automatically be transferred to the defendant's home court: CPR Part 13, Rule 4.
3. The action may be transferred for trial.
4. The court may at any time on application transfer proceedings: CPR Part 30, Rule 2.

When considering transfer the court is to have regard to the criteria in CPR Part 30, Rule 3 including:

a) the financial value of the claim
b) whether it would be more convenient or fair to be heard elsewhere
c) the availability of a judge specialising in the type of case
d) whether the case is complex
e) the importance to the public
f) the facilities at the court for a disabled party or witnesses.
g) the possibility of a declaration of incompatibility under the Human Rights Act 1998.

If the landlord elects to commence proceedings for a sum over £15,000 in the High Court, this may be done in the Central Office regardless of where the premises are located or the defendant resides. Alternatively, if the land-lord wishes to use a district registry, the registry within whose area the demised premises are located or the defendant is resident would often be used but this is not mandatory under the CPR which makes no such distinction. Proceedings commenced in a district registry may be transferred to the Central Office and vice versa: CPR Part 30, Rule 2.

3. COURT PROCEEDINGS

The implementation of the Civil Procedure Rules ("CPR") on 26 April, 1999 brought major changes to court procedures and introduced a "new procedural code". This means that old case law on procedural issues will in many cases have no relevance in the application of the CPR. However, those Rules are set out in plain language and with "sign posts" to refer the reader to other relevant parts of the Rules. The CPR do not affect the substantive law.

The CPR contain less detail than the previous Rules and are supplemented by Practice Directions. The Practice Directions tell the parties what the Court will expect of them.

Overriding Objective

Part 1 of the CPR sets out the overriding objective: the Rules are intended to enable the court to deal with cases justly. Dealing with cases justly will include ensuring the parties are on an equal footing, saving expense and dealing with the case in a way which is proportionate to the amount of money involved, the importance of the case, the complexity of the issues and the financial position of each party. The courts will seek to ensure that cases are dealt with expeditiously and fairly. All Rules must be interpreted in accordance with this overriding objective.

With the overriding objective in mind, the CPR include pre-action protocol for specific types of claim to govern the conduct of the parties before proceedings are issued. Their purpose is to achieve early identification of the issues, disclosure of the evidence and documentation, thereby enabling the parties hopefully to reach an earlier resolution without the need to start court proceedings. At the time of writing there is no protocol specifically for rent arrears cases but the Practice Direction relating to protocols makes it clear that the courts will generally expect parties to all types of litigation to have entered into the spirit of the existing protocols by exchanging information before litigation and generally trying to settle matters before proceedings have begun (see CPR 7.0.3). Further protocols will be introduced over time.

The key elements of the existing protocols are similar and give a good indication of the approach the court is likely to require parties to undertake in the pre-action period. The key elements are:

- A letter of claim setting out the facts, the main allegations, the financial losses claimed, the evidence in support and attaching relevant documents.
- The recipient of the letter of claim should be given three months to consider and respond. That response should be full, dealing with the detailed nature of any defence and any dispute as to the facts. Any relevant documents should also be disclosed. Although there is no reference to this in the CPR, clearly where the claim does not comprise any complex issues and is little more than debt collection the need to wait three months is not appropriate. If the tenant will not pay, delay will not improve this and the landlord may proceed with court action if payment is not forthcoming after a detailed demand.
- The party wishing to instruct an expert (for example in a dilapidations claim) should give the other party the opportunity to agree the appointment of that expert.

Non compliance with the protocol may have the consequence that the party at fault will find it very difficult to obtain an extension of time if proceedings are required and may also be penalised in costs.

It will therefore be essential for a landlord to write a formal and clearly phrased letter before action before commencing proceedings. Any documentation to support the claim requested by the tenant should also be provided. For a precedent letter, see precedent number 7.

In the context of landlord and tenant law and in particular tenant default, a careful regard should however be had to the rules relating to waiver of a breach of covenant. Clearly the landlord should ensure that the steps taken in the pre-action period cannot be construed as amounting to waiver. In such circumstances, it is likely that the protocol will require less pre-action delay (for example, a three month period of consideration after a rent arrears or breeach of alienation covenant claim is made is unlikely to be needed) although again the landlord is likely to be required to give the tenant the opportunity to respond to his allegations.

Commencement

Proceedings will be commenced using a Claim form under CPR Part 7. The landlord must complete and file at court a Part 7 Claim form, service copies and the fee (together with any request for personal service – see below).

The court will issue the Claim form and either send notice of issue to the Claimant giving the claim number and the date of service if the form is to be served by the court, or hand the form back to the Claimant for personal service.

The Claim form must be served within four months of issue (six months if served out of the jurisdiction). A Claimant may issue and serve a Claim form without full Particulars of Claim in the first instance but if served separately, the Particulars of Claim (see below) must be served within 14 days of service of the Claim form.

Response forms must be served with the Particulars of Claim where they are not served with the Claim form. The Defendant's time for responding to the claim runs from the date of service of the Particulars of Claim.

Particulars of Claim

The Particulars of Claim set out the facts giving rise to the cause of action and will set out details of the lease, the rent covenant and the arrears. They may either be served with the Claim form or within 14 days of service of this.

CPR Part 16 specifics what must be contained in the Claim form (Rule 16.2):

(a) A concise statement of the nature of the claim.
(b) The remedy which the Claimant seeks.
(c) A statement of value in accordance with Rule 16.3.
(d) If the Particulars of Claim are not served with the Claim form or contained in it the Claimant must state that Particulars of Claim will follow.
(e) Any representative capacity in which the Claimant is suing.

The contents of the Particulars of Claim are prescribed by Rule 16.4 and must:

(a) include a concise statement of the facts.
(b) set out details of the claim for interest.
(c) be verified by a Statement of Truth: Part 22.
(d) where the claim is based upon a written agreement (as will usually be the case for a claim for arrears under a lease) a copy of the lease constituting the agreement should be attached or served with the Particulars of Claim (or where, unusually, the claim is based upon an oral agreement, the Particulars of Claim should set out the contractual words used and stated by whom, to whom, when and where they were spoken) – see Part 16 Practice Direction 7.3 and 7.4.

Where rent is payable in advance, the full quarter's rent is due even if proceedings are commenced during the quarter.

The CPR require details of any claim for interest. If this is on a contractual basis under the lease this must be set out in the Particulars of Claim. Alternatively the claim may be under the County Courts Act 1984, section 69 or the Supreme Court Act 1981, section 35A (currently at the rate of 8% p.a.).

If the tenant is not the original tenant, it is not necessary to plead the history of assignment. It is sufficient to plead the original demise and that the estate and interest of the lessee is now vested in the tenant by assignment. On the other hand, if the reversion has been assigned, the landlord must show how he acquired title and from whom: *Philips* v *Philips* [1878] 4 QBD 127; *Davis* v *James* [1884 26 CHD 778.

Statement of Truth

All pleadings are called Statements of Case (i.e. Particulars of Claim, Defence and Reply) and must be verified by a Statement of Truth. The form of the Statement of Truth is as follows:-

"[I believe][The Defendant believes] that the facts stated in this Defence are ture."

Verifying a Statement of Case containing a false statement without an honest belief in its truth may give rise to proceedings for contempt of court (Rule 32.14).

A Statement of Truth must be given either by the witness adducing the evidence or by the party or parties' legal representative. In the case of companies, the Statement of Truth may be signed by a person holding a senior position in the company. That person must state the office or position he holds. It will normally include a Director, Secretary, Chief Executive or a Senior Manager. It should be noted that in the case of company landlords, these rules preclude a Statement of Case being verified by a Managing Agent (see Part 22, Practice Direction paragraph 3.11).

See precedent 1 for a specimen Particulars of Claim.

Service

Where the court is to serve any documents this will generally be by first class post. The deemed date of service is two days after the date of posting for all defendants, including limited companies. Bailiff service is not available.

Where a Claim form originally served by post is returned by the post office, the court will send a notice of non-service to the Claimant. It will then be a matter for the Claimant to seek to effect service. The Claimant will receive from the Court the Claim form and response pack etc for the Claimant to serve.

Claimants may effect service of Claim forms themselves (having notified the court that they propose to do so) either by personal service, by post, by fax, by document exchange, or by e-mail. Where the Claimant serves a document, the Claimant must file a Certificate of Service (see Form N215) within seven days of effecting service together with a copy of the document so served attached.

The Rules of Service are set out at CPR Part 6. This specifies the different methods of service:-

(a) **Personal service:** this is effected by leaving it with the individual. If the Defendant refuses to accept the summons it is sufficient service to inform him of the nature of the document and leave it in his presence, even on the floor: *Thomson v Pheney* (1832) 1 DOWL 441. In such circumstances it is better if the document is not in an envelope. A document is served personally on a company or corporation by leaving it with a person holding a senior position within the company. The Practice Direction to Part 6 sets out the meaning of "senior position". A document is served personally on a partnership where partners are being sued in the name of the firm by leaving it with a partner or a person who at the time of service has control or management of the partnership business at its principal place of business. Service on a receptionist or security guard is insufficient: *Amerada Hess* v *Rome* QBD 19 January 2000.

(b) **Service on solicitors.** Where a solicitor is authorized to accept service, any document must be served on him and not by personal service (unless personal service is required by another rule: CPR Rule 6.4 (2).

On occasion it may be necessary to serve on the defendant outside the jurisdiction. In which case an application for permission must be made. See Precedent 16 for a witness statement to support this.

Deemed Date of Service

Service shall be deemed to take place in accordance with the following table.

Method of Service	Deemed Date of Service
First Class Post	Second day after posting
Document Exchange	Second day after left at Document Exchange
Delivering or leaving at Defendant's address	The day after delivery
Fax	Where sent before 4.00 pm, on that day; otherwise the day after the fax was transmitted
Other electronic method (e.g. e-mail)	Second day after day of transmission

Service by Alternative Method

This replaces the previous provisions for "substituted service". Rule 6.8 permits the court to make an order for service by an alternative method not otherwise specified. An application for service by an alternative method requires a formal application supported by written evidence (*i.e.* a Witness Statement) specifying the method of service proposed (*e.g.* service on a third party, advertisement in the press, affixing to premises).

Responding to the Claim

When Particulars of Claim are served they must be served with a Response Pack. This pack will contain an acknowledgement of service, a form of admission and a form of Defence and Counterclaim. The Defendant must respond within 14 days of service of the Particulars of Claim (whether served with the Claim form or subsequently) by one of the following methods:

(a) paying the sums claimed;
(b) filing the form of Admission at court admitting all or part of the claim and, as appropriate, seeking time to pay;
(c) filing the Acknowledgement of Service form; or
(d) serving a Defence.

If the claim is to be defended, the Defence is due within 14 days of service of the Particulars of Claim unless an Acknowledgement of Service is filed within 14 days of service of the of Particulars of Claim in which case the Defence is due 14 days after that, *i.e.* 28 days after service of the Particulars of Claim. The time for service of the Defence may be extended by the parties by up to 28 days only but where this occurs the Defendant must notify the Court in writing (Rule 15.5). Any further extension will require an application to the court for permission under Rule 3.1.

Defence

The Defence must be filed at court and served on all other parties.

Where the Defence states that the amount claimed has been paid, a copy of the Defence is sent to the Claimant by the Court who must notify the court within 28 days of service that payment has been made or that the proceedings should continue as defended. If the Claimant does not reply within the 28 day period the claim will be stayed automatically by the court. Where any party thereafter wishes to take further action they will first have to apply to the court to lift the stay (by making an application under Part 23).

The contents required of a Defence are set out in Rule 16.5. The Defence must expressly state which of the allegations in the Particulars of the Claim are denied, which allegations the Defendant is unable to admit or deny but which the Defendant requires the Claimant to prove, and which allegations are admitted. Where an allegation is denied, the Defendant must state his reasons for doing so and if he intends to put forward a different version of events, he must state his own version. Failure to deal with an allegation where the Defendant does nevertheless set out the nature of his case shall be taken to require the allegation to be proved. However, in a money claim, the Defendant shall be taken to require any allegation relating to the amount of money to be proved unless he expressly admits this. If the Defendant disputes the Statement of Value he must state why and provide his own valuation.

The Defence must also be verified by a Statement of Truth.

If the Defendant has not served an Acknowledgement of Service he must provide an address for service in the jurisdiction.

As referred to above, where proceedings have not been issued in the Defendant's "home court," where the Defendant is an individual who has filed a Defence, the proceedings will be transferred to that "home court". Where there is more than one Defendant, it is the first Defendant to file a Defence which dictates whether and to where automatic transfer will take place. There is no automatic transfer if the first (or only) Defendant to file a Defence is a limited company.

Where a Defendant contends for a defence of set-off this may or may not also be a counterclaim. A counterclaim is a Part 20 claim and will require the issue of a Part 20 claim form which may be made at any time without the court's permission if this is issued before or at the same time as the Defence is filed. Thereafter a counterclaim will require the court's permission.

Reply to Defence

A Claimant who does not file a Reply to the Defence shall not be taken to admit the matters raised in the Defence. A Reply is therefore optional. It is only likely to be necessary where the Claimant wishes to allege facts in answer to the Defence which were not included in his claim. A Reply must be verified by a Statement of Truth pursuant to Part 22.

Judgment in Default

If the Defendant does not reply to the claim, the Claimant may apply for Default Judgment. Where the claim is for a specified amount, there may be judgment for that sum. If the amount claimed is unspecified, then there will he a judgment for liability only. Application for Judgment in Default may be made after the 14 day period has elapsed without any Acknowledgement of Service or Defence having being filed, or, where an Acknowledgement of Service is filed, where no Defence is filed within 14 days thereafter, or an extension agreed: Rules 12.1 and 12.3.

Default Judgment is obtained by the Claimant filing at Court a request in the prescribed form: Rule 12.4. The Default Judgment may include interest where this is claimed in the Particulars of Claim: Rule 12.6. Where there is more than one Defendant the Claimant may obtain Default Judgment against one and proceed with the claim against the other: Rule 12.8. Default Judgment may also be obtained for costs only where the debt (but not costs) is paid: Rule 12.9.

Other Steps in the Proceedings

There will be four "milestones" in any contested court proceedings, namely:

1. ALLOCATION

When a Defence is filed the court will send out a copy of the Defence to the other parties together with an allocation questionnaire specifying a date when that questionnaire is to be returned. Notice of Transfer will be sent out if the case is being automatically transferred to another court. The allocation questionnaire will not be sent out until the last Defence is received where there is more than one Defendant (or the time for the last Defendant to reply has expired). When the allocation questionnaires have been returned (or the period for doing so – 14 days – has expired) the court file will be passed to a procedural Judge for directions and allocation to a track. Cases will be referred to one of the following tracks:-

(a) **Small Claims** – claims valued at less than £5,000 (CPR Part 27)
(b) **Fast Track** – claims valued between £5–15,000 (CPR Part 28)
(c) **Multi Track** – claims valued at over £15,000 (CPR Part 29)

The Directions ordered by the court will vary depending upon the issues and size of the case. These are likely to include the following steps:-

- Disclosure of documents

- Inspection of documents

- Expert evidence (if necessary – but the courts will seek to reduce reliance on experts)

- Service of any further witness statements

In a Small Claims case the court will give standard directions and will fix a trial date.

If however, the claim is on the Fast Track, the court will give directions for the management of the case and again fix a timetable and a trial date. The trial date may be a trial window within which the trial is to take place.

If the claim is on the Multi Track, the court will give bespoke directions for the conduct of the case and will fix a timetable including a case management conference or a pre-trial review (see CPR Part 29).

2. LISTING QUESTIONNAIRE

The next important milestone is the listing questionnaire. It is sent out (in form N170) in both Fast Track and Multi Track cases. The form raises questions about the conduct of the case and will enable the court to keep tight control over case management. The parties are required to complete the listing questionnaire and return it to the court who will then fix the trial date and give any necessary directions. If the questionnaire is not completed or the court believes a hearing is necessary, it may fix a listing hearing (see CPR, Parts 28 Practice Direction 28.5 and 29 Practice Direction 29.8.3).

If neither party files a listing questionnaire the court may order the claim struck out unless these are filed within a period.

3.   PRE-TRIAL REVIEW

In a Multi Track case the court may fix a pre-trial review. This is most often likely to occur after the listing questionnaire has been received. At the pre-trial review the court will consider what additional Directions, if any, are required and the parties should request the court to make any appropriate Directions at that time. Attendance at the pre-trial review by the parties' legal representative is mandatory (Part 29.3), and the client (or a representative of the client with sufficient authority to deal with any issues that arise) may be required to attend: Part 3.1 (2)(c) attend.

As long as the milestones in the proceedings are not affected, the parties may agree to vary time for compliance with Directions or, if necessary, apply to the court.

4.   DISCLOSURE

The rules regarding disclosure (which was previously called "discovery") have been re-worded. It was felt during the review of civil procedure that existing discovery rules radically increased the costs of litigation. The courts will now view applications for additional discovery with greater care and will consider these in the context of proportionality.

Where disclosure is ordered this will be "standard disclosure" which will require a party to disclose documents:

(a)   on which he relies;
(b)   which adversely affect his case, or
(c)   adversely affect another party's case, or
(d)   support another party's case.

The "train of inquiry" test from *Peruvian Guano* used in old, pre-CPR discovery applications is therefore now inapplicable.

Furthermore a party does not now have to undertake all possible steps to locate disclosable documents. The obligation on a party is to make a reasonable search for the documents referred to above. When considering whether a search is reasonable, the court will take account of the number of documents involved, the nature and complexity of the proceedings, the ease and expense of retrieval of the document and the likely significance of any document that might be found during the search (CPR, Part 31.7). The overriding principle of proportionality will apply. A List of Documents (now in the standard form N265) will include a statement by the party giving disclosure setting out the extent of his search.

If a party is dissatisfied with another party's disclosure he may still apply for an order for specific disclosure, specifying the order that he requires the court to make. Such an application must be supported by evidence. Applications are likely to be more rare than previously and the court will take account of all the circumstances and in particular the overriding objective. Expensive satellite litigation concerning disclosure issues is therefore less likely.

Offers to Settle

One of the key thrusts of the CPR procedures is to encourage the parties to settle without pursuing litigation to a final result. The old payment into court regime is therefore retained in the CPR (now known as a Part 36 payment) but the scope of this device is extended to enable a Claimant to make an offer to settle to the Defendant.

Part 36 of the CPR enables an offer to settle to be made by either party in respect of any claim (other than a Defendant's offer to settle a money claim which must be subject to a payment into court in the usual way). The basic principle behind the new provision remains unchanged from previous practice – an offer is made following which the recipient has a 21 day period to consider the offer. If accepted the Claimant recovers his costs to the date of acceptance, but if refused and if the offer is beaten at trial, the offeror receives indemnity costs and interest at 10% above base rate on his money claim (if any) from the date the offer could have been accepted.

Offers to settle can apply to non-monetary aspects of a claim (e.g.) the forfeiture claim) and can also be utilised in the pre-action period. If a pre-action offer to settle is made in respect of a monetary sum, to obtain the benefits of a Part 36 payment offer, this sum must then be paid into court within 14 days of service of the claim form if proceedings are issued: Part 36, Rule 10.

Summary Judgment

Application may be made for summary judgment under Part 24 on the basis that the Defendant has no real prospect of successfully defending the claim and there is no other reason why the case should be disposed of at trial: Rule 24.2. Summary judgment may be sought once the Acknowledgement of Service has been filed or after the Defence. An application for summary judgment must be served at least 14 days before the hearing of the application.

If written evidence (in addition to the statement of case) is required by the applicant, this must he served with or form part of the application. If the Defendant wishes to use written evidence this must be served at least seven days before the hearing and filed at court.

Evidence in reply to this by the applicant is required three days before the hearing: Rule 24.5.

On hearing the application the court may:

a) give judgment on the claim or an issue
b) strike out or dismiss the claim or an issue
c) dismiss the application
d) give directions
e) make a conditional order requiring payment into court or a specified step.

Even if the tenant raises a counterclaim and set-off, it would usually be appropriate, tactically, for the landlord to seek summary judgment in respect of the claim (even if enforcement is suspended), leaving the tenant to pursue his counterclaim.

Interim Payment Order

If the tenant has raised a substantial defence and/or counterclaim, application may, in theory, be made by the landlord for an interim payment order under Part 25. However, an interim payment order is not usually sought if the landlord has commenced proceedings seeking only payment of arrears, as the matter is usually clear-cut and likely to proceed direct to summary judgment.

Amendment

Amendment to proceedings by the addition and/or substitution of parties is governed by CPR Part 19. An application to add or substitute parties may be made by either an existing party or a person who wishes to become a party. Such an application may be made without notice but must be supported by evidence: Rule 19.4. When the Court makes an order for the removal, addition or substitution of a party it may give consequential directions about filing and serving the Claim form on any new Defendant and the management of proceedings: Rule 19.4(6).

Amendment to Statements of Case is governed by Part 17. A party may amend his Statement of Case at any time before it has been served. Once served, a Statement of Case may only be amended if all parties give written consent or the permission of the court is obtained. Where the court's permission is required to amend a Statement of Case, the Applicant should file with the court the application notice and a copy of the Statement of Case with the proposed amendments. The application may either be dealt with at a hearing or; if Rule 23.8 applies, without a hearing.

Procedural Table

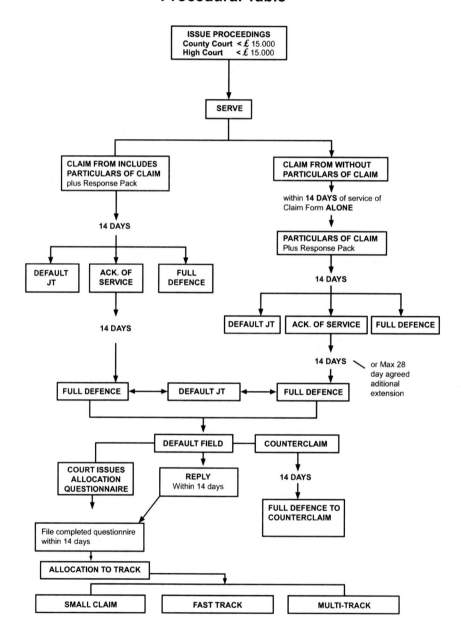

Where the Court's permission to amend is given, the applicant should file with the court within 14 days of the Order the amended Statement of Case and, unless the court otherwise orders, serve this on every other party.

Amendments to a Statement of Case are to be verified by a Statement of Truth unless the court otherwise orders.

Enforcement

Once judgment has been obtained the landlord's solicitor may proceed immediately to take enforcement proceedings, or alternatively may first apply for an order to obtain information from the judgment debtor under CPR Part 71. This is a special court appointment when the tenant is cross-examined in detail on oath as to his financial affairs, assets and liabilities. If the tenant is an individual he will be the person examined, but in the case of a company, a director of the tenant company may be examined. Where an action is proceeding in the High Court the examination will invariably take place in the local county court of the person sought to be examined. Non-attendance may be enforced by committal, which is normally suspended initially to allow the debtor to attend on a subsequent occasion.

See Chapter 14 for further details.

CHAPTER 3
CLAIM FOR POSSESSION

CHAPTER 3
CLAIM FOR POSSESSION

To claim possession the landlord must have a right to forfeit the lease. Such a right must be expressly set out in the lease, i.e. a proviso for re-entry on breach of covenant – otherwise known as a forfeiture clause. A forfeiture clause will not be implied into the lease if, most improbably, one is not expressly included. In such circumstances a landlord may still be able to forfeit if the tenant's default is a breach of a condition upon which the lease was granted.

If the lease is forfeited all interests created out of it will fall, including those of any sub-tenants or mortgagees (subject to any applications for relief that they may make), and the lease will be at an end. It should be borne in mind that once the landlord has embarked upon forfeiture proceedings there is no going back for him. In *GS Fashions Ltd* v *B&Q plc* [1995] 1 WLR 1088, Lightman J held that where a landlord had served court proceedings for forfeiture and the tenant had conceded the landlord's entitlement to possession, it was not then open to the landlord to seek to amend the proceedings by deleting the claim to forfeit.

In order to forfeit a lease an act of re-entry is required by the landlord, either:

1. peaceable re-entry, or
2. court action for possession.

Commencing proceedings will operate as an act of re-entry when the proceedings are served, but the forfeiture will not be final until the court makes a possession order, at which time the forfeiture is backdated to the date of service of the proceedings.

FORFEITURE FOR NON-PAYMENT OF RENT

The landlord must first ascertain that the rent and/or service charges are due in the amount claimed. If the tenant has a legitimate set-off for more then the rent claimed, the landlord may not have a cause of action: *Televantos v McCulloch* [1991] 1 EGLR 123. If the service charges are not reserved as rent, any forfeiture action based on their non-payment must follow the procedure for forfeiture for breach of covenant other than the covenant to pay rent, i.e. the prior service of a Section 146 Notice. Service charges (and indeed other regular payments} are invariably reserved as rent. The landlord's remedies for their non-payment will, therefore, be the same as for unpaid rent. (It should be noted that the restrictions on enforcing non-payment of residential service charges do not apply to commercial service charges.)

Where the service charge or other sums payable are simply subject to a covenant to pay them, forfeiture is available as if a non-rent covenant: *Khar v Delabounty Ltd* [1996] EGGS 183. In such circumstances a section 146 Notice will be needed.

Usually the forfeiture clause will provide that the right to re-enter arises after the expiry of a fixed period (often 14 or 21 days) after the rent fell due. Proceedings for possession cannot be commenced before that period has expired.

If the right to recover the arrears has been assigned to a previous landlord (commonly on a sale of the reversion) the current landlord can nevertheless forfeit in respect of those arrears even though payment of them is not due to him: *Kataria v Safeland plc, The Times* December 3, 1997.

1.   DEMAND FOR PAYMENT

Modern leases almost always provide that a formal demand for payment of the rent is not required. Where this is so, the landlord may proceed to forfeit even if the tenant has had no invoice for the rent: *Railtrack plc v Ohajah* [2000] EGCS 88. If most unusually, the requirement for a demand is not excluded by the lease, under the common law rent must be demanded before a right to forfeit can be exercised. The rent must be demanded at the place specified for payment in the lease or, if no such place is specified, at the demised premises. The demand must be made on the last day for payment before and until sunset for the sum due for the last rental period.

Service of a Claim form in the county court will constitute a demand if the landlord has a right to re-enter for non-payment of rent, and if the rent is over six months in arrear and there are insufficient goods on the premises upon which to distrain: County Courts Act 1984, section 139(1).

In the High Court, section 210 of the Common Law Procedure Act 1852 provides that a formal demand is not required if the landlord has a right to reenter for non-payment of rent, and if one half-year's rent is in arrear and there is no sufficient distress to be found upon the premises to pay all arrears – this suggests that, to be sufficient, distress must satisfy all outstanding arrears and not just the half-year's arrears.

These enactments do not apply in the case of physical re-entry by the landlord: *Railtrack plc* v *Ohajah* (above).

Unless the lease dispenses with the requirement for a demand or the situation falls within the two statutory exceptions referred to above, the landlord must make formal demand for payment of the rent before he can exercise the right to forfeit. Although under the terms of modern leases it is most unlikely that a formal demand will be required, for the sake of completeness the requirements of such a demand are that it must be made:

1. by the landlord or his authorised agent;
2. on the last day available to save the tenant from forfeiture. If the forfeiture clause provides for forfeiture to take effect 14 days after the due date, the demand must therefore he made on the fourteenth day after the date rent is due excluding the day it became due. The demand cannot be made before or after that date;
3. before and at sunset on the appropriate day;
4. at the proper place, i.e. the place for payment specified in the lease or if none is specified at the demised premises;
5. for the precise sum due on that day, i.e. the demand must be for the quarter's rent that is due, not the previous arrears which may have accrued.

Service of a notice under section 146 of the Law of Property Act 1925 is not required before proceedings are commenced claiming possession for non-payment of rent or service charges (or other payments) reserved as rent. However, non-payment of rent or service charges is a once-and-for-all breach of the covenant to pay them and care should, therefore, be taken to ensure these breaches are not waived.

2.   COURT ACTION

Proceedings claiming possession based on non-payment of rent/service charge will be similar to the proceedings outlined in Chapter 2 above save that, in addition to payment of the arrears, the landlord will, of course, be claiming an order for possession based upon the proviso for forfeiture contained in the lease.

A claim for possession of land must be commenced in the county court for the district in which the property is situated. The action may only be started in the High Court if the claimant files a certificate with the Claim Form justifying the claim starting in the High Court because of complicated disputes of fact, points of law of general importance or there is a claim against trespassers and there is a substantial risk of public disturbance or serious harm to persons (CPR 55).

Court proceedings

Possession proceedings in the county court arc by way of fixed date action. CPR Part 55 provides specific rules for possession actions. See also the Practice Direction that accompanies it.

Commencement

The landlord must complete and file at court a claim form in the prescribed form (N11, N11B, N11M or N11R) seeking possession of land, together with Particulars of Claim (they cannot be served separately later) setting out the basis of his claim. Sufficient copies of the Particulars of Claim must be filed so that there is one copy for each Defendant plus one for the court. The landlord must pay the appropriate fee.

Particulars of claim

The Particulars of Claim will plead the facts giving rise to the cause of action, setting out details of the lease, the covenant to pay, the demand (if required), the rent and the arrears and the proviso for reentry. Relevant documents (such as the lease or S. 146 notice) should be attached: P.D.16, 8.3(1). The mandatory requirements of CPR Part 55 Practice Direction 2 state:

In a claim for recovery of land which is commercial premises the Particulars of Claim must:

1 Identify the land sought to be recovered;
2 State whether the claim relates to residential premises;
3 Give full details about the agreement or tenancy, if any, under which the land was held, and any mortgagee;
4 State the ground on which possession is claimed;
5 Give details of every person, who to the best of the Claimant's knowledge, is in possession of the property.

Note:

Where the land includes residential premises (or the commercial premises also have a residential element) there are additional requirements for the Particulars of Claim (Practice Direction 55 paragraph 2.3). This requires the following to be stated:

1. The amount due at the start of the proceedings;
2. In schedule form, the dates when arrears of rent arose, all amounts of rent due, the dates and amounts of all payments made and a running total of the arrears;
3. A daily rate of any rent and interest;
4. Any previous steps taken to recover arrears, with full details of any court proceedings;
5. Any relevant information about the defendant's circumstances, including details about benefits and payments direct;
6. The name of any person known to be entitled to apply for relief from forfeiture. The claimant must file a copy of the Particulars of Claim for service upon such person: Practice Direction 55 paragraph 2.4.

Where rent is payable in advance the full quarter's rent is due even if proceedings are commenced during the quarter. If the landlord wishes to claim interest the Particulars of Claim must include a claim for interest due either under the lease (if it so provides) or, alternatively, under section 69 of the County Courts Act 1984 or section 35A of the Supreme Court Act 1981.

If the tenant is not the original tenant it is not necessary to plead the history of assignments. It is sufficient to plead the original demise and that the estate and interest of the lessee are now vested in the tenant by assignment. The position is otherwise if the reversion has been assigned – see above.

As stated above, where rent is payable in advance the full quarter's rent will be due even if proceedings are commenced before the quarter has expired and even if forfeiture takes place during that quarter. If the tenant fails to vacate, mesne profits can also be claimed from the end of that quarter until the tenant vacates, and accordingly the claim should expressly seek mesne profits from the date of service "until possession be delivered up" at a given rate. If that rate is the same as the current rent for the premises any default judgment may be obtained in due course for a liquidated sum. However, if mesne profits are claimed at a rate higher than the current rent, any default judgment will be for mesne profits "to be assessed" which will necessitate an appointment before a Judge in due course. The reason for this is that it will be necessary for the landlord to adduce evidence (usually from an expert valuer/surveyor) to support his claim for mesne profits at a higher, open market value.

Historically mesne profits have generally been claimed on the basis of the ordinary letting value of the properly and, as has been noted, this has often been at the contractual rate under the forfeited lease. But in two cases, *Ministry of Defence* v *Thompson* [1993] 40 EG 148 and *Ministry of Defence* v *Ashman* (1993) 66 P & CR 195, the Court of Appeal allowed the claims for mesne profits to be calculated on the restitutionary basis by assessing the value to the former occupier of her occupation of the property.

This value was held to be what the local authority would have charged her for a similar property. These cases arose in circumstances which are not typical and it is not thought that they provide any help to commercial landlords.

Where underlessees remain in occupation the landlord, or former landlord as he now is, can maintain a claim for mesne profits for damages for being kept out of his property. The claim will be against the former headleaseholder – even though he has vacated – if the property is still occupied by underlessees or former underlessees: *Viscount Chelsea* v *Hutchinson* [1994] 43 EG 153. No such claim would arise if the underlessecs were statutorily protected.

See **Precedent 2** for specimen Particulars of Claim.

Service

The same rules apply as for service of a claim form seeking payment of unpaid rent – see page 26. The County Court will issue the proceedings as a fixed date action and will fix a date at once for trial to take place not less than 28 days later or trial which will be notified to the parties when the proceedings are issued: Part 55, 5(3).

The proceedings must be served at least 21 days before the hearing: CPR Part 55, 5(3)(c). The court can, however, vary this time: CPR 3.1.

The normal rules in CPR Part 6 regarding service apply to Part 55 claims. Where there is difficulty in effecting service of possession proceedings against trespassers they may be served by affixing them on the premises: CPR 55.6.

If the proceedings are endorsed with the name and address of a person entitled to seek relief the court will also serve a copy of the Particulars of Claim on that person if a spare copy is produced, although the CPR does not require it in commercial cases. Nevertheless it is a prudent step.

As with a claim for unpaid rent, a Response Pack must be served with the Particulars of Claim (see page 26 above). The options open to the Defendant by way of responses are the same, except an acknowledgment of service is not required and CPR Part 10 does not apply. Where a defence is not filed within the time allocated under CPR 15.4 (i.e. 14 days after service of the Particulars of Claim), default judgment under CPR 12 does not apply but the defendant may still take part in the hearing (albeit that the court may take account of this when making a costs order (CPR 55.7). The court is likely to use the first hearing date for giving Directions where the case is disputed and the claim for possession arises on grounds other than arrears of rent.

Judgment in default

Judgment in default is unavailable under CPR 55: see CPR 55.7(4).

OTHER INTERLOCUTORY STEPS IN THE PROCEEDINGS

1. DIRECTIONS:

Most county courts have special fixed date possession lists when numerous possession cases are listed together. Many cases are straightforward rent arrears cases or are undefended. The court listing clerks assume that this is so for all cases. Therefore, there will not normally be time to hear any case where there is a dispute of any substance. Accordingly, if a Defence is filed the future conduct of the proceedings will be governed by directions given at the first hearing.

2. SUMMARY JUDGMENT:

It is possible to obtain summary judgment granting an order for possession of commercial premises under CPR Part 24 as only residential premises are excluded from this procedure: CPR Part 24, Rule 24.3.

3. INTERIM PAYMENT ORDER:

If the tenant has raised a substantial defence and/or counterclaim, application may, in theory, be made by the landlord for an interim payment order (see p 55 below). However, where the landlord is seeking possession for non-payment of rent this would not usually be appropriate as the matter, being a fixed date action, is likely to proceed direct to trial.

4. AMENDMENT:

The same rules apply as for amendment in an action for unpaid rent – see page 33 above.

Relief from forfeiture

County court

Relief from forfeiture for non-payment of rent in county court proceedings is available under sections 138–140 of the County Courts Act 1984.

If the tenant pays all the arrears and costs of the action into court not less than five clear days before the hearing he will obtain automatic relief. This must include all mesne profits due since the court proceedings were issued: *Maryland Estates v Bar Joseph* [1998] 27 EG 142.

If such relief is not obtained, the court will make an order for possession not less than four weeks from the date of the order unless the tenant pays into court all arrears and costs by that date. If payment is made within that time the tenant obtains relief.

The court has power to extend the period specified in the order at any time before possession is recovered.

If the tenant does not obtain automatic relief and does not make payment of the sums due before the date specified in the possession order, he (or anyone claiming under him) can still apply for relief within six months from the landlord's recovery of possession and the court may grant relief on such terms as it sees fit. After six months the tenant will be barred from all relief: section 138(7).

The six-month time limit will also apply strictly to a mortgagee's application for relief: *UDT v Shellpoint Trustees* [1993] EGCS 57.

High Court

If there is at least six months' rent in arrear the tenant will obtain automatic relief by paying all arrears and costs to the landlord or into court before judgment: Common Law Procedure Act 1852, section 212.

If the tenant does not obtain relief in this way before trial, he may apply for relief within six months of the execution of the order for possession: Supreme Court Act 1981, section 38. If he fails to do so he will be barred from all relief: Common Law Procedure Act 1852, section 210. The six months time limit will also apply to a mortgagee (see the UDT case above).

Where the tenant owes less than six months rent, he can apply for relief at any time after the possession order has been made. The six-month time limit does not apply. The court's power arises from its equitable jurisdiction but it will take account of any delay when considering the application for relief: *Thatcher v C H Pearce & Sons (Contractors) Ltd* [1968] 1 WLR 748; *Di Palma v Victoria Square Property Co Ltd* [1984] 1 Ch 346 at p 366.

Procedure for Relief

The application for relief in the county court (or if, rarely, the proceedings are in the High Court) should be made by counterclaim (CPR Part 20) in the landlord's proceedings. If the tenancy is in joint names all joint tenants should join in the application for relief.

Relief is at the discretion of the court upon such terms as the court thinks fit, but is invariably granted where the tenant is prepared to pay the outstanding rent and the landlord's costs unless this would cause injustice. If the landlord has re-let, see *Fuller* v *Judy Properties Ltd* [1992] 14 EG 106 (p xx below).

FORFEITURE FOR BREACHES OTHER THAN NONPAYMENT OF RENT

1.   SECTION 146 NOTICE

Where the tenant is in breach of a covenant other than the covenant to pay rent, the landlord cannot exercise his rights under the forfeiture clause unless he has first served a notice under section 146 of the Law of Property Act 1925 (subject to the exceptions set out in s 146(9) and (10)). Section 146 cannot be excluded by agreement of the parties.

A Section 146 Notice will also be required if the landlord wishes to forfeit the lease for non-payment of service charges or other sums due to the landlord not expressly reserved as rent. Any consultation or certification procedure for service charges set out in the lease must also have been followed. The restrictions in the Housing Act 1996 and generally in relation to residential service charges do not apply to commercial premises.

Once the landlord or his agent has knowledge of the breach, he must ensure that the right to forfeit is not waived (see below). In particular, no further rent should be demanded or accepted.

Contents of Section 146 Notice

The notice must:

* specify the particular breach complained of;
* require it to be remedied if this is possible; and
* require the tenant to make compensation in money for the breach, if the landlord requires such compensation.

See Precedents 4 and 5 for specimen Section 146 Notices. The Section 146 Notice does not have to tell the tenant how he is to remedy the breach: *John Lewis Properties plc* v *Viscount Chelsea* [1993] 34 EG 116. It must however specify the breach: *Adagio Properties Ltd* v *Adagio* [1998] 35 EG 86.

Whether a breach is capable of remedy depends upon the application of the decision in *Savva* v *Houssein* [1996] 47 EG 138. Prior to that case it was thought that the issue of whether a breach could be remedied depended upon the effect it had on the landlord and whether the damage suffered could be remedied. Breach of a positive covenant could usually be remedied.

Negative covenants were not so straightforward. They are more difficult to remedy than positive covenants. Breaches of the alienation covenants had been held to be irremediable, as had breaches of a covenant not to use premises for illegal or immoral purposes: *Rugby School (Governors)* v *Tannahill* [1935] 1 KB 87.

However, in *Savva* the court held that all covenants (other than alienation covenants) are remediable if the mischief caused by the breach can be remedied. This will apply to positive and negative covenants, once and for all and continuing ones.

If a breach can be remedied, the notice must require the tenant to do so. If it cannot be remedied there is no such requirement. If the landlord's solicitor is unsure whether the breach is capable of remedy he should require it to be remedied and include in the Notice the words "if it is capable of remedy".

For breaches capable of remedy, the tenant must be given a reasonable time to remedy them. What is reasonable will depend upon the facts of each case. For example, three months, ordinarily, may be sufficient for a breach of a repairing covenant. On the other hand, six months may be appropriate in relation to a Notice served just before the onset of winter which requires the tenant to attend to substantial works of external decoration. It is important that no specific time limit as such is mentioned in the Notice. If the tenant fails to remedy the breach within a reasonable time of service of the Section 146 Notice and to make compensation in money to the landlord's satisfaction (assuming the landlord requires this), the landlord may proceed to forfeit by peaceable re-entry or the issue of possession proceedings. Even if the breach is incapable of remedy the landlord should wait a short period, say 14 days, before proceeding to forfiet to enable the tenant to consider his position following service of the notice: *Scala House & District Property Co Ltd* v *Forbes* [1974] QB 575. Five days has been held to be too brief: *Courtney Lodge Management Ltd* v *Blake* All ER (D) 30 July.

Service

The Section 146 Notice must be served upon the tenant, or all the tenants if there are more than one. If there has been an unlawful assignment, the

Section 146 Notice should be served on the assignee rather than the assignor because, although unlawful, the assignment will have served to transfer the lease to the assignee: *Fuller* v *Judy Properties Ltd* [1992] 14 EG 106. However, in the case of registered land, the legal estate will not be transferred until registration (*Brown and Root Technology Ltd* v *Sun Alliance Assurance Co Ltd* (1997) *The Times* 27th January), and therefore the assignor must be served. Accordingly, if there is any doubt as to whether an assignment has actually taken place – e.g. in circumstances in which a breach of the alienation covenants may be suspected – the prudent landlord will effect service of the Section 146 Notice on both the suspected assignee and assignor. The Notice does not have to be served on subtenants or mortgagees, but the landlord may wish to do so to alert them to the situation so that, if appropriate, an application for relief from forfeiture can be made.

Service of the Notice should be effected in accordance with section 196 of the Law of Property Act 1925 by:

1. sending the Notice by registered post or recorded delivery addressed to the tenant at his last-known place of abode or business, or
2. leaving it at the tenant's last-known place of abode or business, or
3. affixing it or leaving it for him on the demised premises.

Notices served pursuant to section 196 are served even if not brought to the attention of the recipient (*Kinch* v *Bullard* [1998] 47 EG 140). However, the most satisfactory form of service is the third method, because evidence of service can easily be adduced by the process server or managing agent who effected service. For a specimen letter of instruction, see Precedent 13.

In the case of repairing covenants, section 18(2) of the Landlord and Tenant Act 1927 provides that service of the notice must be known to the tenant, any underlessee or the person who last paid the rent, and the period for remedying the breach runs from the date service became known to him.

Leasehold Property (Repairs) Act 1938

If the lease was originally granted for a period of seven years or more, and more than three years remain unexpired at the date of service of the Section 146 Notice, the notice (in so far as it relates to a breach of the repairing covenants) must comply with the requirements of the Leasehold Property (Repairs) Act 1938. The notice must be served on the tenant at least one month prior to starting proceedings and it must state that the tenant has a right to serve a counter-notice within 28 days of service. If such a counter-notice is served the landlord cannot commence forfeiture proceedings (or sue for dilapidations) without leave of the court. In seeking leave the landlord must establish one of the five grounds in section 1(5) of the Act.

Waiver

When a breach of covenant occurs, the landlord can decide whether to determine the lease or allow it to continue. Once the landlord is on notice of an act or omission that would permit him to determine the lease, he must ensure he does nothing to waive the breach on which he wishes to rely.

The law is complex and great care must be taken:

> "When one approaches the law relating to waiver of forfeiture, one comes upon a field – one might say a minefield – in which it is necessary to tread with diffidence and warily. That is to no small degree due to the number of points in that field that are of a highly technical nature..." (per Sachs J in *Segal Securities Ltd* v *Thoseby* [1963] 1 QB 887 at 897).

The landlord will lose his right to forfeit if he does any act which recognises the continuation of the tenancy after becoming aware of the breach. The landlord must have knowledge of the breach when the alleged act of waiver takes place. Knowledge by a landlord's employee may be sufficient to constitute waiver: *Metropolitan Properties Co Ltd* v *Cordery* (1979) 39 P & CR 10. If the landlord knows of matters which could constitute a breach and makes enquiry of the tenant who falsely persuades him that there has been no breach, this will not constitute waiver: *Chrisdell Ltd* v *Johnson* [1987] 2 ECT.R 123.

The key element in waiver is knowledge of the tacts which give rise-to the right to forfeit. In effect the landlord is put to his election once he becomes aware of a breach of covenant by the tenant; he can either forfeit the lease or alternatively treat the lease as continuing by waiving the breach. Waiver cannot arise from constructive knowledge, such as the advertisement of a winding-up order in the London Gazette: *Official Custodian for Charities* v *Parway Estates Developments Ltd* [1985] Ch 151. But if the landlord knows of facts that give rise to the right to forfeit, he will be taken to know the legal effect of those facts: *David Blackstone Ltd* v *Burnetts (West End) Ltd* [1973] 1 WLR 1487. The fact that the landlord did not intend to waive the breach is irrelevant: *Cornhillie* v *Saha* [1996] 28 HLR 561. It is not necessary for the landlord to have served a section 146 Notice first before he can be said to have waived the breach: *First Penthouse Ltd* v *Channel Hotels and Properties Ltd* [2003] EWHC 2713.

The definitive test of waiver is set out in *Central Estates Belgravia Ltd* v *Woolgar* (No 2) [1972] 3 All ER 610, where it was held that the test is objective. The landlord's intention is immaterial. If the landlord knows of the breach and does an act which is communicated to the tenant and unequivocally recognises that the lease continues (in that case an error by a clerk which led to the rent being demanded) this will constitute waiver. In

John Lewis Properties plc v *Viscount Chelsea* [1993] 34 EG 116 Mummery J held that the receipt of rent by the landlord's bankers would not (had there been a breach of covenant) have amounted to a waiver because the landlord had made it clear by letter that it would not accept or demand rent by reason of the alleged breach of covenant and had later returned the rent paid. The bankers had no authority to make business decisions on behalf of its customer. There had been delay on the part of the landlord in returning to the tenant the rent paid into its bank account but the judge held that the landlord's conduct, objectively considered, had not given the tenant any ground for supposing that the rent had, in fact, been accepted. The onus of proving that the landlord had the requisite knowledge is on the tenant: *Matthews* v *Smallwood* [1910] 1 Ch 777.

Acts of waiver will include demanding or accepting rent (and this cannot be avoided by accepting or demanding on a "without prejudice" basis – see *Expert Clothing Service & Sales Ltd* v *Hillgate House Ltd* [1986] Ch 340). If a payment of money is tendered and accepted as "payment for use and occupation" this may not constitute waiver. But payments tendered as rent cannot be accepted as use and occupation payments without waiving any breach: *Croft* v *Lumley* (1858) 6 HLC 672; 10 ER 1459. Therefore, it is usually safer not to accept any such payments. Other acts of waiver will include entering the premises to carry out repairs, levying distress, granting licences, claiming an injunction, registering notices of assignment, serving Law of Distress (Amendment) Act notices, notices to quit, rent review notices or notices pursuant to section 25 of the Landlord and Tenant Act 1954. Service of a Section 146 Notice is not itself a waiver of a right to forfeit either in respect of that breach or any other breach: *Church Commissioners for England* v *Nodjoumi* (1985) 51 P & CR 155. Without prejudice negotiations or mere inactivity by the landlord (as long as there is no other act recognising the continuance of the lease) will not amount to waiver. Waiver requires a positive act by the landlord that affirms the existence of the tenancy, or conduct by the landlord constituting acquiescence in the breach over a long period: *Wolfe* v *Hogan* [1949] 2 KB 194. Whether acceptance of rent from a surety or by deduction from a rent deposit constitutes waiver is unclear.

If a rent demand is prepared and sent out by the landlord but not received by the tenant, this will not constitute waiver: *Trustees of Henry Smith's Charity* v *Willson* [1983] QB 316. Nor will a demand for insurance premiums not reserved as rent: *Yorkshire Metropolitan Properties Ltd* v *Co-op Retail Services Ltd* [1997] EGCS 57. Distress for rent whether due before or after the breach will constitute waiver: *Green's Case* (1582) Cro Eliz 3; 78 ER 269.

Service of a notice under section 25 of the Landlord and Tenant Act 1954 Part II may constitute waiver. Accordingly, where a breach of covenant occurs towards the end of a lease, the writ seeking forfeiture should be served before the Section 25 Notice. Once the writ has been served the Section 25 Notice opposing a new lease can then be served on the basis that it will take effect if relief from forfeiture is granted.

Waiver will only affect breaches that occurred prior to the act of waiver. If the breach re-occurs or continues thereafter a new cause of action will arise to permit the landlord to make a new election whether or not to forfeit: *Iperion Investments Corporation* v *Broadwalk House Residents Ltd* [1992] 2 EGLR 235.

The effect of a waiver depends on the nature of the breach: breaches of covenant arc either once-and-for-all or continuing breaches (see the table at p 55). A once-and-for-all breach is characterised by a covenant which requires an act to be carried out by a certain time, or a covenant which prohibits an act throughout the term where the breach is not on-going. A continuing breach does not take place at one point but extends over a period or time. A continuing breach is characterised by a covenant that imposes on the tenant a continuing obligation to comply with it and the breach of that obligation is a continuing act or omission. Both the obligation and the breach must, therefore, be of a continuing nature.

If the breach is a continuing one (such as a breach of the repairing covenants), the landlord may waive an earlier breach but his right to forfeit will continue in respect of later breaches after the act of waiver.

For once-and-for-all breaches, waiver will be fatal to the landlord's right to forfeit. Rent should not be demanded or accepted once the breach is known, unless the rent relates to a period prior to the breach of covenant: see the reasoning in *David Blackstone Ltd* v *Burnetts (West End) Ltd* [1973] 1 WLR 1487 and *Capital & City Holdings Ltd* v *Warburg* [1989] 1 EGLR 90, which confirms a landlord may accept rent which fell due before he knew about the right to forfeit. Receipt of rent that accrued due before the breach of covenant will not constitute a waiver of the right to forfeit as that rent is due even if the lease is terminated. Demand or acceptance of rent due in arrear will only constitute waiver of the right to forfeit for the period up to the date that the rent fell due: *Penton* v *Barnett* [1898] 1 QB 276. But demand or acceptance of rent due in advance will waive past and continuing breaches known of at the time of the demand or acceptance: *Segal Securities Ltd* v *Thoseby* (see above). However, a landlord may prefer not to accept any rent, even if it accrued due before the breach, to avoid giving the tenant an argument on waiver, even though, strictly, such acceptance is not a waiver.

If the tenant pays rent direct to the landlord's bank account, will this constitute waiver? In *John Lewis Properties plc* v *Viscount Chelsea* [1993] 34 EG 116 the landlord refused to accept rent for two of three leases. Nevertheless the tenant sent rent for all three tenancies by one cheque to the landlord's bank where the rent was credited to the landlord's account. The landlord repaid the rent relating to the two leases under dispute to the tenant and it was, therefore, held that this did not constitute waiver.

Once forfeiture proceedings have been issued and served, the landlord is considered to have unequivocally decided to determine the lease so that any subsequent act by the landlord will be most unlikely to be treated as waiver: *Civil Service Co-op Society* v *McGrigor's Trustee* [1923] 2 Ch 347. Demanding or accepting rent may, however, be held to be referable to the grant of a new tenancy although rent received from a third party will only amount to re-entry if the landlord had the requisite intention: *Cromwell Developments Ltd* v *Godfrey* [1998] 3 EG 72. Any monies accepted at that time should, therefore, be expressed to be mesne profits to avoid the suggestion of the grant of a new tenancy, or should be the subject of an interim payment order (see p 55).

Effect of forfeiture

Forfeiture determines the lease. Where forfeiture is effected by peaceable re-entry it takes effect from the date the landlord re-enters.

Where forfeiture takes place by court action the lease is forfeited on the date of service of the court proceedings. The subsequent order for possession has retrospective effect to the date of service of the proceedings.

Generally speaking the provisions of the lease come to an end on service of the proceedings and the tenant need not comply with the covenants: *Associated Deliveries Ltd* v *Harrison* (1984) 272 EG 321. The landlord cannot obtain an interlocutory injunction during this period: *Wheeler* v *Keeble (1914) Limited* [1920] 1 Ch 57. Pending an order for possession, there are, however, some covenants which may continue to bind the landlord (such as repairing obligations and quiet enjoyment). Service of the court proceedings seeking for forfeiture does not automatically end the lease but it is an unequivocal election by the landlord to rely on the breach of covenant: *Ivory Gate Ltd* v *Spetale* [1998] EGGS 69. It was put in this way by Stephenson LJ in *Peninsula Maritime Ltd* v *Padseal Ltd* (1981) 259 EG 860:

> "... landlord who has unequivocally elected to determine a lease by serving a writ and forfeiting it cannot himself rely on any covenants of the lease in any shape or form, or any covenants in it, but the tenant who has not elected to determine the lease can do so."

If the tenant obtains relief from forfeiture the lease will be reinstated as if nothing had happened: *Liverpool Properties Ltd* v *Oldbridge Investments Ltd* [1985] 2 EGLR 111. Rent will therefore continue to be due continuing up to (and as a condition of) the relief: *Maryland Estates Ltd* v *Bar*

Joseph [1998] 27 EG 142. If relief is not granted, rent will be due up to the date of service of the procedures (which will include a full quarter's rent if the rent is payable in advance and the relevant due date has passed) and mesne profits from then until the tenant gives up occupation: *Capital and City Holdings Ltd* v *Dean Warburg Ltd* [1989] 1 EGLR 90.

Pending the making of a final possession order or the hearing of the tenant's application for relief, the lease is in a state of limbo. It is not known whether the forfeiture will be effective, whether the breaches of covenant alleged will be proved or relief granted. This has been described as the "twilight" period by Sir Robert Megarry V-C in *Meadows* v *Clerical, Medical and General Life Assurance Society* [1981] 1 Ch 70. The attributes of the lease during this period are unclear, although a tenant who has a subsisting claim for relief still has sufficient interest in it to apply for a new tenancy pursuant to the Landlord and Tenant Act 1954, Part II: *Meadows* v *Clerical, Medical and General Life Assurance Society* (above).

If the tenant does not seek or obtain relief a sub-tenant or mortgagee may apply. Relief granted to a sub-tenant or mortgagee will be by the vesting of a new lease rather than by reinstatement of the old one. Therefore, from the date of forfeiture until the commencement of the new lease, the landlord will be entitled to the income from the premises: *Official Custodian for Charities* v *Mackey* [1985] Ch 168.

It has been suggested that a landlord could withdraw the proceedings and, in effect, cancel the forfeiture at any time until the possession order was made. This would seem to be incorrect if, after service of court proceedings claiming forfeiture, the landlord's right to forfeit is admitted by the tenant in its defence. In those circumstances a landlord cannot claim that the lease is not forfeit, even if his original action was based on a mistake of fact: *G S Fashions Ltd* v *B & Q plc* [1995] 1 WLR 1088. It was held that the decision to forfeit was a once-and-for-all election by the landlord analogous to the acceptance by one party to a contract of a wrongful repudiation by the other. The court did not, however, make any findings relating to the position of a sub-tenant or mortgagee, nor did it decide the effect of a landlord seeking to withdraw from a Forfeiture action in a case where the tenant, in his defence, denied the landlord's right to forfeit.

However, unless the forfeiture is admitted, discontinuance of the proceedings by the landlord *will* reinstate the lease: *Mount Cook Ltd* v *The Media Business Centre Ltd* [2004] EWHC 348 (Ch).

2.   COURT PROCEEDINGS

The procedure to obtain an order for possession following a breach of covenant other than the covenant to pay rent is governed by CPR Part 55 and therefore is identical to the procedure for seeking a possession order based on nonpayment of rent, save that service of the Section 146 Notice must be pleaded.

Application for interim payment order

However, if the tenant has raised a substantial defence and/or counterclaim, application should be made by the landlord for an interim payment order (CPR Part 25 Rule 6). To make such an application the landlord's must satisfy the court that if the case went to trial, the defendant would be held liable (even if the possession claim fails) to pay the landlord for use and occupation of the land. The burden of proof is the civil standard of the balance of probabilities under the previous rules. If there was more than one Defendant the landlord had to prove under the previous court rules that he would obtain an award against a specific Defendant – the application could not be based simply on the fact that the landlord expects to obtain an award against one unspecified Defendant. The CPR make no such provision for interim payments in possession cases but the effect of CPR Part 25 Rule 7 (1) (d) is likely to require this.

Breach of covenant	Once-and-for-all	Continuing	Remediable	Irremediable
Non payment of rent	✓		✓	
Unlawful alienation by assigning/subletting	✓			✓
Insolvency	✓			✓
Unlawful alteration	✓		✓	
Disrepair		✓	✓	
Failure to insure		✓	✓	
Wrongful use		✓	✓	
*Illegal/immoral use	✓	✓		✓

It is not possible to lay down any hard and fast rules for this type of user case. The authorities cannot be distilled into one clear principle. From the landlord's point of view, therefore, it is safest to assume that (a) the breach is once-and-for-all, and (b) it may be capable of remedy

Whenever possible an interim payment order should be sought at the earliest opportunity to establish an income flow for the landlord. The interim payment may be specified to be for a continuing sum to be paid on each of the forthcoming quarter days – the equivalent of future rent.

An application for an interim payment order may be combined, in the alternative, with an application for summary judgment to cover the situation if the application for summary judgment is unsuccessful.

The application must be supported by evidence, and copies of both must be served on the Defendant at least 14 days before the hearing of the application. See Precedents 8 and 9 for a specimen notice of application and evidence in support.

The application may be made at any time after the proceedings have been issued.

Relief

Whether the proceedings are in the High Court or the county court, the tenant may apply for relief pursuant to section 146(2) of the Law of Property Act 1925. The application must be made before the landlord has executed the possession order (unless the judgment is later set aside). If the tenant fails to apply in time he cannot then invoke a right to relief: *Smith* v *Metropolitan City Properties Ltd* [1986] 1 EGLR 52, and see the dicta of Lord Templeman in *Billson* v *Residential Apartments Ltd* [1992] 1 All ER 141 at p 147.

The application for relief is made by counterclaim (CPR Part 20) in the landlord's proceedings. Where there is more than one tenant, they should all join in the application.

Relief may be granted by the court at its discretion on such terms as it thinks fit including costs, expenses and damages. The court will usually grant relief where the tenant has already remedied the breach, or will grant relief conditional upon the tenant remedying within a specific time. In addition the court will usually require the tenant to pay compensation and undertake to comply with any negative covenants: *Hyman* v *Rose* [1912] AC 623.

Relief is likely to be refused if there is no evidence to indicate that the defendant will comply with any conditions the court would impose: *Ellison* v *Residential Apartments Ltd* (No.2) [1993] EGGS 150.

It appears from *Darlington Borough Council* v *Denmark Chemists Ltd* [1993] 02 EG 117, CA that, although in a proper case an appeal court can exercise a fresh discretion under section 146(2) where circumstances have changed, it will not do so if it appears that the tenant would be unlikely or unable to remedy the breach of covenant because, for example, of lack of funds.

Further consideration of relief in specific cases is given in the relevant chapters below Where a tenant seeks relief due to a collateral claim against the landlord, this will only usually be granted if the tenant would be able to remedy the breach (aften payment of rent arrears) even if that collaterial claim fails: *Inntrepreneur Pub Co v Langton* [2000] 8 EG 169.

Some principles, however, can be derived from the following cases:

- *Wilful or deliberate breaches*
  Although the Court may be less inclined to exercise its discretion, there is no rule that relief should only be granted exceptionally in cases where the breach was wilful: *Southern Depot Co Limited v British Railway Board* [1990] 2 EGLR 39.
- *Whether the tenant has made or will make good the breach and is able and willing to fulfil the Lease in the future*
  This may well be relevant for the court to consider if it is going to refuse consent, but cogent evidence will be necessary to support this allega- tion: *Darlington Borough Council v Denmark Chemists Limited* [1993] 1 EGLR 62.
- *The personal hardship that will be suffered by the tenant if relief is not granted*
  This is unlikely to be persuasive as a reason for the tenant to obtain relief especially if the tenant has a claim against another party, such as his so- licitor: *St Marylebone Property Company Limited v Tesco Stores Limited and Patel* [1988] 2 EGLR 40.
- *Although the action was undertaken without the landlord's consent, he could not reasonably have refused consent*
  This will not be determinative as there may be very good reasons why the landlord would be able to withhold consent (such as a refusal to answer reasonable questions: *Sood v Barker* [1991] 1 EGLR 87).
- *Whether the breach has occasioned lasting damage to the landlord*
  This may be relevant: *Ropemaker Properties Limited v Noonhaven Limited* [1989] 2 EGLR 50

COSTS OF FORFEITURE PROCEEDINGS

If a landlord obtains a possession order he will also seek an order for payment of costs by the tenant in the usual way. Section 146(3) of the Law of Property Act 1925 provides that the landlord may recover all reasonable costs and expenses, including those of a solicitor and surveyor employed by the landlord in connection with a breach giving rise to a right of re-entry or forfeiture, even if the tenant obtains relief. The landlord will, therefore, normally obtain an order for payment of costs. At one time this had often been on an indemnity basis, but following the dicta of Lord Templeman in *Billson* (see above) this is now only likely to be on the standard basis unless the lease expressly provides for payment of indemnity costs, or possibly if the breach is deliberate: *Iperion Investments Corporation* v *Broadwalk House Residents Ltd* [1992] 2 EGLR 235. If the lease does provide for payment of indemnity costs, these will usually be ordered: *Church Commissioners for England* v *Ibrahim* [1997] 3 EG 136. In *Billson* v *Residential Apartments Ltd* (No.3) [1993] EGGS 155, costs on the indemnity basis were refused. The court had been critical of the action taken by the tenant but it fell short of the behaviour required to attract an order for costs on the indemnity basis and costs were, therefore, ordered on the standard basis.

If the tenant complies with the Section 146 Notice so that there are no court proceedings, the landlord cannot recover his costs under section 146(3): *Nind* v *Nineteenth Century Building Society* [1894] 2 QB 226. But the landlord will usually seek to get over this difficulty by imposing on the tenant an express covenant in the lease to pay all costs, charges and expenses (including legal costs and any fees payable to a surveyor) incurred by the landlord and incidental to the preparation and service of a Section 146 Notice, notwithstanding that forfeiture is avoided otherwise than by relief granted by the court. In the case of repairs the landlord can recover costs under section 146 (3) only with the leave of the court if the tenant claims the benefit of the Leasehold Property (Repairs) Act 1938 – see section 2 of that Act, and Chapter 19.

However, in an undefended possession claim, fixed costs will only generally apply if one of the grounds for possession is arrears of rent (and whether or not the Possession Order is suspended): see CPR Schedule 2 CCR Order 38 Appendix B Part 2 paragraph D (ii).

Even where the proceedings are defended, the court will look carefully at any claim for costs, particularly if this is not covered by a contractual entitlement under the lease. The courts are keen to ensure that landlords do not incur unreasonable costs for which they then seek an order for payment by the defendant tenant. On the other hand, where the tenant has prolonged proceedings unnecessarily he is unlikely to find favour with the court.

The courts will look carefully at the parties' conduct (including in the pre-action period) when awarding costs that are in the court's discretion (as opposed to those contractually due under the lease), and to take account of the overriding objective and the principle of proportionality.

CHAPTER 4
PEACEABLE RE-ENTRY

CHAPTER 4
PEACEABLE RE-ENTRY

Peaceable re-entry for non-payment of rent or other breach of covenant is a self-help remedy which a landlord may employ without obtaining a court order. Although there have been judicial dicta disapproving of the remedy – in *Billson* v *Residential Apartments Ltd* [1992] 1 All ER 141 it was referred to by Lord Templeman as a "dubious" method of proceeding compared with the "civilised" method of issuing court proceedings – its legality is "beyond question": Lord Denning MR in *McPhail* v *Persons Unknown* [1973] 1 Ch 447. The Law Commission has proposed that it should be abolished but it remains a valid remedy at the date of publication.

CONDITIONS FOR EXERCISING A RIGHT OF PEACEABLE RE-ENTRY

As in any case where the landlord seeks to forfeit, a right to do so must be expressly reserved in the lease, and the grounds for forfeiture have arisen.

Whenever the landlord wishes to re-enter for non-payment of rent or service charges reserved as rent, the sums claimed must have fallen due and been formally demanded, unless the requirement for a formal demand is dispensed with either in the lease or by statute – sec Chapter 3. If the lease dispenses with the need for a formal demand, a landlord may take peaceable re-entry even if the tenant has had no invoice for the rent due: *Railtrack plc* v *Ohajah* [2000] EGCS 88. Moreover, the arrears must really exist: *Televantos* v *McCulloch* [1991] I EGLR 123. However, a landlord may effect peaceable re-entry even if the benefit of the outstanding arrears has been assigned to the landlord's predecessor in title: *Kataria* v *Safeland plc* (1997) *The Times*, December 3.

If the landlord wishes to re-enter for a breach of some other covenant the formalities of service of a notice under section 146 of the Law of Property Act 1925 must have been complied with and, where appropriate, the tenant must have been given a reasonable time to remedy the breach(es) specified unless sub-sections (8)–(10) of section 146 apply.

There must, of course, have been no waiver by the landlord of the breach of covenant. Demand and/or acceptance of rent which accrued due before the grounds for forfeiture arose, and the issue and service of court proceedings, and obtaining judgment will not constitute waiver of the right to peaceably re-enter: *Re a Debtor* (No. 13/A/10 of 1995) [1995] 41 EG 142.

RE-ENTRY

There must be some final and unequivocal act by the landlord to constitute actual re-entry: *Hone* v *Daejan Properties* [1976] 2 EGLR 10. Entry for another purpose – for example, securing the premises if the tenant has left – is not sufficient: *Relvok Properties Ltd* v *Dixon* (1972) 25 P & CR 1. The landlord does not need to evict the tenant as such; he must merely re-enter. Leases often provide that re-entry on part of the demised premises will constitute re-entry of the whole. Otherwise a landlord cannot re-enter only part of the premises, leaving part of the demise extant.

Re-entry is generally effected by changing the locks to exclude the tenant from the premises: *Eaton Square Properties Ltd* v *Beveridge* [1993] EGCS 91. A practical approach for effecting peaceable re-entry is set out below (see page 68).

The grant of a new lease of the premises to a third party may constitute forfeiture: *Redleaf Investments Ltd* v *Talbot* (1994) *The Times*, 5 May.

Re-letting the demised premises to a sub-tenant will be a sufficient act of re-entry to forfeit the lease to the tenant. Allowing the subtenant to remain in occupation on the same terms as his current subtenancy is, apparently, insufficient to constitute re-entry: *Ashton* v *Sobelman* [1987] 1 WLR 177. The landlord should, therefore, make it clear to the sub-tenant that he is granting him a new lease, albeit on the same or similar terms.

STATUTORY RESTRICTIONS

The restrictions on effecting peaceable re-entry of residential property are considerably wider than those applying to commercial premises. Physical re-entry of commercial premises is restricted by the following statutory provisions:

1.   CRIMINAL LAW ACT 1977, S 6

Any person who, without lawful authority to do so, uses or threatens violence for the purpose of securing entry into any premises either for himself or for someone else commits an offence if:

1. there is someone present on the premises at the time who is opposed to the entry which the violence is intended to secure, and
2. the person using or threatening the violence knows that that is the case.

A right to forfeit by re-entry will not constitute "lawful authority" for the purposes of the Act and accordingly, in practice, where the tenant or his representative is present on the premises violence must be avoided. This does not prevent forcible re-entry, merely violence. In practice, if there is someone present at the premises it would be wise not to attempt peaceable re-entry until the premises are unoccupied.

There is little judicial guidance as to what will constitute violence. It will be a question of fact in each case. Violence can be against a person or the property. Breaking open a door is likely to constitute violence (*Hemmings* v *Stoke Poges Golf Club* [1920] 1 KB 720), but breaking a small pane of glass to effect entry, using a credit card to slip the locks, or removing padlocks or bars (see *Williams* v *Taperell* (1892) 8 TLR 241) is not likely to be violence. Indeed the *Williams* case also seems to suggest that cutting through boards preventing entry through a door will be acceptable, although this would appear to be close to the dividing line. Breaking locks has been held to be lawful: *Razzaq* v *Pala* [1997] 38 EG 157.

Breach of section 6 may lead to criminal liability, but if no more than reasonable force is used it is thought that no claim for civil damages is likely to arise (see *Hemmings* v *Stoke Poges Golf Club* above), and although the landlord may have committed a crime, the re-entry will be effective.

2. INSOLVENCY

Prior to the Insolvency Act 2000 there were several cases dealing with whether forfeiture by peaceable re-entry (and/or levying distress) was restricted by the Insolvency Act 1986. Although the cases initially prohibited this, subsequent cases made it plain that a right of re-entry did not constitute enforcement of a security and was therefore permissible.

The position has now been clarified by the 2000 Act.

The landlord's right to rely on the remedy of peaceable re-entry is now as follows.

Companies:

1. After a petition for an administration order has been presented and during the period for which an administration order is in force: the landlord's right to take peaceable re-entry may only be pursued with the consent of the administrator or the leave of the court.

2. The landlord's right to proceed where there is a compulsory winding up order is the same as under an administration order.
3. There is no restriction when an administrative receiver or Law of Property Act receiver has been appointed (although note that post-15 September 2003 most floating charges can only be enforced by administration so the restrictions in 1. above apply).
4. Peaceable entry may not be pursued without the leave of the court during the moratorium for small companies (as defined in section 247 Companies Act 1985) or once a CVA has been approved by creditors. It may be used prior to the CVA being approved or for post-CVA new debts.

Individuals:

Peacable re-entry remains available in bankruptcy cases. In *McMullen & Sons Ltd* v *Cerrone* (1993) 66 P & CR 351 the court held that distress did not amount to "other legal process" under section 252 of the Insolvency Act, and that accordingly distress was not prohibited. It was said that "proceedings" was confined to judicial proceedings and the reference to "other legal process" covered only judicial enforcement proceedings or process. Applied to cases of peaceable re-entry, the potential restrictions under the Insolvency Act will be substantially diminished. In *Re a Debtor No 13A 10 of 1995* [1995] 41 EG 142, the *McMullen* approach was adopted and the court held that peaceable re-entry did not constitute "other proceedings...execution... or other legal process". Accordingly section 252 did not prevent peaceable re-entry.

During the moratorium for individuals exploring an IVA, peaceable entry may not be taken without the leave of the court and may not be taken after that moratorium when the IVA has been approved by creditors. It may be used for a post-IVA new debt. (see section 252 as amended by the Insolvency Act 2000).

3.   LEASEHOLD PROPERTY (REPAIRS) ACT 1938

Where the landlord wishes to proceed by peaceable re-entry following a breach of repairing covenants in the lease, he cannot do so if the Act applies, as section 1(3) prevents forfeiture by action or otherwise without leave of the court. Peaceable re-entry will, therefore, be permissible only if leave is first obtained.

4.   PROTECTION FROM EVICTION ACT 1977, S 2

Enforcement of a right of forfeiture is prohibited by section 2 other than by court proceedings if any person is lawfully residing in premises "let as a dwelling". Ordinarily this provision will have no application to commercial leases, but there may be instances where a commercial lease has a mixed business and residential use. Will such a lease be protected by section 2? It is submitted that the test will be to consider the purpose of the letting, which must have been mainly for residential use for section 2 to apply. Accordingly the section may not prohibit peaceable re-entry where the premises comprise a shop with flat above: *Pulleng* v *Curren* (1980) 44 P & CR 58.

5. HUMAN RIGHTS ACT 1998

The Human Rights Act 1998 came into force on 2 October 2000. It incorporates into English law the European Convention on Human Rights. It has been said that the exercise of a right of peaceable re-entry engages three rights under the Act namely:

- Article 6 (1):
  "In the determination of his civil rights and obligations . . . everyone is entitled to a fair and public hearing within a reasonable time by an independent and impartial tribunal established by law".
- Article 8:
  "Everyone has the right to respect for his private life [and] his home . . .".
- Article 1 of the First Protocol:
  "Every natural or legal person is entitled to the peaceful enjoyment of his possessions. No one shall be deprived of his possessions except in the public interest and subject to the conditions provided for by law and by the general principles of international law...".

As forfeiture involves a determination of a tenant's rights it is said that the procedural requirements of Article 6 are engaged. However, as a right to forfeiture arises only if a tenant is in default, it is highly arguable that there is no dispute (or "contestation") and as the tenant must show he has a reasonable claim in domestic law, arguably Article 6 does not apply. This is particularly so because where a landlord has re-entered wrongfully a claim for damages is available: *South Tottenham Land Securities* v *R & A Millett (Shops)* [1983] 2 EGLR 122. Furthermore, in cases of wrongful re-entry domestic law provides a remedy and indeed the tenant remains able to seek relief from forfeiture.

As far as Article 8 is concerned, the European Court has held that the concept of a "home" is capable of being extended to business premises: *Nienietz* v *Germany* (1992) 16 EHRR 97. However in that case it was stated that business premises would have less intense protection. In any event, a landlord would expect to be able to rely on the qualifications to Article 8 rights by arguing that as the interference with a tenant's rights was in accordance with the law (because it was pursuant to a contractual right and did not offend against any other law), that it was to pursue a legitimate aim (namely the right of the landlord to receive rent which is itself protected by Article 1 of the First Protocol: *Mellacher* v *Austria* (1989) 12 EHRR 391; and the interference was necessary and proportionate because there was a good reason for the action and there were existing safeguards under English law.

The principal concern of Article 1 of the First Protocol is to protect individuals against actions of the state. Therefore it is to be expected that a court would be unlikely to rule that peaceable re-entry was a breach of this Article particularly as the court would be balancing the tenant's right to occupation with the landlord's right to receive rent. Furthermore the re-entry would be for a legitimate purpose (namely to allow a landlord to re-enter premises where the tenant was not paying rent and make them available for re-letting) and the re-entry would not impose an excessive burden (in that it was envisaged by the original lease).

Although the arguments relating to peaceable re-entry have not as yet been tested by the courts, it is highly arguable that peaceable re-entry does not constitute a breach of the Human Rights Act.

THE MERITS OF PHYSICAL RE-ENTRY

Although there are a number of potential benefits for a landlord forfeiting by peaceable re-entry, there are also several possible drawbacks which must be considered.

Following the decision in *Billson* v *Residential Apartments Ltd* [1992] 1 All ER 141, a landlord should think carefully when repossessing the premises without a court order.

The advantage of being able to get the premises back quickly and cheaply knowing that there is virtually no possibility of an application for relief being made, let alone succeeding, has now gone. Indeed, there may even be a disadvantage in physically retaking possession. In cases of relief from forfeiture where court proceedings are involved the landlord knows more or less where he stands in terms of how long he will have to wait for any application for relief to be made. In the *Billson* situation however – and even where the breach is nonpayment of rent – the landlord cannot be sure how long the courts will allow the tenant to apply for relief except that it will probably be about six months. The period within which an application may be made is not entirely clear (see p 69 below). However, a tenant who delays may find relief is refused: *Somers Mews Investments* v *Miller* 29.1.1982 (unrep). It has been suggested that relief would not he granted if the landlord had re-let. However, it would now seem that in the case of a re-letting to a tenant who has no notice of the previous tenant's application, any relief subsequently granted to the tenant will be on the basis that he is given an interest as the immediate reversioner to the new tenant. The new tenant will be entitled to remain in occupation but must pay rent to the old tenant, who will in turn be liable for rent under his now revived lease to the landlord. If the landlord has obtained a premium on the grant of the new lease this will become due to the tenant – see *Fuller* v *Judy Properties Ltd* [1992] 14 EG 106. Although the landlord may be anxious to re-let the premises, he will have to make full disclosure of the background situation to any prospective new tenant(s) who may well be nervous about taking a new lease in such an open-ended situation. Alternatively, earlier case authority had suggested that third party rights created by a new letting may defeat the claim for relief: *Silverman v AFCO (UK)* [1988] 1 EGLR 51.

Alternatively, the tenant (or those claiming under him such as a mortgagee) may be able to elect to take an unencumbered lease: *Bank of Ireland Home Mortgages v South Lodge Developments* [1996] I EGLR 91 (see page 238)

Moreover, the landlord could be faced with a substantial claim for damages if it was shown subsequently that his re-entry was unlawful (*South Tottenham Land Securities v R + A Millett* [1984] 1 WLR 710), and even if he retakes possession after the tenant has departed he could still find himself in possession of the former tenant's goods and have to decide how to deal with them – see Chapter 14 below.

If the tenant applied for an injunction to be allowed back into the premises pending the outcome of his application for relief it may be difficult for the landlord to resist such application. It has been suggested that court proceedings afford the landlord a locus poenitentiae – an opportunity of changing his mind and not actually going for possession by discontinuing the proceedings after service of the writ. This opportunity is not available to a landlord who proceeds by peaceable re-entry which takes effect at once. However, it is submitted that this argument does not stand up to close scrutiny – on being served with the writ the tenant could vacate immediately (see dicta of Lord Templeman in *Billson*, [1992] 1 All ER 141 at pp 144–145).

In a depressed market it is also doubtful whether the argument that the tenant, having been physically excluded from premises, is likely to be more willing to remedy a breach of covenant, will necessarily apply: the tenant may simply accept that the lease is at an end. Equally, whilst it is, in theory, possible for the landlord to get into a direct and new relationship with the sub-tenant(s) at a much earlier stage, this is still against the background that the tenant may get relief and thereby upset any new arrangements with subtenants.

Once the lease has been forfeited the right of distress is no longer available, even for arrears pre-dating the forfeiture: *Murgatroyd v Silkstone & Dodworth Coal & Iron Co Ltd* (1895) 65 LJ Ch 111.

The landlord will also need to consider the position regarding any goods belonging to the tenant that will remain on the premises (see page XXX). However, if there are valuable tenant's fixtures on the property, the landlord may want to take peaceable re-entry as the tenant will not be entitled to return to reclaim them: *Re Palmeiro* [1999] 38 EG 195 (applying *Pugh v Artou* (1869) LR 8 Eq 626).

Against that has to be balanced the fact that, in a case where the premises have been abandoned and/or where there is little or no prospect of the tenant seeking relief, it would seem to be a waste of time (possibly months) and legal costs to go through the formalities of court proceedings and retaking the premises through the bailiff or sheriff's officer.

The factor that is likely to decide the matter will, it is submitted, be the occupancy situation at the premises. If tenants and subtenants are in actual occupation then, on any view, peaceable re-entry is going to be difficult and is probably best avoided. Only where the premises are vacant is peaceable re-entry often likely to be the appropriate way of regaining possession for the landlord.

AS A METHOD OF ENFORCEMENT OF A COURT ORDER

If the landlord has obtained a court order for possession and if there is no residential element, the landlord can enter without waiting for a formal warrant or writ of possession. But he must use no more force than necessary *(Aglionby v Cohen* [1955] 1 QB 558) and the provisions of section 6 of the Criminal Law Act 1977 will apply. Further, enforcing a right of re-entry consequent upon an order for possession requires actual eviction of the tenant. In some cases this may require the attendance of several persons, which may constitute an offence under section 6 or a riot. Where the premises are occupied, the attendance of either the sheriff's officer or the county court bailiff is, therefore, more likely to achieve re-entry without risk of allegations of breaches of section 6 or riot or damage to/loss of the tenant's goods at the premises.

ON THE TERMINATION OF A LEASE

If a lease of commercial premises which is not protected by the Landlord & Tenant Act 1954 Part II (for example, if the protection of the Act is excluded) comes to an end, or indeed if a licence determines, there is no need for a landlord to obtain a possession Order. This would only be necessary if there was a residential occupier in the premises or if there were individuals in occupation opposed to re-entry. Absent those facts, the landlord may peaceably re-enter at the termination of an unprotected lease or licence.

RE-ENTRY IN PRACTICE

There is little judicial guidance as to how peaceable re-entry should be effected. However, the prudent landlord would be well advised to take the following steps:

1. A letter should be written to the tenant stating that if, for example, all arrears of rent are not paid within a specified time the landlord proposes to proceed to forfeit the lease. The method of forfeiture should not he specified. If the breach complained of requires service of a Section 146 Notice; this should be served and the tenant given time to remedy the breach.

2. Assuming the default continues, inform the police that the landlord is going to re-enter on a certain day and at a certain time. If they attend, this should ensure that the procedure can continue notwithstanding persons in occupation.

3. Select a quiet time to re-enter when the possibility of resistance is least – at night, very early in the morning or at weekends.

4. The landlord or his agent should attend at the premises, making a special visit with the express purpose of forfeiting the lease. If anyone is encountered on the visit (such as a sub-tenant or employee of the tenant) they should be told the purpose of the visit. The landlord or agent should then peaceably re-enter using minimum force and, without using violence to the premises, walk through them to effect re-entry and change the locks.

5. Attend with a locksmith. If keys are not available the locksmith may be able to effect non-violent entry by picking the lock or making use of a credit card. Once entry has been effected the locksmith can then change the locks.

6. Put a notice on the premises explaining that peaceable re-entry has been effected, giving a contact name and a warning that entry onto the premises is not permitted without the written permission of the landlord or his solicitors/agents – see Precedent 6.

7. Write to the tenant and any sub-tenants explaining that on a certain date forfeiture was effected by peaceable re-entry and that the lease is, therefore, at an end. Say that unless there is an application for relief from forfeiture within 14 days the landlord proposes to re-let the premises.

8. Make a note of precisely how and when forfeiture was effected. The agent should take a notebook with him when he re-enters and should record there and then exactly what steps he took. The notes may then be used in evidence in any future court proceedings.

RELIEF FROM FORFEITURE

Physical re-entry has the same effect as forfeiture by court proceedings. Subject to any application for relief by the tenant, a sub-tenant or mortgagee, the lease is determined at the date of re-entry together with any interests created under it including the rights of any former assignees: *Eaton Square*

Properties Ltd v *Beveridge* (see above). Obligations under covenants also end on re-entry: *Wheeler* v *Keeble* [1920] 1 Ch 57.

For non-payment of rent the tenant will have to rely on the court's inherent equitable jurisdiction and apply for relief without undue delay, and probably within six months by analogy with section 210 of the Common Law Procedure Act 1852 – see *Thatcher* v *C H Pearce & Sons (Contractors) Ltd* [1968] 1 WLR 748. In the county court, section 139(2) of the County Courts Act 1984 specifically provides that relief can be given provided application is made within six months from re-entry, and this applies to sub-tenants and mortgagees as well as tenants.

Until the House of Lords decision in *Billson* v *Residential Apartments Ltd* [1992] 1 All ER 141 it had been thought that the courts could not grant relief from forfeiture for other breaches of covenant once the landlord had completed the act of forfeiture by peaceable re-entry, because section 146(2) of the Law of Property Act 1925 provides that relief may be sought where the landlord is "proceeding" by action or otherwise to enforce a right of re-entry. It was said that once the landlord had re-entered he was no longer "proceeding". This would make a subtenant or mortgagee vulnerable as they may not know of the service of a Section 146 Notice until after the landlord had re-entered, by which time it would be too late to apply for relief.

The House of Lords, in *Billson*, said that this was incorrect. An application for relief could still be made by a tenant or anyone claiming under him after the landlord had re-entered. There is no formal time limit for the application, although the limit in the Common Law Procedure Act 1852 – six months from the date of execution – is probably as good a guide as any, and delay in making an application would be taken into account by the court in deciding whether to grant relief.

If relief is granted it will be retrospective to the date of forfeiture. If the tenant has remedied or undertakes to remedy the breach, the court will usually order relief but the tenant will ordinarily be responsible for the costs of the proceedings: *Fuller* v *Judy Properties Ltd* [1992] 14 EG 106 – although not indemnity costs: *Billson* v *Residential Apartments Ltd* (above), unless (possibly) the breach of covenant was deliberate: *Iperion Investments Corporation* v *Broadwalk House Residents Ltd* [1992] 2 EGLR 235.

Relief is available to a judgment creditor who holds a charging order over the tenant's interest in the premises: *Croydon (Unique) Limited* v *Wright* Butterworths case reports; 29.7.99. See also *Ladup Ltd* v *Williams and Glyn's Bank plc* [1985] 1 WLR 851, and *Bland* v *Ingram's Estates* [2000] All ER(D) 2441.

Remedies Table

Legal Status of Tenant	Remedies		
	Distress	Forfeiture	
		Peaceable Re-entry	By Court Action
IVA	NO unless leave	NO unless leave	NO unless leave
Bankruptcy	YES But subject to limits as to amounts. 347 IA 1986	YES *Re A Debtor No 13 A* [1993] 41 EG 142	YES s. 285 IA 1986 & *Ezekiel* v *Orakpol* [1977] QB 260
Administration	NO – unless leave	NO – unless leave or consent	NO – unless leave
Receivership	YES	YES	YES
Compulsory Liquidation	NO – unless leave	NO – unless leave	NO – unless leave, but seek "Blue Jeans Order" for possession
CVA (large companies).*YES		YES	YES unless aggred

* But may depend on wording of the CVA

CHAPTER 5
DISTRESS

CHAPTER 5
DISTRESS

Distress is an ancient remedy which enables a landlord, as soon as the rent is overdue, to enter the demised premises (not any other premises), seize the goods on the premises, sell them and take the rent owing out of the proceeds of sale.

It can be an extremely effective, fairly cheap and speedy method of obtaining payment. On the other hand, it can have drawbacks which are considered later. The mere threat by a landlord to resort to what some regard as a draconian measure is often sufficient to obtain immediate payment.

The law of distress is extremely complicated, and the advice to a landlord who wishes to distrain is that he must use the services of a responsible and respectable certificated bailiff, who is a member of the Certificated Bailiffs' Association of England and Wales. An individual landlord can, in theory, levy the distress himself, but a company or other corporate landlord must use a certificated bailiff: *Hogarth* v *Jennings* [1892] 1 QB 907.

Apart from anything else, the actual process of distraining can be unpleasant, which is another reason for employing a certificated bailiff.

Although the remedy continues to be available at present, it has been criticised by the courts and the Law Commission, and it is arguably a breach of the Human Rights Act (see below). How long it survives, or survives unrestricted, remains to be seen.

THE FOUR REQUIREMENTS

Leave to distrain is not necessary in relation to commercial premises. There are, nevertheless, four main requirements which have to be satisfied before distress can be levied:

1. There has to be a letting, i.e a current landlord and tenant relationship. A licence is not sufficient.

2. The rent must be agreed. Ordinarily this will be expressed in the lease or tenancy agreement hut it will be sufficient if it has been agreed orally.
3. The rent must be in arrear, if only by one day.
4. The tenancy must still be in existence so that, for example, there could be no distress if notice to quit had expired. Nor can the landlord distrain for rent which has been the subject of a prior judgment, or after he has forfeited the lease.

DEFENCES

Unless expressly excluded by the lease, equitable set-off is available against a claim to levy distress: see *Fuller v Happy Shopper Markets Ltd* [2001] All ER (D) 156 (Feb). In *Eller v Grovecrest Investments Ltd* [1994] 27 EG 139 a tenant who had complained of the landlord's breaches of covenant and acts of nuisance withheld his rent. He was able to obtain an injunction restraining the levying of distress against his goods. Therefore where a tenant has a valid claim entitling the tenant to exercise a right of set-off against the rent, the rent will not be in arrear and thus there is no right to distrain.

If the amount of the rent is the subject of an appeal it would seem that it does not have the necessary degree of certainty to be the subject of a distress: *Eren v Tranmac Ltd*, 25 November 1993, Court of Appeal (unreported).

DISTRAINABLE RENT

The landlord can distrain for arrears of rent which have accrued due over the previous six years. A landlord cannot levy distress against the goods of an assignee in respect of arrears of rent due before the assignment and owed by the assignor: *Wharfland Ltd v South London Co-operative Building Co Ltd*: [1995] 30 EG 95.

SERVICE CHARGES

Whether the landlord can distrain for service charges is unclear. In *Concorde Graphics Ltd v Andromeda Investments SA* (1982) 265 EG 386, Vinelott J considered that a landlord could distrain for service charges but held, on the facts, that distress could not be levied because the amount of the service charge was in dispute – rent can only be distrained for if it is for a sum certain. Although most leases say that service charges are reserved as rent and can be recovered as rent and distrained for, it is by no means certain that labelling service charges in that way will have the desired effect. It may provide the landlord with a contractual right of distress, but this could hardly prejudice the rights of third parties whose goods can be distrained for rent. It is also possible that the purported contractual right to distrain would have to be registered under the Bills of Sale Acts 1878 to 1882, which lay down conditions in relation to agreements which purport to give rights over personal chattels in order to secure debts. In the case of a company tenant, section 396 of the Companies Act 1985 provides that an agreement entered into by a company which is the equivalent of a bill of sale executed by an individual has to be registered as a charge over the company's property, otherwise it will be void against the liquidator, administrator or creditor of the company.

It seems that an inclusive rent in which there is an element for, say, the use of furniture, is distrainable: *Rousou* v *Photi* [1940] 2 KB 379.

TENANT IN COMPULSORY LIQUIDATION

1.   LANDLORD DISTRAINS BEFORE A WINDING-UP PETITION IS PRESENTED

After the petition is presented the company, any creditor or contributory can apply to the court to stay the distress: Insolvency Act 1986, section 126.

After the winding-up order has been made, the landlord will have to apply to the court to continue the distress. He will need leave of court to sell the goods: Insolvency Act 1986, section 130. Leave will usually be granted.

2.   LANDLORD DISTRAINS AFTER THE WINDING-UP PETITION IS PRESENTED

The distress is void: Insolvency Act 1986, section 128. But the landlord may apply for and obtain leave under section 130 of the Act.

Leave is unlikely to be granted in relation to rent that fell due prior to the winding-up.

Leave will usually be given in respect of rent that fell due during the period of the liquidation, but only for the apportioned amount from the date of presentation of the petition.

VOLUNTARY LIQUIDATION

There is no restriction on the landlord's right to distrain, but under section 112 of the 1986 Act the liquidator or any contributory or creditor can apply to the court to impose a stay on any distress. As with compulsory liquidation, leave will probably be given to complete a distress begun before the liquidation but not if the distress was commenced after liquidation in respect of rent which was due before liquidation: *Re Margot Bywaters Ltd* [1942] Ch 121. Leave will probably be given to continue a distress which was started after liquidation in respect of amounts which fell due whilst the liquidator had the property.

BANKRUPTCY

1.   INDIVIDUAL VOLUNTARY ARRANGEMENTS

Section 252 of the Insolvency Act 1986 (as amended by the 2000 Act) provides that once an interim order has been made "no other proceedings, and no execution or other legal process, may be commenced or continued against the debtor or his property except with the leave of the court". It was thought that the levying of distress is not caught by the phrase "or other legal process" and so the landlord, in that case, was entitled to continue with a distress, even though an interim order had been made. However section 252(2)(aa) and (b) now provides that distress and peaceable re-entry are prohibited (without leave) when an order has been made, and when pending (section 253).

2.   RENT DUE BEFORE BANKRUPTCY

Even though the tenant is made bankrupt, the landlord can still distrain, but not for arrears that go back for more than six months before the bankruptcy order is made. If the landlord distrains after a petition has been presented but before the order is made, any monies recovered which are in excess of the six months' rent are to be held for the bankrupt's estate: Insolvency Act 1986, section 347(2).

3.   RENT DUE AFTER BANKRUPTCY

The landlord can distrain for all the rent due after bankruptcy if the trustee in bankruptcy remains in possession and renders himself liable by not disclaiming the lease: *Re Binns, ex parte Hale* [1875] 1 Ch D 285.

LIQUIDATION, BANKRUPTCY AND PREFERENTIAL CREDITORS

If the landlord distrains and then within three months the tenant is wound up or made bankrupt, the landlord will have to hold the goods or the proceeds of sale to satisfy preferential claims for rates, taxes, salaries and wages etc. to the extent that the company's property/the bankrupt's estate is insufficient to meet the preferential debts: Insolvency Act 1986, sections 176 and 347(3). The landlord will however rank as a preferential creditor to the extent of the funds paid over to the estate: section 347 (4).

ADMINISTRATION

Distress cannot be levied against a company in administration except with the leave of the court or, following the administration order, with the leave of the court or the consent of the administrator: Insolvency Act 1986, section 43 of Schedule B1.

COMPANY VOLUNTARY ARRANGEMENTS

The Insolvency Act 2000 imposes a 28 day moratorium in relation to small companies between the presentation of the proposal and the creditors' meeting. The stay can be extended by two months. During the stay a landlord may not levy distress. A small company is defined under section 247 Companies Act 1985 as having:

- a turnover not exceeding £2.8m;
- a balance sheet not exceeding £1.4m; and
- not more than 50 employees.

RECEIVERSHIP

There is no restriction on the landlord distraining against goods on the demised premises even though the goods are subject to a floating charge and a receiver has been appointed.

However, after 15 September 2003, most floating charges may only be enforced by the appointment of an administrator in which case the use of distress is limited as set out above.

PROCEDURE

There is no requirement for a landlord to give notice of his intention to distrain. Ordinarily he will merely instruct a certificated bailiff by means of a warrant. A corporation can only levy distress by a certified bailiff.

Distress can be levied on any day after the rent falls due (except Sunday) between sunrise and sunset. The fact that the rent is payable in advance makes no difference.

Distress is effected by entering the premises, seizing the relevant goods, and securing the goods (known as "impounding"). The bailiff does not have to touch or put a notice on the goods. A notice affixed to the door of the premises notifying the distress against the goods in sufficient both to effect the distress and to give the tenant the required notice of the distress. The bailiff will however usually make an inventory and take photographs of the goods.

The landlord or certificated bailiff cannot enter the premises by force, unless the bailiff is seeking to re-enter to remove goods previously seized and entry is intentionally refused: *Khazandi* v *Faircharm Investments* and *McLeod* v *Butterwick* (1998) The Times March 12. Having once obtained entry, the bailiff can seize and impound the goods on the premises. The restriction on the use of forceful entry applies only to the outer door, not any inner, locked doors.

Although the bailiff may impound the goods away from the premises (in which case the place of impounding must be identified), distress is usually effected by constructive seizure, namely leaving the goods on the premises. If the rent arrears are not paid within 5 days of the seizure, the goods distrained against may be sold at the best price obtainable. Until the goods have been sold (regardless of whether the 5 days have passed or not), the tenant has the rights to tender the rent arrears and costs and so secure the release of the goods (known as the tenant's right to replevy the goods). The tenant may make a written request to extend this 5 day period to 15 days.

In theory, the distrainor can take all goods found on the demised premises, whether or not they belong to the tenant. In practice, this general rule has been considerably watered down both by common law and by statute, and there are numerous restrictions as to which of the tenant's and third party's goods may be taken. Moreover, the distrainor cannot take all the goods on the premises but only those of sufficient value to cover the arrears of rent and recoverable costs.

Goods that are privileged – usually but not always belonging to the tenant – are divided between those which are absolutely privileged, which cannot be taken at all, and those which are conditionally privileged, which can only be taken if there are insufficient other goods upon which distress can be levied. The categories of goods which cannot be taken are both long and complicated. Moreover, in some cases, there is an overlap between the various classes of goods.

1.   ABSOLUTE PRIVILEGE

Goods which are absolutely privileged include:

- perishable articles;
- fixtures;
- wearing apparel and bedding of the tenant and his family, up to the value of £100, and tools and implements of his trade up to £150;
- loose money.

2.   QUALIFIED PRIVILEGE

The goods to which this privilege attaches include:

- all tools and implements of a man's trade – not necessarily the tenant's;
- beasts of the plough, agisted animals and growing crops.

It will be seen that this exemption applies mainly in the agricultural context.

3.   THIRD PARTY GOODS

This is, in practice, the most important category of exempted goods. Again, there is a long list of third party goods which are absolutely privileged. Strictly speaking the goods cannot be taken but inevitably, because it is not always immediately obvious that they are privileged, they will sometimes be seized and many of the statutes which confer the privilege also provide a procedure enabling the owner to recover his property. In particular, goods belonging to under-tenants, lodgers and strangers are privileged under the Law of Distress (Amendment) Act 1908.

Third parties have a right to serve a notice claiming their ownership of goods that have been seized but, subject to that, the landlord will be able to sell the goods five days after impounding them. He must obtain the best net price for them but does not have to hold an auction.

WRONGFUL DISTRESS

The consequences of a wrongful distress can be fairly severe for both land-lord and certificated bailiff and will vary, as will the tenant's remedies, according to the nature of the impropriety.

A distress may be illegal, irregular or excessive.

An illegal distress is one which is unlawful from the beginning, e.g. where the landlord distrains when there arc no rent arrears, or forces an entry or takes privileged goods. There are a number of remedies available to the ten-ant or third party, including rescuing the goods, replevin – getting them back through the county court, damages, and the tenant can recover double the value of the goods sold if no rent was in arrear. In addition it must always be remembered that because this type of distress was void *ab initio*, no title to the goods has ever been acquired and consequently no title can be trans-ferred on sale, so that the owner can always proceed against the purchaser in conversion.

Distress is irregular where the entry and seizure were lawful but there is then some irregularity in the way the distress is conducted. The tenant's remedy is to sue for damage suffered.

An excessive distress occurs when the value of the goods taken is clearly more than the outstanding rent. Again, the tenant's remedy is to sue for damages.

MERITS OF DISTRAINING

As has been mentioned, there can be certain drawbacks from the landlord's point of view. If the distress is illegal, irregular or excessive the penalties can be fairly harsh, and inevitably the exercise of the remedy brings to an end whatever goodwill there may have been between landlord and tenant. More-over, from a legal point of view, the levying of distress can waive any breach of covenant.

Whatever criticisms there have been of distress, the fact remains that it can be a most effective and speedy remedy which has considerable attractions from a landlord's point of view. It effectively gives priority to landlords over other creditors. It is quick and reasonably cheap. The fees of the certificated bailiff, vary from about 5% to 10% of the actual monies recovered: see the Distraint by Collectors (Fees, Costs and Charges) (Amendment) Regulations 1995 for details of fees.

A full description of distress is to be found in the Green Paper *Enforcement Review Consultation Paper 5: Distress for Rent* from which it will be seen that the Law Commission has recommended that the remedy should be significantly changed. Further proposals are set out in a second Green Paper entitled *Towards Effective Enforcement – A Single Piece of Bailiff law and a regulatory structure for Enforcement.*

HUMAN RIGHTS ACT – THE END OF THE ROAD FOR DISTRESS?

The Human Rights Act 1998 came into force on 2 October 2000. It incorporates into English law the European Convention on Human Rights. It has been said that the exercise of the right of distress infringes the Human Rights Act. This has not as yet been decided by the court. One reported case (*Fuller* v *Happy Shopper Markets Limited* [2001] All ER (D) 156 (Feb)) referred to distress as " the ancient (and perhaps anachronistic) self-help remedy" which involved the serious interference with the right of the tenant under the European Convention on Human Rights. However, distress was not prohibited in that case on those grounds. The court simply commented *per curiam* that the Human Rights implications of levying distress had to be in the forefront of the mind of the landlord before he proceeded with it and the landlord had to satisfy himself that taking action by means of distress was in accordance with the law.

The legality of distress is said to be open to challenge on the basis that it engages the following rights under the Human Rights Act:

- Article 1 of Protocol 1 which gives the right to peaceful enjoyment of ones possession.
- Article 6 which contains the right to a fair trial.
- Article 8 which provides for protection for one's private and family life, home and correspondence...

As distress involves an interference with a tenant's rights to enjoy his goods, it is said that this breaches Article 1 of Protocol 1. However, it must not be forgotten that the tenant is in arrears of rent and there are penalties for wrongful restraint. It is arguable therefore that the tenant's position is not worsened by a landlord levying distress. Against this, however, is the fact that distress does not provide the tenant with any choice over which goods are seized.

Distress is also said to breach Article 6. The court's permission is not required before the remedy is exercised. Furthermore, there is clear potential for goods to be sold before the tenant or owner has an opportunity to make an application to the court to challenge any illegal, irregular or excessive distress.

The Article 8 protection for private and family life, the home and correspondence, has been held to extend to business premises: *Nienietz* v *Germany* (1992) 16 EHRR 97. However, a landlord would expect to be able to rely on the qualifications to Article 8 rights by arguing that any interference with the tenant's rights is in accordance with the law, that the remedy is used in pursuit of a legitimate aim (namely the right of a landlord to receive rent), and that the interference is necessary and proportionate to safeguard the landlord's rights.

These arguments suggest that distress offends against the Human Rights Act have been advanced by many commentators, but have not, as yet, been decided by the courts. It is, however, clear that the Human Rights Act gives ample scope for a tenant to argue that distress breaches his human rights.

CHAPTER 6
SURETIES

CHAPTER 6
SURETIES

Most commercial leases contain a covenant by one or more sureties guaranteeing the tenant's obligations under the lease. Typically the surety will covenant that the tenant will pay the rent and perform the other covenants and that the surety will make good the landlord's losses if the tenant is in default.

There is a great deal of learning about the obligations and rights of sureties and guarantors. In the context of the landlord and tenant situation, much of it will be of academic interest only because a well-drawn surety covenant will displace the common law rules which tend to favour the guarantor at the expense of the creditor, i.e the landlord.

The extent of the surety's obligations is always a question of construction of the actual covenant.

GUARANTEE OR INDEMNITY?

Although, as we shall see, the distinction between a guarantee and an indemnity may be somewhat artificial where a lease is concerned, nevertheless the theory is that a guarantee is a "secondary" liability whereas an indemnity constitutes a "primary" obligation.

Again the distinction between the two is a question of construction of the wording that has been used. In practice the covenant is usually drawn in terms which are sufficiently wide to include both a guarantee and an indemnity. Whilst the lease is continuing the liability will often be that of a guarantor, but once the liability of the tenant has crystallised the likelihood is that the covenant will be in the nature of an indemnity.

There are some practical consequences of the distinction.

Section 4 of the Statute of Frauds 1677 provides that a guarantee must be in writing or evidenced in writing and signed by the guarantor or his agent. There are no formal requirements for an indemnity.

The secondary nature of the liability under a guarantee means that if, for some reason, the tenant's covenants are void or unenforceable then the guarantee itself will also be unenforceable. Moreover, if the liability of the tenant is discharged for some reason (other than by disclaimer where the guarantor's liability continues – see page 212) then the liability of the guarantor, being co-extensive with the liability of the tenant, will also be discharged. In neither case would the primary liability under an indemnity be affected by the invalidity of the main contract or the discharge of the principal debtor.

GENERAL PRINCIPLES

Before discussing specific problems in the landlord and tenant situation, it may be helpful to consider first some principles which apply to surety contracts generally.

The traditional approach of the courts is that the contract is to be construed in favour of the surety, and that no liability is to be imposed on him which is not clearly and distinctly covered by the agreement. The reasons for this are twofold.

The contract will, generally speaking, be prepared by those advising the creditor and consequently the maxim *contra proferentem* will apply – in case of doubt the covenant will be construed in favour of the surety and against the creditor. Secondly, it would seem that account is also taken of the fact that although the surety may have come to some arrangement with the debtor he is guaranteeing, as often as not the surety enters into the contract on a purely gratuitous basis and receives nothing in return.

But if these factors are not present – if the contract was not drafted by the creditor, or if the surety receives some benefit from the debtor – then it is possible that the court would not construe the contract in that way. Moreover, there have been indications that the courts may not always adopt the principle of strict construction against the creditor. In *Johnsey Estates Ltd v Webb and others* [1990] 19 EG 84, Mr Justice Millett rejected this rule of construction put forward on behalf of the surety. He said:

> "Lastly, it was submitted on behalf of the defendants that if there is an ambiguity or doubt upon the meaning of the suretyship covenant I should construe it in favour of the defendants and against the plaintiffs. Certainly it is true that neither equity nor law will put a construction on a contract of guarantee which results in imposing on the surety any greater obligation than that which on the strictest construction of the instrument he must be said expressly to have undertaken: see *Eastern Counties Building Society v Russell* [1947] 1 All ER 500.

On the other hand, the words have to be fairly construed in their context and in accordance with their proper meaning without in any way favouring the guarantor, who is not placed in any more favourable position in this regard than any other contracting party. The so-called rule of construction is very much a matter of last resort."

In *Jaskel v Sophie Nursery Products Ltd* [1993] EGCS 42, the Court of Appeal had to construe the effect of a lease and a supplementary agreement in which the tenant agreed to pay a rent deposit. In the lease from L to T the sureties guaranteed T's liability (for rent) and they signed the supplementary deed under which T agreed to pay a rent deposit but they were not parties to it. On default by T the sureties argued that they were not responsible for a deposit as it was in a separate deed. The Court of Appeal held that there were no grounds for allowing the lease and the supplementary agreement to be construed as one document and the sureties could not be expected to assume obligations which were not spelt out. The supplemental deed did not contain the full recital of the covenants of the lease itself which it would have had to have had if the sureties were to be liable. Accordingly the sureties had guaranteed only the rent and could not be asked to top up the rent deposit.

VARIATION

1.   AT COMMON LAW

Another important principle is that any variation in the terms of the agreement between the creditor and the debtor which *could* prejudice the surety will, unless he agrees to the variation, discharge him from liability: *Holme v Brunskill* (1877–78) 3 QBD 495. The most obvious example is where the creditor agrees to give the principal debtor extra time to pay and there is a binding agreement to this effect. The thinking behind this rule is highly artificial. It is that by giving the debtor extra time, the creditor deprives the surety of the right the surety has to use the name of the creditor to sue the principal debtor. If this right is suspended for only a very short time and although the surety suffers no damage whatsoever it does, in theory, mean that the surety's right to pay off the creditor and sue the principal debtor for an indemnity is prejudiced because the surety cannot sue until the time has expired. However, the operation of this rule will not always mean the surety is released. In *West Horndon Industrial Park Ltd v Phoenix Timber Group plc* [1995] 20 EG 137 and *Howard de Walden Estates Ltd v Pasta Place Ltd* [1995] 22 EG 143, the sureties were released but not in *Metropolitan Properties Co (Regis) Ltd v Bartholomew* [1995] 14 EG 143.

In the *Howard de Walden* case the court held that in deciding if a variation is substantial or prejudicial to the surety, the Court must view this objectively, not by looking to see if in fact there has been a material prejudice.

The practical effect of these rules is now considerably reduced because every well-drawn contract of suretyship provides that the surety will not be released by any neglect or forbearance by the landlord in enforcing the tenant covenants and expressly permits variation of the obligations and the giving of time without discharging the surety.

2.   BY STATUTE

As we shall see (p 105 below), section 18 of the Landlord and Tenant (Covenants) Act 1995 provides that following assignment a former tenant will not be liable to pay any amount that is referable to a subsequent, "relevant variation" of the tenant covenants. This provision also applies to a guarantor of a former tenant whose liability under the guarantee is not wholly discharged by the variation. Section 25 of the Act prohibits any contracting out.

Bearing in mind that the extent of the liability of the surety will always be a question of construction of the particular covenant, we turn to the main questions that arise in the landlord and tenant situation.

PERIOD OF LIABILITY

Generally speaking a surety will be answerable only for liabilities arising during the contractual term: *Junction Estates Ltd* v *Cope* (1974) 27 P & CR 482; *A Plesser & Co Ltd* v *Davis* (1983) 267 EG 1039.

But the covenant may be drawn so as to extend liability to cover matters arising during the period of the statutory extension of the tenancy under section 24 of the Landlord and Tenant Act 1954: *A Plesser & Co Ltd* v *Davis* (above). Furthermore, the surety may be liable in damages if the tenant holds over unlawfully: *Associated Dairies Ltd* v *Pierce* (1983) 265 EG 127.

A surety to a lease will remain liable to pay arrears of rent and service charge which accrue due after service of forfeiture proceedings. Mere service of forfeiture proceedings will not in itself end the surety's liability: *Ivory Gate Ltd* v *Spetale* [1998] 27 EG 139. When the liability ends (if it does) will depend on the outcome of the proceedings (i.e. whether the lease is forfeited or relief granted).

If the lease is surrendered this will usually end the surety's liability: *BSE Trading Ltd* v *Hands* [1996] EGCS 99.

Section 17 of the Landlord and Tenant (Covenants) Act 1995 (see page 105 below) applies not only to a former tenant but also his guarantor. A landlord will not be able to recover any fixed charge from such guarantor unless, within six months of the charge becoming due, he serves on the guarantor a notice informing him that the charge is now due and that the landlord intends to recover the amount specified in the notice and any interest payable.

TIME LIMIT

A claim for rent must be brought within six years – see section 19 of the Limitation Act 1980: *Romain* v *Scuba TV Limited* (1995) *The Times* November 22. The definition of rent in section 38 includes a rent charge and rent service. Claims other than those for unpaid rent will be subject to the normal limitation period of 12 years which is applicable to any document under seal (section 8 of the Limitation Act 1980).

RENT REVIEW

A lease may provide for a surety to be involved in the review procedure or he may be a director of the tenant company. But if the surety has no say in the negotiations between landlord and tenant he will, nevertheless, be bound by the variation in rent since it will, presumably, take effect in accordance with and be contemplated by the terms of the lease. Moreover it has been held that, even after the lease has come to an end, the surety will be liable for the increased rent which arose under an earlier rent review but which was not activated until after the lease had ended: *Torminster Properties Ltd* v *Green* [1983] 1 WLR 676.

CONDITIONS PRECEDENT TO ENFORCEABILITY OF GUARANTOR'S LIABILITY

It is sometimes suggested that the guarantor has an argument that, before he can be made liable to the landlord, he can require the landlord to enforce his remedies against the principal debtor, the tenant. But there appears to be no clear authority supporting this proposition. Even if there were, the likelihood is that the surety would be required to indemnify the landlord for the risk, expense and delay of proceeding first against the tenant. Of course the surety contract might, improbably, provide that the creditor must first pursue the principal debtor, or that the surety is not to be liable until after demand has been made of him or he has been given notice of the debtor's default. In practice many standard-form guarantees exclude any such preconditions.

A guarantor of a former tenant will not be liable to the landlord unless he has been served with a notice under section 17 of the Landlord and Tenant (Covenants) Act 1995 as mentioned above.

PURCHASER OF THE REVERSION

The benefit of a surety covenant may be expressly assigned by the landlord to the purchaser of his interest but, apart from that, it seems the benefit of the covenant can be enforced by an assignee of the reversion by virtue of section 62 of the Law of Property Act 1925. This is because the covenant "touches and concerns" the land: *Kumar* v *Dunning* [1987] 3 WLR 1167; *P & A Swift Investments* v *Combined English Stores Group plc* [1989] AC 632.

But section 3 of the Landlord and Tenant (Covenants) Act 1995 provides that the benefit and burden of all landlord and tenant covenants will automatically pass to an assignee of the lease or reversion unless a covenant is "expressed to be personal to any person". Section 4 provides for the automatic transfer of the benefit of the landlord's right of re-entry on the assignment of the reversion. Sections 6 and 7 of the Act enable a landlord and a former landlord to apply to be released from their covenants on the assignment of the reversion. The procedure is set out in section 8 but, briefly, it involves the service of a prescribed form of notice on the tenant either before or within four weeks of the assignment. The landlord will be released if the tenant does not, within four weeks of service of the notice, object to the release or if he serves on the landlord a notice in writing consenting to the release. If the tenant does object the landlord can apply to the county court for a declaration that it is reasonable for the landlord to be released.

INSOLVENCY OF TENANT – DISCLAIMER OF LEASE

Where the liquidator or trustee in bankruptcy of an insolvent tenant disclaims the lease the disclaimer operates to determine "the rights, interests and liabilities" of the current tenant: Insolvency Act 1986, section 178; section 315 for personal bankruptcy.

However, the termination of the liabilities of the insolvent tenant does not affect the obligations of a guarantor of that tenant to the landlord, whether he be the original tenant or an assignee: *Hindcastle Limited* v *Barbara Attenborough Associates Limited* [1996] 1 EGLR 94.

Where the insolvent tenant is not the original tenant, it must be remembered that under the Landlord and Tenant (Covenants) Act 1995 the landlord will, additionally, have to show that he has complied with the notice procedure of section 17 of the Act if he wishes to pursue a former tenant or his guarantor – see page 105 below.

DEATH OR INSOLVENCY OF THE SURETY

Again it will be a question of looking at the wording of the covenant, but the likelihood is that the death of the surety will not discharge his liability. Generally speaking the parties will be taken to have intended that the liability of the guarantor should continue throughout the lease, and it would be contrary to that intention for the guarantor's liability to be brought to an end by his death: *Lloyd's* v *Harper* (1880) 16 Ch D 290.

If the surety becomes insolvent the landlord will prove in the bankruptcy or winding-up for arrears of rent, service charges and other liabilities which have accrued due. The lease may contain a provision entitling the landlord to call for an acceptable substitute surety.

CHAPTER 7

ORIGINAL TENANT/ASSIGNEE LIABILITY

CHAPTER 7
ORIGINAL TENANT/ASSIGNEE LIABILITY

The Landlord and Tenant (Covenants) Act 1995 altered the law relating to the continuing liability of original tenants and assignees who gave direct covenants to the landlord. The Act came into force on 1 January 1996. However, it is necessary to consider the law as it stood before the end of 1995 and then look at the position under the Act – an understanding of the "old law" is essential for an appreciation of the changes brought about by the Act.

Although it has always been possible for an original tenant to contract out of his liability for matters arising after he has disposed of the lease, this is something that has hardly been encountered and, in the absence of such contracting out, the rules are, briefly, as follows.

PRIVITY OF CONTRACT

The original tenant is liable, by virtue of the doctrine of privity of contract, for all matters which arise during the existence of the contract, i.e. the lease, even after the lease has been assigned. An assignee who gives the landlord a direct covenant to be liable under the tenant covenants for the remainder of the term is in the same position. Moreover an assignee who covenants with the landlord to pay the rents reserved by the lease will be liable, under that contract, (as will his surety) for rent that accrues due after he himself has reassigned the lease. His liability will extend to the whole of the term of the lease and not just the period during which the lease remains vested in him: *Estates Gazette Ltd* v *Benjamin Restaurants Ltd* [1994] 26 EG 140.

The assignee of a pre-1996 lease is, however, liable to his assignor by way of indemnity for sums paid by him in default: *Scottish and Newcastle plc* v *Raguz* [2003] 41 EG 179.

PRIVITY OF ESTATE

An assignee of the leasehold interest who does not enter into a direct covenant with the landlord is liable, by virtue of the doctrine of privity of estate, only for matters which arise during the time he holds the lease. Rent payable in arrear is apportionable so that if a subsequent assignee fails to pay a quarter's rent, his assignor will be liable to pay that part of the quarter's rent which relates to the period up to the date of the assignment. It is also possible for an assignee to be saddled with a liability that arose before he acquired the lease. If a breach of covenant started before the assignee took his assignment and is continuing during the period of the assignee's owner-ship of the lease, the assignee may have to remedy the breach in order to prevent the landlord forfeiting.

Many examples have been given of the harshness of the privity of contract/ original tenant rule. Take the case of a 25-year lease. The original tenant may hold the lease only for a year or so before assigning it on, but then, many years later, may suddenly be faced with a claim from the landlord calling upon him to pay rent or deal with dilapidations which have arisen only in the last year or so.

EXTENT OF THE LIABILITY

The original tenant is liable not only for the rent as originally laid down in the lease, but also for the rent as subsequently fixed in any rent review. An attempt to argue that an original lessee was not bound by an agreement reached between the landlord and assignee was unsuccessful in *GUS Property Management Ltd v Texas Homecare Ltd* [1993] 27 EG 130. At review the landlord and assignee agreed that that revised rent should be £210,000 per annum for three years and £220,000 for each of the remaining two years. The original tenant argued that what had been agreed was a deviation from the rent review provisions in the lease which did not provide for a "stepped" revised rent. It was held that the agreement made between the landlord and the assignee had been made with a view to implementing and giving effect to the review provisions, not to reach an agreement outside them. An assignee stands in the place of the original lessee and is authorised to do whatever the original lessee might have done. There was nothing in the wording of the lease to take the case outside the ordinary principles. More-over, if the lease contains an option for renewal or extension and the option is exercised by a subsequent assignee, the original tenant will be liable into the whole of the period of the extension: *Baker v Merckel* [1960] 1 QB 657, CA.

The original tenant will not, however, be responsible for a subsequent variation which is of a nature that is not contemplated by the terms of the lease: *Beegas Nominees Ltd* v *BMP Petroleum Ltd* [1998] 31 EG 96.

The original tenant is not liable for matters arising during the statutory continuation of the tenancy under the Landlord and Tenant Act 1954. In *City of London Corporation* v *Fell* [1993] 3 WLR 1164, the House of Lords held that Part II of the 1954 Act imposed liability only on the landlord and the occupying tenant. It did not expressly impose liability on the original tenant where, following an assignment, arrears of rent had accrued after the expiry of the contractual term. The continued tenancy was capable of existing in law independently of the original contract and so no such liability needed to be, nor was it to be, implied.

VARIATION OF LEASE

What is the position if an assignee agrees a material or substantial variation of the lease with the landlord? The situation is not entirely clear, but a fundamental variation by an increase in the premises or the term would almost certainly result in an implied surrender of the lease and re-grant, which would in turn release the original tenant. Other variations not contemplated by the original lease will not be binding on him: *Friends' Provident Life Office* v *British Railways Board* [1995] 48 EG 106, *Beegas Nominees* v *BHP Petroleum* (see above). Variation may also release the liability of any guarantor (see Chapter 6).

RELEASE OF CURRENT TENANT

If a landlord, without any qualification or reservation, releases the current tenant, e.g. on accepting a settlement or surrender of the lease from him, this will have the effect of releasing the original tenant and any assignees or sureties who gave the landlord a direct covenant: *Deanplan Ltd* v *Mahmoud* [1993] Ch 151. See also the test in *Watts* v *Lord Aldington* (1993) *The Times* 16th December: has a right to sue been reserved?

DEATH

The death of the original tenant will not discharge his liability and a landlord will be able to claim against his estate.

INSOLVENCY

If the tenant is made bankrupt or goes into liquidation the landlord will be able to prove his claim in the bankruptcy/winding-up. Moreover a landlord may be able to persuade the court to make an order under section 651 and/or section 653 of the Companies Act 1985 reinstating a company which had previously been dissolved. In *Stanhope Pension Trust* v *Registrar of Companies* [1993] NPC 169; [1994] BCC 84 a lease granted to F was assigned by F and then assigned twice more before the liquidators of the ultimate assignee disclaimed the lease. In the meantime F had also been wound up but L applied to the court to have the dissolution of F rendered void under section 651 so as to enable F to exercise a right of indemnity for the rent against subsequent solvent assignees. The Court of Appeal held that F should be restored to the register but it also said that where, as here, the making of an order under section 651 directly affected the rights of a third party, i.e. the assignees, they were entitled to be joined.

If the trustee in bankruptcy or liquidator of an assignee disclaims the lease the original tenant and any sureties will still remain liable to the landlord but may be able to claim a vesting order.

VOLUNTARY ARRANGEMENTS

Although a landlord will be bound by the terms of a voluntary arrangement of which he has had notice and in respect of which he was entitled to vote at the creditors' meeting, this will not relieve the original tenant of his liability for rent as he will be an outsider to the voluntary arrangement and will be unable to derive any assistance from its terms: *R A Securities Ltd* v *Mercantile Credit Co Ltd* [1994] NPC 76; (1994) 2 BCC 598.

PAYMENT BY GUARANTORS

The landlord will have to give credit to the original tenant for sums paid in relation to rent by guarantors. The landlord, and not the original tenant, is in a position to appropriate the benefit of payments made by guarantors although, if he appropriated them to sums not yet due, he would have to pay interest: *Milverton Group Ltd* v *Warner World Ltd* [1994] NPC 64. In this case it was also held that a payment made by a surety to obtain his release from all future liability under his surety covenant does not serve to release the tenant from any future arrears that accrue due.

POSSIBLE DEFENCES?

In *Norwich Union Life Insurance Society* v *Low Profile Fashions Ltd* [1992] 21 EG 104, the original tenant assigned the lease to the first assignee who subsequently assigned to the second assignee. The original tenant did not choose the second assignee and had no control over the assignment to him. The second assignee fell into arrear with the rent and other monies due. There was then a third assignment of the lease at a premium, which enabled the second assignee to discharge part of the monies owing to the landlord. When the second assignee was compulsorily wound up the landlord sued the original tenant. On behalf of the original tenant it was argued that there was to be implied into the lease a term that, in relation to its dealings with the second or subsequent assignees, the landlord would take reasonable care to ensure that such an assignee was financially able to meet the rent and service payments due under the lease, and secondly that, since the tenant's continuing liability to the landlord arose from privity of contract, the court should apply an equitable doctrine restraining the landlord from pursuing its remedy against the tenant when, because of the existence of alternative remedies against the second assignee and a surety, it was wholly unreasonable for the landlord to pursue its remedy against the tenant. The Court of Appeal rejected both these arguments and commented that the perceived injustice, so far as the original tenant was concerned, should be the subject of reform by legislation. It was not appropriate to try to develop the law on a case-by-case basis. The advantage of legislation was that it would be enacted following the considered recommendations of the Law Commission in their report *Landlord and Tenant Law: Privity of Contract and Estate* (Law Com No 174), which had been made after widespread consultation with parties who may be affected by changes in the law.

LANDLORD AND TENANT (COVENANTS) ACT 1995

The Government accepted the Law Commission's recommendations for new leases and the Commission's scheme forms the backbone of the reforms introduced by the Act which came into force on 1 January 1996. It deals with both new and existing leases.

1.   NEW LEASES (GRANTED ON OR AFTER 1 JANUARY 1996 – SEE S 1)

The main purpose of the Act is to bring to an end the ongoing liability of original tenants and those assignees who have given direct covenants to the landlord.

Release of tenant (s 5)

Following assignment the tenant is released from the tenant covenants and ceases to be entitled to the benefit of the landlord covenants.

If the assignment is of part only of the premises the release and cessation apply only to the covenants that relate to the part of the premises assigned.

The section applies not only to original tenants but also to assignees who have given direct covenants to the landlord to be liable for matters arising after they themselves have assigned.

Excluded assignments (s 11)

Section 5 does not affect assignments in breach of covenant or by operation of law. But a tenant who was not discharged because the assignment was excluded will be released as from the next assignment (if any) which is not an excluded assignment.

Authorised guarantee agreements (s 16)

If the tenancy contains a covenant against assignment (absolute or qualified) whereby the assignment cannot take place without the landlord's consent, he may require a tenant who is being released from a tenant covenant to enter into an agreement guaranteeing the performance of the covenant by the assignee. The authorised guarantee agreement cannot:

- require the tenant to guarantee somebody other than the assignee
- impose liability on the tenant for any period after the assignee is released.

The agreement can, however:

- make the tenant liable as sole or principal debtor in respect of any obligation owed by the assignee;
- make the tenant liable as guarantor of the assignee's performance of the relevant tenant covenant. But the tenant's liabilities as guarantor cannot be more onerous than his liabilities as sole or principal debtor;
- require the tenant, if the tenancy is disclaimed, to take a new tenancy of the premises. The term of the new tenancy must not expire later than the term of the tenancy assigned by the tenant and its tenant covenants must be no more onerous that those of the assigned tenancy.

A former tenant who was not previously discharged may subsequently be released by the making of a non-excluded assignment. The landlord may then require the former tenant (as well as the assignor) to enter into an authorised guarantee agreement whereby the former tenant guarantees the performance of the tenant covenants by the assignee under the non-excluded assignment.

The section specifically declares that the general law of guarantees (particularly with regard to the release of sureties) applies to authorised guarantee agreements.

Landlord's consent to assignments (s 22)

New subsections (1A) to (1E) are to be inserted after section 19(1) Landlord and Tenant Act 1927.

A landlord and tenant will be able to enter into an agreement specifying

- any circumstances in which the landlord can withhold his consent to an assignment; or
- any conditions subject to which such consent may be granted.

The landlord will be acting reasonably if he withholds his consent on the ground that any such circumstances exist – assuming, of course, that they do exist. If he gives his consent subject to any such conditions, he will not be regarded as giving it subject to unreasonable conditions. Section 1 Landlord and Tenant Act 1988 (p 132 below) will have effect subject to these provisions.

The agreement between landlord and tenant need not be contained in the lease and it can be made at any time before the application for licence to assign is made.

Where the agreement allows the landlord (or any other person) to determine the circumstances in which consent can be withheld or the conditions subject to which consent may be granted, the agreement must provide that the power of determination is to be exercised reasonably or that the tenant is to have an unrestricted right of appeal to an independent person whose decision is final.

Section 19 (l)(b) of the 1927 Act, which is concerned with building leases (see page 132 below), will have no effect in relation to any assignment of a building lease which is granted on or after the date the 1995 Act comes into force. Residential leases are not caught by these new subsections.

2.   NEW AND EXISTING LEASES

Notice to former tenant or his guarantor (s 17)

A landlord will not be able to recover any fixed charge from a former tenant or his guarantor unless, within six months of the charge becoming due, he serves on that person a notice informing him:

- that the charge is now due; and
- that the landlord intends to recover the amount specified in the notice and any interest payable.

Notice to the current tenant or his guarantor is not needed. Nor is it necessary to serve the former tenant with a Section 17 Notice if the landlord is only taking action against that former tenant's guarantor: *Cheverell Estates* v *Hains* [1998] 2 EG 127.

If a guarantor's obligation to make payment only falls due under the lease when demand is made of him, the six months period only begins to run when demand is made: *Romain* v *Scuba TV Ltd* [1996] EG 126.

If the landlord does however serve notice under Section 17 on a former tenant and then pursues him for payment, the former tenant may still look to his assignee to repay him. In such circumstances, the former tenant is not required himself to serve a Section 17 notice on the assignee: *M W Kellogg Ltd* v *F Tobin* (unreported, April 8, 1997). However, the former tenant can only recover payments made after receipt of a valid Section 17 Notice; payments made by him to the landlord voluntarily before a Section 17 Notice is served are not recoverable from the assignee: *Kellogg*.

The landlord cannot recover more than is specified in the notice unless:

- it transpires that more is due under the fixed charge than was specified in the notice;
- the notice mentioned that possibility; and
- within three months of the increased amount being determined the landlord serves a further notice saying that he intends to recover the greater amount (plus any interest payable).

A fixed charge that became due before the date the Act came into force will he treated as having become due on that date.

"Fixed charge" means:

— rent
— service charge as defined by section 18 Landlord and Tenant Act 1985 (disregarding the word "dwelling") and
— any liquidated sum payable by the tenant for breach of a tenant covenant (*e.g.* Section 146 Notice costs, a debt due under *Jervis* v *Harris* – see page 123)

A notice will not be invalid even if it includes items that are subsequently found not to be due to the landlord: *Commercial Union* v *Moustafa* (see below).

"Landlord" includes anyone who can enforce payment of the fixed charge.

The form of notice to be given pursuant to section 17 is prescribed by the Landlord and Tenant (Covenants) Act 1995 (Notices) Regulations 1995.

Service of a Section 17 Notice should be effected in accordance with Section 23 Landlord & Tenant Act 1927 by:

1. Personal service; or
2. Leaving the Notice at the last known place of abode in England & Wales of the person to be served including any business address); or
3. By recorded delivery or registered post to the last known address. Postal service will be deemed to be effected 7 days after the posting on an individual and 2 days after posting on a company.

Service may be affected by recorded delivery to the recipients' last known place of abode, and will be validly served in this manner even if not received: *Commercial Union Life Assurance Co Ltd* v *Moustafa* [1999] 24 EG 155.

Variation of the tenant covenants (s 18)

Following assignment a former tenant will not be liable to pay any amount that is referable to a subsequent variation of the tenant covenants – a "relevant variation". A former tenant is somebody who has entered into an authorised guarantee agreement or who remains bound by privity of contract.

The provision also applies to a guarantor of a former tenant whose liability under the guarantee is not wholly discharged by the variation. A "relevant variation" is one which the landlord has an absolute right to resist and which was made on or after 1 January 1996. Earlier variations will be governed by *Friends' Provident* (above).

Overriding leases (s 19)

The former tenant (or his guarantor) who has had to make full payment in accordance with section 17 – described in the Act as "the claimant"– can require the landlord to grant him an overriding lease of the premises. He will then become the landlord of the assignee whose liability he has made good for a period of three days longer than the unexpired residue of the term of the lease. If the landlord is himself a tenant and unable to grant this extra three days, the overriding lease will be for the maximum period he can grant. He will thus be able to exercise the various landlord's remedies against the defaulting assignee. The claimant must make a request for an overriding lease to the landlord.

There is no prescribed form but the request must:

- be in writing and
- specify the payment which triggers the entitlement to the lease and
- be made within 12 months of making the payment

The landlord must then grant the lease within a reasonable time whereupon the claimant must deliver to the landlord a duly executed counterpart. The claimant must also pay the landlord's costs of and incidental to the grant of the lease.

If there is more than one claimant for an overriding lease, the first claim in time will be entitled to the lease (rather than the first payment made).

No overriding lease will arise if payment is made before a Section 17 Notice is served or if the contractual term of the lease has expired (even if the tenant is holding over under the Landlord and Tenant Act 1954, Part II).

Further reference should be made to sections 19 and 20 of the Act for the detailed provisions and requirements of the statutory overriding lease.

Contracting out (s 25)

Any agreement that purports to restrict the operation of the Act is void.

LANDLORD & TENANT (CONVENANTS) ACT 1995 PROCEDURES

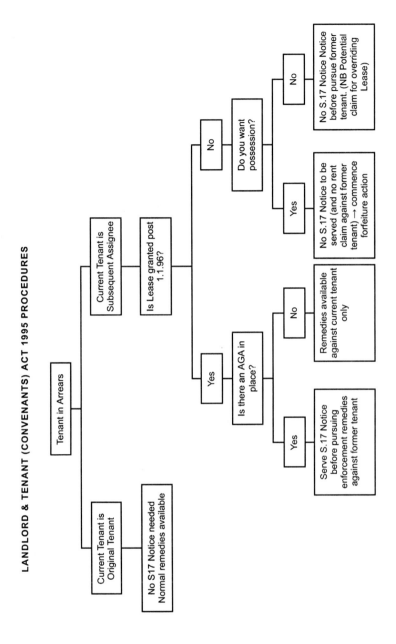

CHAPTER 8

DILAPIDATIONS

CHAPTER 8
DILAPIDATIONS

Most claims by landlords for disrepair are made at the end of the lease when the landlord serves a terminal schedule of dilapidations on the outgoing or former tenant. As often as not, these claims are eventually settled.

In a typical situation at the end of the lease, the landlord will serve a substantial terminal schedule and there will then be lengthy negotiations between the parties. There may well be proceedings issued by the landlord and a payment into court by the tenant. Almost certainly the tenant will make some form of without prejudice offer. Although such cases do occasionally end up with a court hearing, the vast majority are settled for considerably less than was originally being claimed.

This book does not set out to examine the finer points of landlord and tenant law. Reference should be made to the standard texts for a detailed exposition of all the rules of common law, statute and the construction of particular repairing covenants. The intention here is to give an outline of the rudimentary principles of the law in relation to the tenant's repairing obligations, and then proceed to an examination of the remedies available to the landlord for the breach of those obligations.

NO EXPRESS COVENANT

If, most improbably, the lease does not contain a tenant's repairing covenant, his liability will arise under the doctrine of waste or under an implied obligation in his contract with the landlord to use the premises in a tenant-like manner. Putting the matter very generally, a tenant would be liable for waste if he did or omitted to do something which caused lasting damage to the nature of the premises to the detriment of the landlord. The duty to use the property in a tenant-like manner means, in effect, that the tenant "must take proper care of the place": *Warren v Keen* [1954] 1 QB 15 at p 20, per Denning LJ.

Alternatively, a covenant by the landlord to keep the premises in repair may be implied if the use of the premises would otherwise be impossible (*Liverpool City Council v Irvin* [1976] 1 EGLR 53) or if there is a correlative obligation, such as a payment for the cost of keeping the premises in repair: *Barrett v Lounora (1982) Ltd* [1988] 2 EGLR 54. Such a covenant will, however, only be implied rarely: *Duke of Westminster v Guild* [1983] 2 EGLR 37, *Adami v Lincoln Grange Mangement Ltd* [1998] 1 EGLR 58.

All written modern tenancy agreements contain some form of tenant's repairing obligation, so the doctrine of waste and the contractual implied term are likely to arise only in relation to oral tenancies.

EXPRESS COVENANTS

The nature and extent of the tenant's liability under his express covenants is a matter of construction.

MEANING OF "REPAIR"

A considerable body of case law has built up concerning the extent of the tenant's obligations to repair. This book is concerned primarily with the action a landlord can take when a tenant is in default of his repairing obligations. It is not possible to give an exhaustive account of all the authorities. Nevertheless the following principles can be distilled from the cases:

1.   DEFINITION

"Repair involves the renewal of subsidiary parts; it does not involve renewal of the whole": *Anstruther-Gough-Calthorpe v McOscar* [1924] 1 KB 716 at p 734, per Atkin I.J. But renewing subordinate parts over a period of time may result in replacing the whole.

2.   STANDARD OF REPAIR

This will vary from property to property. Regard must be had to the age and nature of the premises at the start of the lease, but an obligation to repair carries with it a duty to put the premises into repair if they are not already in repair: *Proudfoot v Hart* (1890) 25 QBD 42.

In that Case it was said the standard of repair contemplated by the covenant is that which "having regard to the age, character, and locality of the premises would make them reasonably fit for the occupation of a reasonably minded tenant of the class likely to take them". This approach to the standard of repair required has recently been adopted and confirmed in *Mason v TotalFinaElf UK Ltd* [2003] EWHC 1604.

When considering the standard of repair the length of term is relevant. The standard of repair under a short lease may not be as high as under a long lease.

If the premises are destroyed, the normal repairing covenant will oblige the tenant to rebuild (*Matthey* v *Curling* [1922] 2 AC 180) unless the premises were destroyed as a result of enemy action: Landlord and Tenant (War Damage) Act 1939.

Although the extent of the tenant's repairing obligation is always a question of fact and degree, at the end of the day the test is whether what he is being asked to do can properly be described as repair. The tenant is not obliged to give back to the landlord something wholly different from what was demised: *Ravenseft Properties Ltd* v *Davstone (Holdings) Ltd* [1980] QB 12.

3.   IMPROVEMENTS AND INHERENT DEFECTS

The ordinary repairing obligation does not oblige the tenant to improve the property. Substantial works to a building may, at first blush, appear to constitute an improvement. But if the property is not made so different from what it was they will be regarded as a repair. See, for example, *New England Properties Ltd* v *Portsmouth New Shops Ltd* [1993] 23 EG 130 (a landlord's covenant). If the property is flawed the tenant may or may not be obliged to carry out repairs necessitated by the defect and correct the fault. The test will always be the same, i.e. the tenant is not obliged to make the property substantially different from what it was.

If the additional work required would not materially alter the nature of the property, then the tenant will have to remedy the defect because that will constitute a repair. But there must have been disrepair, i.e. deterioration, so the tenant cannot be required to replace an item which is in repair with another item which will, indirectly, cure a defect which has existed since the building was built: *Post Office* v *Aquarius Properties Ltd* [1987] 1 All ER 1055.

In *Credit Suisse* v *Beegas Nominees* [1993] EGCS 157, the judge had to consider a landlord's covenant to maintain, repair, amend and renew the walls of the building so as to keep them in good and tenantable condition". He held that that meant that all the cladding had to be stripped off and replaced so as to make the building watertight even though it had been subject to leaks prior to the tenancy in question.

Renewal of parts of a building which in themselves amount to an improvement may still constitute a repair: *Minja Properties Ltd* v *Cussins* [1998] 2 EGLR 52.

Repair of air-conditioning plant can be a particular area of concern. However, even if the plant has reached the end of its recommended lifespan, evidence of defects of malfunction is needed for it to fall within the repair covenant: *Fluor Daniel Properties Ltd* v *Shortlands Investments Ltd* [2001] EGCS 8.

4.   METHOD OF REPAIR

If a repair can be undertaken by a variety of methods, it is a matter for the person carrying out the work (not the paying party) to choose which to adopt. If the tenant does the work he can therefore do the minimum needed for a proper job. If the landlord does it, he does not have to use the cheapest method, as long as what he does is reasonable: *Plough Investments* v *Manchester* CC [1989] 1 EGLR 244. However, this does not permit an alternative solution to be used which does not effect the necessary repair: *Creska* v *Hammersmith & Fulham BC* [1998] 37 EG 165, (in that case the tenant installed storage heaters rather than repair the underfloor heating system: this did not constitute acceptable repair).

5.   PARTICULAR COVENANTS

The obligation to repair means to keep the property in substantial repair, and this is so whether the expression used is "tenantable repair", "good repair", "habitable repair" or "sufficient repair".

"Good tenantable repair" means the state of repair appropriate to the premises concerned having regard to their age, character and locality and the sort of tenant who would be likely to take them: *Proudfoot* v *Hart* (1890) 25 QBD 42.

"To repair and renew" is said to be the same as to keep in repair. The addition of "renew" apparently adds nothing to the ordinary obligation: *Collins* v *Flynn* [1963] 2 All ER 1068; *Halliard Property Co Ltd* v *Nicholas Clarke Investments Ltd* (1983) 269 EG 1257. But for an alternative view see *Norwich Union Life Insurance Society* v *British Railways Board* [1987] 2 EGLR 137.

6.   FIXTURES AND FITTINGS

Items on the premises will be either a chattel (i.e. a fitting), or a fixture which will become part of the premises. An item which is a fixture will become part of the landlord's property and therefore subject as part of the premises to the liabilities in the lease both to keep the premises in repair and yield up in repair. Such an item which is a fixture cannot be removed by the tenant at the end of the lease. This is the position even if the landlord has forfeited by peaceable re-entry: *Re Palmiero* [1999] EG 195.

A chattel however remains the tenant's property but consequently there is also an obligation on the tenant to remove it at the end of the lease. If the tenant fails to do so the landlord may claim damages for failure to yield up with vacant possession, or (as appropriate) as further disrepair.
Whether an item becomes a fixture depends on the degree and object of the annexation: *Elitestone Ltd v Morris* [1997] 27 EG 116

7.   WHEN DOES THE OBLIGATION ARISE?

A covenant to repair obliges the covenantor to keep the premises in repair at all times and a breach occurs as soon as there is default in this: *Loria v Hammer* [1989] 2 ECLR 249. However, where it is the landlord who covenants to repair, the breach only arises when he is on notice as to the existence of the defect: *British Telecommunications Plc v Sunlife Assurance Society PLC* [1995] EGCS 139.

COVENANTS TO REINSTATE

A covenant to reinstate may arise at the end of the lease or on the operation of a break clause. It may be a stand alone covenant or may arise under the covenant restricting alterations or pursuant to a licence for alterations which runs with the land. Break clauses are often conditional upon the tenant having complied with the covenants in the lease including any reinstatement covenant. The Courts have interpreted reinstatement covenants strictly. For example in *Camden Theatre v London Scottish Properties Ltd* [1984] (unreported) a covenant to reinstate with gold leaf was held not to have been complied with where gold paint only was used.

A covenant to reinstate is not subject to the limitation imposed by section 18(1) of the Landlord & Tenant Act 1927. The measure of the Landlord's loss will therefore be the cost of undertaking the works – where the Landlord actually carries out this work. It the remedial works are not undertaken, the measure of damages will be the diminution in the value of the reversion: *James v Hutton and J Cooke and Sons Ltd* [1950] 1 KB 9.

ENVIRONMENTAL LIABILITIES

Liability for environmental matters may arise as a result of action taken by the regulatory authorities under statutes such as the Environmental Protection Act 1990 or the Water Resources Act 1991, as a result of common law liabilities in negligence, nuisance or the principle in *Rylands* v *Fletcher*, or pursuant to the lease. An examination in detail of the liability for environmental matters (in particular contaminated land) under the Environmental Protection Act and Water Resources Act goes beyond the ambit of this book. That legislation does however enable the Environment Agency to prosecute for example those who have caused or knowingly permitted polluting material to enter controlled waters, or to cause or knowingly permit land to be in such a condition that it is regarding as contaminated land within the meaning of the Environmental Protection Act. Action may be taken against the freehold owner, tenant or occupier who may also face a claim under the Environmental Protection Act for statutory nuisance.

However, irrespective of the liability which may arise under the legislation, tenants may face liabilities to landlords under the terms of their lease. Many older leases were not drafted with environmental liabilities in mind. The wording is therefore sufficiently wide in many cases so that any particular liability is likely to fall within the wording of one or more of the following tenant's covenants:

a) Repair
b) Service Charge
c) The obligation to comply with statute
d) The obligation not to commit nuisance or waste
e) An obligation to pay for of outgoings in respect of the premises

Although environmental liabilities have now been foreseen for some years, even new leases may be drafted in such a way as to leave such liability on the tenant. It will therefore be important to examine the provisions of the lease to assess their applicability to any particular situation where environmental liabilities arise.

DISABILITY DISCRIMINATION ACT

From 1 October 2003 service providers will be obliged under the Disability Discrimination Act to make "reasonable adjustments" in relation to any physical features on premises which could operate as physical barriers to access by disabled people. Such adjustments may just require a change in working practices but could also require changes to physical features.

The Act does not distinguish between owners and occupiers but occupiers will normally be the "service provider" as it is they whom the public will be visiting. In a multi-let building however, the landlord may often be the service provider.

From the tenant's perspective, if he is a service provider he will need to consider making alterations. If these are prohibited under the lease then the Act will apply a provision to the effect that they may be made with the landlord's written consent, not to be unreasonably withheld.

Where the landlord carries out work, he may well be able to recover the cost of this from the tenant as most modern leases include the cost of works "required by statute".

Equally a landlord may well be able to argue that a tenant is obliged to carry out adjustment work where the tenant's repair obligations include an obligation to carry out works required by statute. New leases will no doubt include an express obligation to this effect.

REMEDIES FOR TENANT'S BREACH OF REPAIRING COVENANTS

The landlord's remedies are:

- damages;
- forfeiture;
- entering and executing the repairs;
- injunction.

LEASEHOLD PROPERTY (REPAIRS) ACT 1938

This Act, which applies only to repairing covenants, may prevent the landlord from starting proceedings for damages or forfeiture without leave of the court.

The Act applies where the lease was granted for a term of seven years or more and where there are at least three years of the term still to go.

In such a case the landlord cannot proceed to forfeit or sue for damages without first giving notice under section 146 of the Law of Property Act 1925 informing the tenant of his right to serve a counter-notice claiming the benefit of the Act. If the tenant serves a counter-notice within 28 days, no further proceedings by action or otherwise may be taken unless the court gives leave.

To obtain leave, the landlord will have to establish one of the five grounds specified in section 1(5) of the Act. They are:

1. that if immediate repairs are not carried out there will be a substantial diminution in the value of the reversion or that there has already been such a diminution;
2. that immediate repairs are necessary to comply with an enactment, court order or requirement of a statutory authority;
3. where the tenant does not occupy the whole of the premises, that immediate repairs are needed in the interests of the occupier;
4. that the cost of immediate repairs would be small compared to the cost of postponing the works;
5. that there are special circumstances which make it just and equitable that leave should be given.

The relevant date upon which the landlord has to establish one or more of the grounds specified in section 1(5) is the date of the application for leave to bring forfeiture proceedings: *Landmaster Properties Ltd* v *Thackeray Property Services* [2003] EWHC 959.

It used to be thought that the landlord had only to show a strong prima facie case that one of the grounds under the Act could be established but, in *Associated British Ports* v *C H Bailey plc* [1990] 1 All ER 929, the House of Lords held that that was not enough. The landlord must prove the ground alleged on the balance of probabilities. Repairs costing £600,000 were required to a derelict dry dock. The tenant argued, successfully, that as the lease still had 62 years to run the damage to the landlord's reversion was minimal.

The court can, if it refuses to grant leave, impose conditions on the tenant: *Allsopp* v *DHSS* (1988) NPC 30. Moreover, the court has an overriding, unfettered discretion: *Land Securities plc* v *Receiver for the Metropolitan Police District* [1983] 1 WLR 439.

Where the lease enables the landlord to enter and do repairs in default of the tenant carrying them out under his obligations, and provides for the recovery, by the landlord, of the cost of those repairs, an action for the cost is for a contract debt and is not subject to the 1938 Act: *Hamilton* v *Martell Securities Ltd* [1984] Ch 266; *Colchester Estates (Cardiff)* v *Carlton Industries plc* [1986] Ch 80; *Elite Investments Ltd* v *T I Bainbridge Silencers Ltd* (1986) 280 EG 1001; and especially *Jervis* v *Harris* [1996] 10 EG 159.

The right to enter and repair as confirmed by *Jervis* is an important weapon in the landlord's armoury (for further details see page 123 below).

INITIAL REPAIRS

The 1938 Act does not apply where the tenant is under an obligation to put the premises into repair on taking possession or within a reasonable time thereafter.

AN ACTION FOR DAMAGES

No Section 146 Notice is required in respect of terminal dilapidations, i.e. failure to yield up in repair. A Section 146 Notice is, nevertheless, sometimes served before a lease is about to expire and, provided the lease contains the necessary covenant by the tenant, the landlord should be able to claim as a contract debt his costs and expenses in relation to and in contemplation of the preparation and service of the Section 146 Notice: *Bader Properties Ltd* v *Linley Property Investments Ltd* (1967) 19 P 8c CR 620. The landlord must start proceedings in the county court where the damages claimed are less than £15,000. Otherwise he may begin in the High Court. Complicated dilapidations claims are often started in or transferred to the Technology and Construction Court.

Once he has issued proceedings, the landlord can use the summary judgment procedure under Part 24 of the Civil Procedure Rules if he considers there is no defence, coupling that with an application for an interim payment under Part 25.

THE MEASURE OF DAMAGES AT COMMON LAW

The damages which a landlord may recover for breach of a repairing covenant are subject to special statutory rules. In order to understand these rules, it is necessary to consider the position at common law and then to consider the changes effected by statute.

ACTION BROUGHT BEFORE THE EXPIRY OF THE LEASE

The measure of damages is the dimunition in the sale value of the reversion which has resulted from the breach: *Conquest* v *Ebbetts* [1896] AC 490. This is the amount by which the market value of the landlord's interest is reduced by the disrepair. Accordingly the measure of damages will be less if the action is brought during the term rather than at the end of the lease.

ACTION BROUGHT AT THE END OF THE LEASE

The measure of damages is based on the tenant's covenant to yield up the premises in repair. At common law the measure of damages is the actual cost of carrying out the repairs necessary to put the premises into the state of repair required by the covenant: *Joyner* v *Weeks* [1891] 2 QB 31. This would apply even if the premises were to be pulled down, so that the repairs were valueless. A Landlord could also claim for loss of rent for the period of the repairs: *Woods* v *Pope* (1835) 6 C & P 782.

LANDLORD AND TENANT ACT 1927, S 18(1)

Pursuant to this section, damages for breach of a covenant to keep or put premises in repair during the currency of a lease, or to leave or put premises in repair at the end of a lease, cannot exceed the amount (if any) by which the value of the reversion in the premises is diminished owing to the breach.

It is convenient to set out section 18(1) of the Landlord and Tenant Act 1927 in full:

> "Damages for a breach of covenant or agreement to keep or put premises in repair during the currency of a Lease, or to leave or put premises in repair at the termination of a Lease, whether such covenant or agreement is expressed or implied, and whether general or specific shall in no case exceed the amount (if any) by which the value of the reversion (whether immediate or not) in the premises is diminished owing to the breach of such covenant or agreement as aforesaid; and in particular, no damage shall be recovered for a breach of any such covenant or agreement to leave or put premises in repair at the termination of a Lease, if it is shown that the premises, in whatever state of repair they might be, would at or shortly after the termination of the tenancy have been or be pulled down, or such structural alterations made therein as would render valueless the repairs covered by the covenant or agreement."

This means in particular that no damages can be recovered if it is shown that the premises would, at or shortly after the end of the tenancy, have been or be pulled down, or structural alterations made to them as would render the repairs valueless.

The section imposes a "ceiling" on the amount of the damages which can be recovered. The section is divided into two "limbs".

The first limb imposes a diminution in value of the reversion "ceiling" and applies to actions brought both during the term and at the end of the term.

The second limb applies only in relation to actions brought at the end of the term: *Re King* [1962] 1 WLR 632. Under the second limb no damages whatever will be recovered if the landlord would pull down or so alter the premises that the works would be rendered valueless: *Cunliffe v Goodman* [1950] 2 KB 237. The correct approach is to assess damages on the basis of the amount recoverable at common law and then to ascertain the diminution in value of the reversion. The lesser of the two sums will be the recoverable amount. The diminution in the value of the reversion is assessed at the expiry date of the lease and involves two valuations of the landlord's interest. The first is a valuation based on the assumption that the premises are in the state that they would have been in if the tenant had performed his repairing obligations. The second valuation will be the valuation of the premises in their actual state and condition at that date: *Mason v TotalFinaElf UK Ltd* [2003] EWHC 1604.

1.   ACTION BROUGHT DURING THE TERM

The measure of damages is still the diminution in value.

2.   ACTION BROUGHT AT THE END OF THE TERM

Section 18 has affected the measure of damages for terminal dilapidations. If the cost of repairs exceeds the diminution in value, the measure of damages is restricted to the diminution. Loss of rent and other heads of damages can still he claimed, but the total damages cannot exceed the section 18 "ceiling".

Whilst the measure is the diminution in a term-end action, the cost or estimated cost of the repairs is highly relevant. The landlord will, therefore, produce both evidence as to the cost of repairs and evidence as to the diminution in value of the reversion (based upon evidence showing the repaired and unrepaired values of the reversion). Failure to produce evidence of the diminution in the value of the reversion may cause the claim to fail: *Mather v Barclays Bank plc* [1987] 2 EGLR 254.

The cost of repairs may well be the proper measure of damages or, at any rate, a useful guide: *Jones v Herxheimer* [1950] 2 KB 106; *Smiley v Townsend* [1950] 2 KB 311; *Haviland v Long* [1962] 2 QB 80; *Drummond v S & U Stores Ltd* (1980) 258 EG 1293. The measure of damages is to be assessed at the date of the determination of the lease: *Jaquin v Holland* [1960] 1 WLR 258.

If there is a sub-tenant in occupation with repairing obligations, who is protected by Part II of the Landlord and Tenant Act 1954, there may then be no diminution in value: *Family Management v Gray* (1980) 253 EG 369 and *Crown Estate Commissioners v Town Investments Ltd* (1992) 8 EG

111. Even though repairs are required to the premises the landlord will be deemed to suffer no damage to his reversion, because section 34(1)(a) of the Act fixes the rent of the new tenancy at the full open market rent irrespective of the effect the occupation of the tenant might have had.

The fact that the landlord has re-let to a new tenant who will carry out repairs does not provide a defence to the former tenant by reducing the diminution in value: *Haviland* v *Long* [1952] 2 QB 80.

3.   HEADS OF DAMAGE

The heads of damage (subject always to the section 18 limit) can include not only the costs of repair but also:

1. loss of rent;
2. solicitors' and surveyors' costs if the lease so provides: *Lloyds Bank Ltd* v *Lake* [1961] 1 WLR 884;
3. value added tax if the landlord is not registered for VAT: *Drummond* v *S &U Stores Ltd* (1980) 258 EG 1293. But in *Elite Investments Ltd* v *T I Bainbridge Silencers Ltd* (No 2) (1987) 283 EG 747, it was held that VAT should be added to damages for breach of covenant to repair, where the landlord is not registered, only if there is a realistic option that the works will in fact be done;
4. service charges; rates.

An interesting case which shows the inter-action between the damages recoverable at common law and under the section 18 "ceiling" is *Culworth Estates Ltd* v *The Society of Licensed Victuallers* [1991] 2 EGLR 54. The landlord, rather than repairing or redeveloping the property, decided to sell it to a developer. Judge Peter Crawford QC, sitting as a High Court judge, described section 18 as falling into two limbs. As to the first limb he said it "...does not provide a substitution for the common law quantum of damages. It sets a limit to the quantum of damages". He held that the landlords could recover the full, agreed cost of repairs together with professional fees and loss of rent. He found that the landlords had no settled intention to redevelop and so the second limb of section 18(1) had no application. The loss in value of their reversion was at least as great as, or greater than, the cost of the work and, therefore, the whole of the damages were awarded.

4.   THE COST OF REINSTATING

Provided the covenant in question is outside the provisions of section 18, there may well be cases where the cost of reinstatement is the measure of damage and is larger than the diminution in value of the reversion. In *Eyre* v *Rae* [1947] 1 KB 567 the premises were converted into five flats in breach of a covenant to use as a private dwelling-house. It was argued that there was no loss because the landlord would receive back premises which were more valuable since they could be let at a higher rent. Nevertheless, it was held that the landlord was entitled to the full cost of restoring the premises to a single home and the loss of rents during the period of the works. See also on similar facts *Westminster v Swinton* [1948] 1 KB 524.

5.   AGREED LUMP SUM

If the parties agree that the tenant will pay to the landlord a lump sum by way of agreed damages for dilapidations, the court will usually enforce this as a binding legal agreement. If the agreement is silent on the point, it may be implied that the agreement covers all disrepair except for any substantial further disrepair occurring between the date of the agreement and the date the tenant vacates; *Southern Counties Agricultural Trading Society Ltd v Green & Carter Ltd* (1983) 266 EG 715.

RIGHT TO ENTER AND REPAIR

The landlord does not have a right to enter and repair upon the tenant's default unless the right is expressly reserved in the lease: *Yelloly v Morley* (1910) 27 TLR 20; *Regional Properties Ltd v City of London Real Property Co Ltd* [1980] 257 EGM 64.

The clause usually provides for notice to be served by the landlord requiring the repairs to be carried out within a specified time – usually three months – failing which the landlord can enter and repair at the tenant's cost. A contractual notice can be served together with a Section 146 Notice.

If the clause provides that the cost of the works can be recovered as a debt (and not damages), there will be no need to serve notice under the Leasehold Property (Repairs) Act before the landlord carries out the work: *Colchester Estates (Cardiff) v Carlton Industries plc* [1986] Ch 80; *Hamilton v Martell Securities Ltd* [1984] 1 All ER 665; *Elite Investments Ltd v T I Bainbridge Silencers Ltd* [1986] 280 EG 1001; and especially *Jervis v Harris* [1996] 10 KG 159. Nor will the restriction on damages in the Landlord and Tenant Act 1927, s.18 apply.

The *Jervis* case is the seminal exposition of the law on this point. It confirmed once and for all that where the lease reserves the right for the landlord to enter and carry out works and then charge them to the tenant, the landlord's claim is one for debt, rather than damages. Leave under the 1938 Act is therefore not required. Nor is such a provision an unenforceable penalty. This gives the landlord a powerful weapon.

When considering the use of this power, the lease should be checked to ensure that the disrepair is the responsibility of the tenant. Notice should then be served on the tenant requiring him to undertake the work necessary to comply with the covenants in the lease. If the tenant defaults, the landlord should seek access to carry out the works. If this is refused, the landlord may seek an injunction to prevent the tenant prohibiting access. However, in some cases the court may refuse to grant an injunction if the damage to the tenant is serious and damages would form an appropriate alternative remedy: *Hammersmith and Fulham London Borough Council* v *Creska Ltd* [1999] PLSCS 159.

Once the landlord has undertaken the repairs, the cost of these will constitute a debt due from the tenant which may be enforced by Court action, insolvency proceedings or (where this sum is reserved as rent) distress. Assuming the proviso for forfeiture is widely drawn, failure to comply with the obligation may also amount to a ground for forfeiture.

The benefit of this right to enter and repair as a remedy for the landlord is strengthened by the fact that the restriction on damages set out in section 18 of the 1927 Act does not apply. The value of the landlord's claim is not limited to the diminution in the value of the landlord's reversion. Instead, the common law applies and the landlord will be entitled to the full cost of repair. Therefore, it will benefit landlords to threaten to exercise their rights under *Jervis* before the end of the term of the lease rather than suing the tenant for terminal dilap- idations as the latter will be capped by section 18 whereas the former will not. Faced with the prospect of disruption to his business before the end of the lease, and having to pay the repair costs in full, many tenants are likely to do a deal with the landlord. The landlord in such circumstances is likely to achieve a far better result than he would have done if he had had to take action and face the cap under section 18 of the 1927 Act.

INJUNCTION

Hill v *Barclay* (1810) 16 Ves Jun 402 is usually cited as authority for saying that a landlord cannot enforce a tenant's repairing covenant by a mandatory injunction, and an injunction will not normally be an appropriate remedy to deal with a tenant's breach of repairing covenant.

A claim for specific performance is usually unlikely to be granted since the courts will not usually be prepared to oversee a building contract. However, the order can be made against a landlord: *Jeune* v *Queen's Cross Properties Ltd* [1974] Ch 97; *Francis* v *Cowlcliffe Ltd* (1976) 33 P & CR 368.

A landlord may in rare circumstances obtain an order for specific performance against the tenant if damages would be an inappropriate remedy: *Rainbow Estates Ltd* v *Tokenhold Ltd* [1998] 24 EG 123. In that case the order was made because of serious disrepair and the absence in the lease of a proviso for forfeiture. Where there is a right of re-entry, or the landlord is entitled to enter and carry out the works, a court is still unlikely to grant specific preference.

FORFEITURE

See Chapters 3 and 4 above.

TERMINAL DILAPIDATIONS CLAIMS

The draft Pre-Action Protocol for terminal dilapidations claims prepared by the Property Litigation Association and published in 2002, sets out best practice in identifying the relevant issues before cases come to court. A party which refuses to follow the protocol runs the risk of adverse costs orders.

The protocol seeks to ensure that as much information about the claim is exchanged as soon as possible. This is particularly important in the light of the specific statutory limit on the recovery of damages.

Section 18(1) of the Landlord and Tenant Act 1927 limits a landlord's claim against a tenant for a breach of repairing obligations to the amount by which its reversionary interest has diminished in value due to the disrepair. Where a landlord intends to demolish or redevelop the property, it will not be entitled to recover any damages for breach of repairing obligations as these are rendered obsolete by the development plans.

Sometimes a landlord will carry out the works of repair itself on the expiry of a lease, with the aim of re-letting the property as soon as possible. In such circumstances, the cost of the works, together with lost rent during the time taken to carry out the works will be the amount of damages sought by a landlord and the *prima facie* measure of loss.

However, where a landlord has not carried out the works, but intends them to be carried out at a later stage, the protocol requires the landlord to state when it intends to do the work and what steps it has taken.

Also relevant is the cap in section 18(1) of the Landlord and Tenant Act 1927, when considering whether or not the cost of the works will exceed the amount by which the value of the landlord's interest has diminished due to the disrepair.

On occasions, the diminution in the value of the reversion will be less than the cost of putting the premises back into repair, so a landlord will not be entitled to recover more than that, even if a fully-detailed and costed schedule of dilap- idations has been prepared setting out all the tenant's breaches of its repairing obligations, ostensibly giving rise to a substantial claim.

In *Ultraworth Limited* v *General Accident Fire and Life Assurance Group Plc* [2000] 2 EGLR 115) the risks of not obtaining such evidence at an early stage and pursuing a dilapidations claim without it were seen. The parties reached agreement in connection with the cost of some of the works, but not others. The matter proceeded to court and the landlord sold the property during the course of the action. The court took the view that the property would only have been of interest to a developer and that the disrepair had not caused a diminution in the value of the reversion, therefore the landlord had not suffered any recoverable loss and in consequence had no claim. In such a situation a landlord is likely to be ordered to pay the costs of the legal proceedings.

Landlords should, as a preliminary step following the preparation of a costed schedule of dilapidations, obtain a section 18(1) valuation as an overview of a claim for dilapidations to establish whether the cost of the repairs exceeds any diminution in value of its reversionary interest, taking into account the potential of the property.

CHAPTER 9

UNLAWFUL ASSIGNMENTS AND SUB-LETTING

CHAPTER 9
UNLAWFUL ASSIGNMENTS AND SUB-LETTING

Unless the lease expressly prohibits alienation, at common law the tenant's entitlement to assign or sub-let is unrestricted. However, all modern commercial leases invariably contain covenants restricting disposition by the tenant. The covenants may be absolute or qualified, may restrict alienation of the whole or part of the premises (or both), and may be a mixture of the following common restrictions.

COVENANT AGAINST ASSIGNMENT

This covenant prevents the tenant from disposing of his entire interest under the lease but does not stop him sub-letting the premises in whole or in part. An involuntary assignment (such as on the death or bankruptcy of the tenant) will not be a breach of the covenant. There will be no breach unless there is a legal assignment – for an equitable assignment see "Covenant against parting with possession" below. The execution of a declaration of trust, the deposit of the lease for security or allowing another into possession will not be breaches of the covenant.

A covenant not to assign or sub-let runs with the land and binds any assignee even if there is no direct covenant between the assignee and the landlord. It will not bind a sub-tenant unless there is a direct covenant in which the sub-tenant covenants with the head landlord that he will not assign or sub-underlet without the head landlord's consent. Any such requirement will be subject to the provisions of section 19 of the Landlord and Tenant Act 1927 and the Landlord and Tenant Act 1988 (see below).

A covenant prohibiting assignment of part of the premises prevents an assignment of the whole: *Field* v *Barkworth* [1986] 1 All ER 362.

COVENANT AGAINST SUB-LETTING

A covenant against sub-letting is invariably included in modern commercial leases. Depending upon the wording of the covenant, it may not prevent the tenant granting a licence to occupy. It is uncertain whether an assignment constitutes a breach of this covenant. It seems that a covenant against underletting simpliciter will not prevent assignment: *Re Doyle and O'Hara's Contract* [1899] 1 IR 113. But a prohibition against underletting for all or part of the term will have that effect: *Greenaway* v *Adams* (1806)12 Ves 395. Unless there is a specific covenant enabling the tenant to charge the lease, a covenant against sub-letting will often prevent the tenant from mortgaging the premises, because a mortgage of a leasehold interest operates either by way of sublease or by way of legal charge which takes effect as if a sublease had been created. *Re Good's Lease* [1954] 1 All ER 275 suggests, however, that there may be no breach where the mortgage is by way of legal charge.

A covenant against sub-letting is broken if the tenant parts with exclusive possession of all or (if the lease so provides) part of the property, to a sub-tenant. If the lease does not prohibit sub-letting of part, such a sub-letting will not breach a covenant prohibiting subletting of the whole, unless a number of sub-lettings of parts result in the whole building being sub-let: *Chatterton* v *Terrell* [1923] AC 578. If the covenant prohibits sub-letting of part, sub-letting of the whole will be a breach of the covenant: *Field* v *Barkworth* [1986] 1 All ER 362; *Troop* v *Gibson* [1986] 1 EGLR 1.

Sub-letting the premises for a term expiring after the date of the term held by the tenant operates as an assignment: *Milmo* v *Carreras* [1946] KB 306; even if the sub-tenancy is granted orally: *Parc Battersea Ltd* v *Hutchinson* [1999] 22 EG 149.

COVENANT AGAINST PARTING WITH POSSESSION

A covenant prohibiting the tenant parting with possession of the premises prevents the tenant assigning or sub-letting, or allowing another into occupation even if there is no formal assignment.

An equitable assignment will be a breach of this covenant. The covenant will also often expressly prohibit sharing possession. If it does not, the covenant will be broken only if the tenant is totally out of possession, not if be retains possession and is simply permitting someone else to share occupation with him: *Lam Kee Ying Sdn Bbd* v *Lam Sbes Tong* [1975] AC 247.

Permitting somebody else to use the premises if the tenant retains legal possession will therefore not constitute a breach of this covenant, as a breach requires the complete exclusion of the tenant. It is important to consider the facts of a particular case to ascertain whether the tenant has indeed given up legal possession. Investigations by the landlord may include checking the name of the subscriber for public utilities supplied to the premises, checking by whom the rent is paid, and inspecting the premises themselves to ascertain, for example, whether the tenant's or someone else's name is exhibited at the premises. However a properly drafted lease will normally prevent the tenant retaining possession but allowing others to use the premises if there is a covenant prohibiting sharing.

COVENANT AGAINST SHARING POSSESSION

This covenant is often combined with a covenant against parting with possession, but is wider than one which simply prohibits parting with possession. A covenant prohibiting sharing possession will often be construed as prohibiting sharing both the use and the occupation of the premises: *Tulapam Properties Ltd* v *De Almeida* (1981) 260 EG 919. However, there is no precise test of the meaning of "sharing occupation": *Mean Fiddler Holdings Ltd* v *London Borough of Islington* [2003] 19 EG 120.

COVENANT PROHIBITING CHARGING THE DEMISED PREMISES

As mentioned above, a mortgage may take effect as a sub-demise which will invariably be prohibited by the covenant against subletting. However there is often a specific provision in the lease allowing the tenant to charge the premises, subject to the landlord's prior consent.

ABSOLUTE OR QUALIFIED COVENANT

Alienation covenants are either absolute (i.e. prohibiting all dispositions), qualified (i.e. prohibiting alienation without the landlord's prior consent) or fully qualified (i.e. a qualified covenant with the addition of the words "such consent not to be unreasonably withheld").

If the lease contains an absolute prohibition but the tenant wishes to assign, sub-let etc. he may request permission from the landlord. The landlord has no obligation to consent and it is entirely within his absolute discretion whether or not he does.

A qualified covenant is subject to the following statutory provisions.

1.   LANDLORD AND TENANT ACT 1927, S 19(1)(A)

If the alienation covenant provides that any disposition requires the land-lord's consent, the covenant is deemed to be subject to a proviso that consent is not to be unreasonably withheld. It is not possible to contract out of this provision, although the landlord may require the tenant to pay his legal or other expenses incurred in connection with that consent.

2.   LANDLORD AND TENANT ACT 1927, S 19(1)(B) – BUILDING LEASES

Section 19(l)(b) provides, in effect, that a building lease granted for more than 40 years by a lessor who is not a public body is freely assignable etc. more than seven years before the end of the term even if it contains a qualified covenant against alienation. But written notice of the disposition must be given to the landlord within six months. If the lease provides that on a dis-position the tenant must procure that the assignee enters into a direct covenant with the landlord, the landlord can insist on the direct covenant being obtained, notwithstanding the provisions of section 19(l)(b) which do not require consent itself: *Vaux Group plc* v *Lilly* [1991] 1 EGLR 60.

3.   LANDLORD AND TENANT (COVENANTS) ACT 1995 (S 22)

This section provides that, in relation to new tenancies i.e. those granted on or after 1 January 1996, new subsections (1A to 1E) are to be inserted after section 19(1) Landlord and Tenant Act 1927.

Under the new law a landlord and tenant will be able to enter into an agree-ment specifying

- any circumstances in which the landlord can withhold his consent to an assignment; or
- any conditions subject to which such consent may be granted.

The landlord will be acting reasonably if he withholds his consent on the ground that any such circumstances exist – assuming, of course, that they do exist. If he gives his consent subject to any such conditions, he will not be regarded as giving it subject to unreasonable conditions. Section 1 of the Landlord and Tenant Act 1988 (see below) will have effect subject to these provisions.

The agreement between landlord and tenant need not be contained in the lease and it can be made at any time before the application for licence to assign is made.

Where the agreement allows the landlord (or any other person) to determine the circumstances in which consent can be withheld or the conditions subject to which consent may be granted, the agreement must provide that the power of determination is to be exercised reasonably or that the tenant is to have an unrestricted right of appeal to an independent person whose decision is final.

Section 19(1)(b) of the 1927 Act, which is concerned with building leases (see above), will have no effect in relation to any assignment of a building lease which is granted on or after 1 January 1996. Residential leases are not caught by these subsections.

4.   LAW OF PROPERTY ACT 1925, S 144

Unless the lease states to the contrary, this section provides that no fine or sum of money is payable for the landlord's consent. The provision does not prevent the landlord requiring payment of his reasonable legal or other expenses, nor, it is thought, the payment of a returnable deposit. The lease may require the assignee to enter into a direct covenant with the landlord to pay the rent and perform the covenants. The landlord cannot demand an increased rent, as this will almost certainly be regarded as a fine: *Jenkins* v *Price* [1907] 2 Ch 229.

5.   LANDLORD AND TENANT ACT 1988

A qualified covenant against assigning, underletting, charging or parting with possession is subject to the provisions of the Landlord and Tenant Act 1988. This Act provides a framework of duties and obligations which will apply to applications for consent.

If the tenant makes a *written* application to the landlord for consent to alienate, the Act provides, at section 1(3) that:

1. the landlord must give consent unless it is reasonable not to do so;
2. consent must be given in writing within a reasonable time of the tenant's application;
3. any reasonable conditions the landlord wishes to impose must be notified to the tenant within a reasonable time;
4. if the landlord proposes to refuse consent he must give notice in writing to the tenant of that refusal and the reasons in writing within a reasonable time of receipt of the tenant's application.

Similar obligations apply to an application by a sub-tenant which is subject to the consent of the head landlord (s 3).

If the landlord, having received the application, cannot give consent without the consent of some other person (for example, a superior landlord), section 2 of the Act imposes a duty upon any person who has received a written application to take such steps as are reasonable to secure the receipt within a reasonable time by the other person of a copy of the application. The person to whom the application is passed then himself comes under the duties set out in section 1(3) of the Act, and, if applicable, the duty to pass on the application to any superior landlord whose consent is required.

Section 4 creates a liability in damages for a landlord in breach of the provisions of the Act. It is therefore in the landlord's interest to deal with applications for consent expeditiously. The Act places the burden of proof on the landlord to show that he responded within a reasonable time and that any grounds for refusal are reasonable (s 1(6)).

REASONABLE TIME

The Act does not specify the time within which a landlord must respond to the tenant's request, either to consent or to object to the proposed transaction. It was originally suggested that 28 days would be appropriate (and there has been judicial reference to this period: *Dong Bang Minerva (UK) Ltd* v *Davina Ltd* [1994] EGCS 104 and [1996] 31 EG 87) but this was not included in the Act. There is therefore no statutory fixed period, and what constitutes a reasonable time will depend upon the facts of each case: *Go West Ltd* v *Spigarolo* [2003] All ER (D) 331 Jan, where the court held that what amounts to a reasonable time will be assessed by reference to the circumstances of the particular case, not any longer objective standard. It has been held that a period of three months before the landlord responded to the request was too long: *Midland Bank plc* v *Chart Enterprises Inc* [1990] 44 EG 68. However, the court did make it clear, in that case, that the landlord is entitled to take time to consider whether there may be an existing breach of covenant and to pursue any appropriate enquiries. Further the following comments of Mumby J in *Go West* should be noted: "I find it hard to imagine that a period of ... almost four months could ever be acceptable, save perhaps in the most unusual and complex situations ... it may be that the reasonable time ... will sometimes have to be measured in weeks rather than days; but, even in complicated cases, it should be measured in weeks rather than months." In *NCR Ltd* v *Riverland Portfolio No 1 Ltd* [2005] EWCA Civ 312 it was held that in an uncomplicated transaction, a period of 2–3 weeks from receipt of the tenant's full case for consent was not unreasonable.

REASONABLENESS OF REFUSAL

Section 1 (5) of the Act provides that a landlord's refusal will only be reasonable in a case where if consent were withheld, and the tenant completed the transaction, the tenant would be in breach of covenant. In the application of this provision, the pre-existing authorities concerning reasonableness will not be ignored – see dicta of Lord Justice Stuart-Smith in *Air India* v *Balabel* [1993] 30 EG 90.

The leading case is *International Drilling Fluids Ltd* v *Louisville Investments (Uxbridge) Ltd* [1986] Ch 513. The Court of Appeal set out seven principles to be taken into account when considering whether consent had been reasonably or unreasonably withheld. One of these has now been superseded by the Act, which has expressly provided that the burden of proving reasonableness is on the landlord. The remaining criteria are:

1. the purpose of a covenant restricting assignment is to protect the landlord from having his premises used or occupied in an undesirable way or by an undesirable tenant;
2. the landlord is not entitled to refuse his consent on grounds which have nothing to do with the landlord and tenant relationship in regard to the subject-matter of the lease;
3. the landlord does not have to prove that the conclusions which led him to refuse consent were justified if they were conclusions which in the circumstances might be reached by a reasonable man;
4. it may be reasonable to refuse consent because of the intended use of the premises even if that use is not expressly prohibited by the lease;
5. a landlord need usually consider only his own interests, but in certain circumstances a refusal of consent may cause disproportionate harm to the tenant and in those circumstances a refusal may be unreasonable;
6. reasonableness is to be decided as a question of fact in all the circumstances.

Although these criteria were laid down in the context of a covenant against assignment, it is thought that they will apply to any alienation covenant and it has been held that they do apply to sub-lettings: *Straudley Investments Ltd* v *Mount Eden Land Ltd* [1996] EGCS 153. In addition the following two criteria will also apply:

1. it will be reasonable to refuse if it is necessary to prevent the tenant acting to the prejudice of the landlord
2. it will be unreasonable to impose a term which enhances the landlord's control.

If the landlord refuses consent for more than one reason and it is subsequently found that one of the reasons relied on was unreasonable, this will not taint the reasonableness of the refusal on other grounds: *BRS Northern Ltd* v *Temple Heights Ltd* [1998] 2 EGLR 182 and *British Bakeries (Midlands) Ltd* v *Michael Testler and Co Ltd* [1986] 1 EGLR 64. It was also held in the *British Bakeries* case that the test of what is reasonable is an objective one: could a reasonable landlord have withheld consent for such reason(s)? This has now been expressly approved as the test: *Kened Ltd* v *Connie Investments Ltd* [1997] 4 EG 141.

In *Air India* v *Balabel* (above), the Court of Appeal confirmed that the 1988 Act does not require a landlord to justify, as a matter of fact, the matters relied upon in refusing consent. It also confirmed that in deciding this issue the judge should not rely upon any matters arising subsequent to the refusal of consent by the landlord.

Before the 1988 Act, the landlord could rely on all the reasons he had taken into account, even if these had not all been communicated to the tenant at the time. He could, it was thought, rely on these reasons at the trial in any court proceedings even though they had not previously been notified to the tenant: *Lovelock* v *Margo* [1963] 2 QB 786. But they had to be reasons that actually influenced the landlord: *Orlando Investments Ltd* v *Grosvenor Estate Belgravia* [1989] 43 EG 175. However, since the 1988 Act, the court will no longer permit a landlord to rely on reasons which have not been communicated to the tenant – the Act provides a positive duty on the landlord to give the reasons for his refusal. The landlord can only rely on reasons actually given to the tenant in writing and in reasonable time; oral reasons are insufficient: *Footwear Group* v *Amplight Properties* [1998] 25 EG 171.

In a case which pre-dates the Act, *Bromley Park Gardens Estates Ltd* v *Moss* [1982] 2 All ER 890; [1982] 1 WLR 1019, the Court of Appeal held that the date for deciding the reasonableness or otherwise of the landlord's refusal of consent is the date he makes his decision (or the date of disposition if the tenant proceeds without licence) and not the date of the hearing. This approach has been confirmed, so far as the Act is concerned, by the decision in *CIN Properties* v *Gill* [1993] 38 EG 152. The court also confirmed that the reasonableness of the landlord's refusal will be judged on the circumstances existing and known to the landlord at the time of his decision. See also *Blockbuster Entertainment Ltd* v *Leakcliffe Properties Ltd* [1997] 8 EG 139. The court will not allow the landlord to adduce evidence of matters that only came to his attention after consent had been refused (in the *CIN* case evidence of the poor financial state of the proposed assignee). See also on this issue *Straudley Investments Ltd* v *Mount Eden Land Ltd supra*. However, the landlord can elaborate on his stated grounds: *Ashworth Frazer Ltd* v *Gloucester City Council (No 2)* [2001] 46 EG 180.

PROCEDURE FOR APPLICATIONS UNDER THE LANDLORD AND TENANT ACT 1988

1. Tenant's request for consent to alienate must be made in writing and served either as provided for in the lease or under section 23 of the Landlord and Tenant Act 1927 (in practice, by recorded delivery).
2. If the consent of a superior landlord is required, the land lord should pass the application to him within a reasonable time.
3. The landlord's solicitor may request an undertaking from the proposed assignor's solicitor to pay the landlord's reasonable legal costs. If further information is required, such as financial references for the proposed assignee, these should be requested as soon as possible, preferably in writing.
4. The landlord must respond within a reasonable time in writing, either giving consent (and if applicable stating any reasonable conditions) or, if consent is refused, setting out the reasons which should include all relevant grounds for refusal: *Blockbuster Entertainment* (above). As stated above, a refusal should state all grounds that the landlord has in contemplation. However, this does not require that a letter that sets out all aspects of the landlord's view. As stated by Lord Rodger in the *Ashworth Frazer* case: " ... the degree of detail contained in such a letter is likely to depend to a large extent on what is said by the Tenant in the application to which the Landlord is responding. In practice a dialogue may develop. Once the Landlord has stated in writing the ground on which he refuses consent, he cannot later rely on any other ground. That does not mean to say that, when seeking to show that it was reasonable for him not to consent on the stated ground, he is confined to what he has said in his letter. Section 1(6)(c) [of the Landlord & Tenant Act 1988] contains no such restriction, and rightly so. Otherwise, instead of being a straightforward practical document, the notice containing the Landlord's reasons for withholding consent would soon become a battleground for litigants and an increasingly sophisticated playground for Conveyancers. Such cannot have been the intention of Parliament in enacting the legislation."
5. The landlords consent should he recorded in writing, preferably by a formal licence. This will usually include a covenant from the assignee directly with the landlord to comply with all the covenants in the lease. It is possible to give consent in correspondence, even if marked "subject to licence": *Next plc v NFU Mutual Insurance Co Ltd* [1997] EGCS 181. Landlords' agents should therefore take care with the drafting of correspondence as any requirement for express written consent can be by letter, and does not require a formal deed to be binding: *Aubergine Enterprises v Lakewood International* [2002] EWCA Civ 177. Once given, consent cannot be withdrawn.

Correspondence relating to the grant of licences to assign (or alterations) is often marked "Subject to Licence" and "Without Prejudice". Many practitioners will feel that this gives them the protection necessary to ensure that consent is not given until the formal licence documentation is completed. However, a recent Court of Appeal decision has highlighted that this may not always be the case: *Aubergine Investments Limited* v *Lakewood International Limited* [2002] EWCA Civ 177. In that case the sale of long leasehold premises required the landlord's prior written consent to assign, such consent not to be unreasonably withheld and (under the terms of the lease) there were certain conditions to be satisfied.

When consent was requested, the landlord's agent responded marking the letter "subject to contract" and "without prejudice" and stating that the landlord "will be prepared in principle to grant a licence for the assignment of the lease". The reply went on to refer to the landlord's solicitors dealing with the formalities of the licence.

The purchaser subsequently had difficulty in obtaining the necessary funds to complete. By the contractual completion date, both the landlord's agents and the landlord's solicitors had indicated that the landlord would grant consent "in principle" and "subject to licence".

In view of its financial difficulties, the purchaser sought to rescind the contract pursuant to Standard Condition 8.3.4 and requested return of the deposit pursuant to Condition 7.2(a). The purchaser contended that the landlord's consent had not been obtained.

At first instance the judge held that Standard Condition 8.3 did not require the landlord's consent to be in writing. That was rejected by the Court of Appeal who confirmed that the consent required by the lease must be a prior written consent, however, the Court held that the appropriate consent had been given here by virtue of the letter from the landlord's solicitors enclosing an engrossment of the licence for execution by the purchaser and indicating that consent was agreed "in principle". The Court held that the qualification "in principle" did not mean that the landlord was seeking to rely on any reasonable grounds for refusing consent.

Clearly it is no longer safe to refer to consent being granted "in principle" unless it is unequivocally intended to constitute the necessary consent. If it is not, a different form of words will have to be used and it should be spelt out expressly that consent is not to be given until all formalities have been complied with. Indeed, it would be sensible to spell out precisely what is required in terms of documentation etc. (including any specific requirements for consent under the lease) in order for consent to be treated as granted. All correspondence should be headed "subject to completion of formal licence" and a disclaimer inserted in any initial letter making it plain that agents or other advisers do not have authority to grant consent.

SOME TYPICAL REASONS FOR REFUSAL OF CONSENT

Note: a specimen letter of refusal is at Precedent 19.

1.   INFORMATION

A landlord is entitled to know the nature of the transaction. He is also entitled to financial information about the proposed assignee *(Norwich Union Life Insurance Ltd* v *Shopmoor Ltd* EG Legal Notes 13.12.97) including, for example, accounts for companies and financial references from former landlords, bankers or others with knowledge of the financial standing of the proposed assignee/subtenant. References need to be carefully scrutinised. They may not be acceptable if the information is not current, if any financial statistics are unaudited, if the writer disclaims liability for the reference, if the writer is unqualified, if the reference is too brief (e.g. standard bank reference), or because income is stated without corresponding expenditure. However, a landlord may he acting unreasonably if he delays in making a request for information, or requests information that is not necessary to deal reasonably with the application for consent.

The landlord is entitled to all particulars that concern him: *Kened Ltd* v *Connie Investments Ltd* (see above). The landlord is entitled to know the true nature of the transaction (often through being provided with Heads of Terms) but he is not automatically entitled to require to see a copy of the proposed assignment or underlease unless the lease specifies this or there are special circumstances: *Dong Bang Minerva (UK) Ltd* v *Davina Ltd* (see above). If a copy of such a document is required, the request should be dealt with as a condition of consent and not as a pre-condition of considering the application.

2.   COLLATERAL ADVANTAGE

It is unreasonable for the landlord to seek to obtain a collateral advantage as a condition for giving or a reason for withholding consent. Examples would be to procure a surrender of the lease *(Bromley Park* above), to obtain a variation of the lease *(Roux Restaurants Ltd* v *Jaison Property Development Co Ltd* [1996] EGCS 118), to obtain a rent deposit from a sub-tenant held in the joint names of the landlord and the tenant *(Straudley Investments Ltd* v *Mount Eden Land Ltd* – see above), or to prevent the proposed assignee leaving another property of the landlord where he was the

tenant: *Re Gibbs and Houlder Bros and Co Ltd's Lease* [1925] Ch 57564.
Even where a covenant includes express conditions, these may not be used
to secure a collateral advantage: *Mount Eden Land Ltd* v *Towerstone Ltd*
[2002] 31 EG 97.

3.   GOOD ESTATE MANAGEMENT/TENANT MIX POLICY

A landlord may reasonably refuse consent for reasons of good estate management: *Viscount Tredegar* v *Harwood* [1929] AC 72. This is a vague
concept, and the actual management reason must be given. Often it is because of a policy adopted by the landlord for his estate, but that policy cannot
be used to refuse consent on reasonable grounds if it seeks to achieve for the
landlord an uncovenanted advantage: *Rayburn* v *Wolf* (1985) 50 P & CR
463. Refusal based on a diminution in the investment value is reasonable:
Ponderosa International Developments Inc v *Pengap Securites (Bristol)
Ltd* (see below). Difficulty in letting other premises is also a reasonable reason for refusal of consent: *F. W. Woolworth* v *Charlwood Alliance Properties* [1987] 1 EGLR 53.

An increasingly important part of estate management is to maintain tenant
mix, either to ensure "grouping" of similar businesses or to avoid unhelpful
competition. To maximise the prospects of successfully relying on such a
policy the landlord should ensure that he has an express policy on this issue,
although this is not essential and previous conduct may be taken to demonstrate this: *Moss Bros Group plc* v *CSC Properties Ltd* [1999] EGGS 47.

The courts have held that a landlord may reasonably object to a proposed
assignment to maintain this tenant mix policy to prevent competing uses
(*Chelsfield MH Investments* v *British Gas plc* [1995] NPC 169), or to prevent a particular style of use that was incompatible with existing businesses
(*Crown Estate Commissioners* v *Signet Group plc* [1996] 2 EGLR 200,
where the landlord's estate management policy was upheld).

4.   STATUS OF ASSIGNEE OR SURETY

A landlord may reasonably refuse consent because of the poor financial
standing of the proposed assignee or because of a relevant personal
reason: *Re Gibbs and Houlder Bros and Co Ltd's Lease* [1925] Ch 575. The
test usually applied in that the tenant should have net profits at a level of
three times the rent: *British Bakeries* v *Michael Testier* (see above). But this
rule of thumb must not be applied "blindly": *Footwear Group* v *Amplight
Properties* (see above).

It has been argued that it is reasonable to refuse consent where the proposed
surety is resident outside England and Wales, albeit within a country that is

a signatory to the Brussels Convention, as enforcement would be slightly more difficult. This was rejected as not being a reason that a reasonable landlord would rely on as sufficient to withhold consent: *Vered Ltd v Connie Investments Ltd* [1997] 4 EG 141.

5.   STATUS OF SUB-TENANT

It has been said that the status of a sub-tenant is of less importance to the head landlord as there is no direct relationship. It is submitted that this may not be correct, because the tenant may require continued payment of rent to enable him to keep up the payments due in turn to the head landlord and, in due course, any sub-tenant may be in direct relationship with the head landlord under the Landlord and Tenant Act 1954, Part II. It has been held that it is not reasonable to refuse consent to a sub-letting at less than the open market rent although this will affect the landlord's reversion: *Blockbuster Entertainment Ltd v Leakcliff Properties Ltd* [1996] EGGS 151.

6.   COLOUR, RACE OR ETHNIC ORIGIN AND SEX

It is unreasonable to refuse consent based on colour, race or ethnic origin: Race Relations Act 1976, section 24(1). Section 31 of the Sex Discrimination Act 1975 makes similar provision with regard to discrimination on grounds of sex.

7.   USER OR ANTICIPATED BREACH OF COVENANT

A landlord may reasonably refuse consent if the proposed assignee/subtenant intends to use die premises in a way that will inevitably result in a breach of the user covenant, or if the proposed use would be detrimental to the premises – see *Re Gibbs and Houlder Bros and Co Ltd's Lease* [1925] Ch 575. But suppose the landlord fears that the proposed assignee/sub-lessee will breach the user clause. It was thought that if, following alienation, the landlord will be able to enforce the user covenant, (i.e. giving consent will not waive his rights and estop him from taking action under the clause), he will be unable to refuse consent. This was particularly so as the landlord can in any event expressly reserve his rights in relation to enforcing the covenant. However, the House of Lords have now confirmed that a landlord may refuse consent if he reasonably fears that the assignee will breach the user covenants: *Ashworth Frazer Ltd v Gloucester City Council (No2)* [2001] 46 EG 180.

There may also be circumstances where a landlord can reasonably object to a proposed use, even if it is not one that is expressly prohibited by the lease: *Bridewell Hospital (Governors) v Faulkener* (1892) 8 TLR 637. The landlord is less likely to be able to refuse consent if the user clause is narrowly drawn so that the tenant may be unable to assign: *Bates* v *Donaldson* [1896] 2 QB 241; *International Drilling Fluids Ltd* v *Louiseville Investments (Uxbridge) Ltd* [1986] Ch 513.

8. COMPETING USE

The landlord may reasonably object if the use proposed by the assignee/sub-tenant will compete with the landlord or the neighbouring premises: *Whiteminster Estates Ltd* v *Hodges Menswear Ltd* (1974) 232 EG 715.

9. STATUTORY PROTECTION

It may be possible for the landlord to refuse consent if the proposed assignee/sub-tenant would be entitled to claim statutory protection. But the courts have said that there is no universal rule that consent may reasonably be refused on this basis. Each case must be examined on its own facts: *Lee* v *K Carter Ltd* [1949] 1 KB 85; *Bickel* v *Duke of Westminster* [I977] 1 QB 517. It is reasonable to refuse consent to assign to an assignee who would obtain protection when the lease has almost expired (see *Lee* above), or if the assignee would be able to claim the protection of the Leasehold Reform Act (see *Bickel* above). It has also been held to be reasonable to refuse consent if the proposed assignee would be entitled to claim the protection of the Landlord and Tenant Act 1954, Part II: *Re Cooper's Lease* (1968) 19 P & CR 541.

If the lease still has some time to go, it is less likely to be reasonable for the landlord to refuse consent: *Thomas Bookman Ltd* v *Nathan* [1955] 2 All ER 821.

10. DIRECT COVENANTS

The landlord may be able to require an assignee to enter into a direct covenant with him to comply with the terms of the lease. For leases granted on or after 1 January 1996 see Chapter 7 and pages 101-105. But it is probably unreasonable to require a sub-tenant to enter into a direct covenant with the head landlord to pay rent: *Balfour* v *Kensington Gardens Mansions Ltd* (1932) 49 TLR 29.

The lease may expressly require that any assignee (or sub-tenant) enters into direct covenants with the landlord. In those circumstances the landlord can obviously insist upon compliance with that requirement. A provision of this nature does not imply that the landlord has a duty to take reasonable care to ensure that second or subsequent assignees are able to pay the rent and other monies due under the lease: *Norwich Union Life Insurance Society* v *Low Profile Fashions Ltd* [1992] 21 EG 104.

11. COMPARABLE STATUS OF EXISTING TENANT

The landlord may seek to object to an assignment because he considers that the status of the assignee is not as good as that of the current tenant. It may be reasonable to refuse consent on this basis, but only if the change of tenant is likely to cause real damage to the landlord: *Ponderosa International Developments Inc* v *Pengap Securities (Bristol) Ltd* [1986] 1 EGLR 66. The landlord cannot reasonably refuse consent to assign to an existing tenant of another property he owns on the ground that it will then be difficult to re-let that other property: *Re Gibbs and Boulder Bros and Co Ltd's Lease* [1925] Ch 575.

However, the landlord can reasonably refuse consent to an application to reassign the lease to the original tenant to enable that tenant to activate a personal break clause: *Olympia & York Canary Wharf Ltd* v *Oil Property Investments Ltd* [1994] 29 EG 121. A lease allowed the original tenant to operate a break clause. On assignment of the lease it was made clear that the assignee did not have the benefit of the clause. The assignee went into administrative receivership and paid no rent which, by now, was more than the market rental value of the premises. The assignee sought to assign the lease back to the original tenant and the landlord refused consent as this was being done so that the original tenant could operate the break clause. The Court of Appeal confirmed that the landlord was acting reasonably in refusing consent.

12. UNDERTAKING FOR COSTS

The landlord may seek payment of his legal or other costs incurred in connection with the grant of consent. Invariably the landlord's solicitor will require an undertaking for costs from the assignor's solicitor. The Law Society Council has expressed no view whether there is a legal obligation to pay those costs (although s 19 of the 1927 Act certainly permits a request by the landlord as a condition of consent), but the Council has confirmed that it is not improper to request such an undertaking (Council statement 19.12.84). Arguably it may be unreasonable to insist upon an undertaking if the lease expressly provides for payment of the costs by the tenant.

This practice was considered by the court in *Dong Bang Minerva (UK) Ltd* v *Davina Ltd* (see above). The landlord sought a solicitor's undertaking for costs of £4,500, including the costs of his mortgagee and the costs of instructing a surveyor to consider the question of dilapidations. The landlord contended that he did not have to take any steps to consider the application for consent until the undertaking was given. This contention seemed to be rejected by the judge at first instance, but she did not have to decide it finally or whether a solicitor's undertaking could be required, as she held that the undertaking sought must be reasonable and that the costs sum contended for here was not. This was confirmed on appeal. The court accepted that in some cases a solicitor's undertaking could be required because of the easier enforcement it provided. It may be more appropriate to make the payment of costs a condition attaching to the consent.

13. SUBSISTING BREACH OF COVENANT

A landlord may reasonably refuse consent if there is a subsisting breach of covenant. However the breach must be substantial: *Orlando Investments Ltd* v *Grosvenor Estate Belgravia* (see above). In the *Orlando* case the landlord required the proposed assignee to give a direct covenant to him supported by a performance bond to remedy certain substantial disrepair. The court held that where there are substantial breaches of the repairing covenant it is not unreasonable for the landlord to refuse consent unless he can be reasonably satisfied that the proposed assignee will remedy them. However, in the *Straudley Investments* case (see above) the court held it was unreasonable to refuse consent based on breaches of the repairing covenant as the landlord could still seek to enforce the obligation under that covenant after the assignment.

This contrasts with *Beale* v *Worth* [1993] EGGS 135, where the Court of Appeal held that for a continuing breach of covenant to repair to provide grounds for a landlord's refusal to allow assignment of the lease, it must be extensive and longstanding. A mere dispute with a tenant did not suffice. Nor will mere sloppy practice by the tenant: *Mount Cook Land Ltd* v *Hartley* [2000] EGCS 26. It is therefore difficult to extrapolate a consistent approach and each case must be viewed on its own facts.

14. REFUSAL OF CONSENT BY SUPERIOR LANDLORD

If a superior landlord unreasonably withholds consent, this will not permit the direct landlord to refuse consent as he could nevertheless proceed with the assignment. A refusal of consent on this ground will therefore be unreasonable: *Vienit Ltd* v *W Williams & Sons (Bread Street) Ltd* [1958] 3 All ER 621.

15. LANDLORD AND TENANT ACT 1927, S 19 (LA)

If the landlord and tenant have made an agreement pursuant to this new provision (inserted by the Landlord and Tenant (Covenants) Act 1995) then the landlord will not be unreasonably withholding his consent on the ground that any of the relevant circumstances exist – assuming, of course, that they do exist – and if he gives his consent subject to any of the relevant conditions, he will not be regarded as giving it subject to unreasonable conditions. See page 104 above.

16.   SURETY

If the landlord seeks to refuse consent unless a surety is provided (and there was not previously one) this may be unreasonable: *Taylor Brothers (Groceries) Limited* v *Covent Garden Properties Limited* [1959] 1 All ER 728

17.   MARKET RENT

Alieniation provisions often prohibit subletting at less than the market rent. This may be less than passing rent if it can still be shown to represent the current market value: *Clinton Cards (Essex) Ltd* v *Sun Alliance & London Assurance Co Ltd* [2002] 37 EG 154.

If, however, the lease prohibits subletting at less than the passing rent, a collateral agreement between the tenants and the subtenant will be read together with the sublease, and in such circumstances a landlord might reasonably refuse consent on the grounds that the passing rent was not being met: *Allied Dunbar Assurance plc* v *Homebase Ltd* [2002] EWCA Civ 666; [2002] 27 EG 144. As the collateral deed is part of the full picture, the landlord is entitled to see it.

18.   EFFECT ON THE VALUE OF THE LANDLORD'S INTEREST

It has been held that it is reasonable for a landlord to refuse consent because of his concerns regadsing the effect of the underletting on the value of the lanslord's interest in the premises: *NCR Ltd* v *Riverland Properties No 1 Ltd* [2005] EWCA Civ 312.

REMEDIES FOR BREACH

1.   FOR LANDLORD

The precise terms of the alienation covenants must be checked to ensure that the anticipated breach is prohibited by the lease. The burden is on the landlord to prove the breach and the covenant will be strictly construed against him.

Alienation in breach of covenant will still serve to vest the legal estate in the assignee/sub-tenant, but the landlord will have the right to forfeit the lease and/or seek damages for breach of covenant: *Old Grovebury Manor Farm Ltd* v *W Seymour Plant Sales and Hire Ltd* (No 2) (1979) 252 EG 1103 (subsequently approved by dicta of the House of Lords in *Linden Garden Trust Ltd* v *Lenesta Sludge Disposals Ltd* [1994] 1 AC 85 at pp.107–109). The Section 146 Notice should, therefore, be served on the assignee/sub-tenant: *Fuller* v *Judy Properties Ltd* [1992] 14 EG 106.

However, in the case of registered land if the assignment is not registered at the Land Registry, the legal estate will not be transferred and will remain vested in the assignor: *Brown and Root Technology Limited* v *Sun Alliance and London Assurance Company Limited* (1997) *The Times* 27th January. In such a situation, the Section 146 Notice should therefore also be served on the Assignor. In these circumstances, the breach of covenant is likely to be a breach of the covenant against sharing or parting with possession as the legal estate will not have been transferred. The assignor will also remain liable for the rent and performance of the covenants. Once the assignment is registered, the transfer of the legal estate will take effect on the date of receipt by the assignment of the Land Registry: Rule 83 Land Registration Rules.

UNDERTAKING

On occasion the landlord may decide that he does not have a sufficiently strong case to pursue a claim for forfeiture. Alternatively, he may take the view that having served the Section 146 Notice, and having received a contrite response from the tenant, an undertaking not to breach the covenants in the future is sufficient. This does of course also provide additional ammunition for the landlord in the future if he needs to take action against the tenant for a subsequent breach. (A precedent undertaking is at Precedent 17.)

FORFEITURE

Notice under section 146 of the Law of Property Act 1925 must be served. A breach of the alienation covenant is irremediable and so the Section 146 Notice need not require it to be remedied. Such a breach is a once-and-for-all breach and it is therefore important to ensure that the breach is not waived. A stop should be put on the rent and nothing should be done which is consistent with the continuation of the lease. Knowledge by an agent/employee of the landlord will constitute knowledge by the landlord: *Metropolitan Properties Co Ltd* v *Cordery* (1979) 251 EG 567.

After service of the Section 146 Notice, the landlord can forfeit by peaceable re-entry or proceedings. As the breach is irremediable there is no need to wait a reasonable time before proceeding.

But a short time should be allowed to permit the tenant to consider what action to take. Fourteen days was held to be appropriate in *Scala House and District Property Co Ltd* v *Forbes* [1974] 1 QB 575. It is not dependant on any terms a tenant may have negotiated with a third party: *Albany Holdings Ltd* v *Crown Estate Commissioners* [2003] All ER (D) 18 Jun.

The tenant, a sub-tenant or mortgagee may apply for relief from forfeiture. Where it can be shown that the landlord has suffered damage, the court is likely to order forfeiture: *Crown Estate Commissioners* v *Signet Group plc* [1996] 2 EGLR 200. However, the refusal of forfeiture in respect of wilful breaches seen in cases such as *Shiloh Spinners Ltd* v *Harding* [1973] AC 691, is now more often replaced with a more lenient approach: *Mount Cook Land Ltd* v *Hartley* (see above).

INJUNCTION/DAMAGES

A landlord who has advance knowledge of an intended unauthorised alienation may apply for an injunction and damages.

The injunction will usually be sought before an intended breach of the alienation covenants to prevent that breach. But a mandatory injunction may also be obtained, after a breach of such a covenant, against the tenant for breach of a contractual obligation and against the unlawful sub-tenant for inducing a breach of covenant: *Hemingway Securities Ltd* v *Dunraven Ltd* [1995] 09 EG 322. In that case the court order also required the sub-tenant to surrender the sub-lease granted in breach of covenant.

2.   FOR TENANT

If the landlord is unreasonably withholding consent, the tenant may proceed with the proposed alienation. Clearly this is a risky strategy. Alternatively, the tenant may apply to the court for a declaration that the landlord is unreasonably withholding consent: section 53(l)(a) Landlord and Tenant Act 1954. If the tenant proposes to rely upon the 1988 Act, consent to alienation must first have been sought in writing. If there is no written application for consent, the Act will not apply and the lease will be liable to forfeiture.

A landlord who fails to comply with the provisions of the 1988 Act is liable to a claim in damages (s 4). But damages will not be awarded where the tenant has suffered no loss: *Clinton Cards (Essex) Ltd* v *Sun Alliance & London Assurance Co Ltd* [2002] 37 EG 154.

In *S Ayers* v *Longacre Securities Ltd* [1994] 11 CL 243, the landlord withheld consent for seven months. It was declared that consent had unreasonably been withheld, not throughout the whole period, but for one month only, and damages were awarded to the tenant, assessed on the basis of (a) one month's interest on the purchase monies he was kept out of at the rate of his overdraft facility less (b) the benefit of the trading profits the tenant had made during the one-month period.

Exemplary damages may be awarded: *Design Progression Ltd* v *Thurloe Properties Ltd* [2004] 10 EG 184. In that case the landlord deliberately prevaricated because the rent under the lease was below market rate and the landlord would have preferred to grant a new lease. The effect of the prevarication was that the potential assignee found alternative premises. The court characterised the landlord's behavious as deplorable and awarded £25,000 by way of exemplary damages.

Tenants may seek exemplary damages where the landlord has acted unreasonably, and that behaviour displays features that merit punishment. An obvious example is where a landlord has acted in a way calculated to make a profit which would otherwise exceed any compensation he may have to pay to the tenant.

The normal rules with regard to exemplary damages are that they will be moderate, reflect the means of the party against whom they are awarded, the conduct of that party and the level of other compensation.

CHAPTER 10

UNAUTHORISED ALTERATIONS

CHAPTER 10
UNAUTHORISED ALTERATIONS

If there is no express covenant in the lease prohibiting alterations, the only common law restriction is that the tenant must not commit waste or breach the repairing covenants.

The covenant against alterations may be absolute (prohibiting any alterations) or qualified (prohibiting alterations without the landlord's consent).

What constitutes an alteration is often not defined in a lease. However it has been held that to amount to an alteration, works must affect the form or structure of the building: *Bickmore* v *Dimmer* [1903] 1 Ch 158.

QUALIFIED COVENANTS

Section 19(2) of the Landlord and Tenant Act 1927 implies into the covenant a provision that the landlord's consent must not be unreasonably withheld for any alterations which are improvements. What constitutes an improvement must be considered on the facts of each case. It will not necessarily increase the value of the premises. Whether the works will be an improvement is to be viewed from the tenant's point of view: *Lambert* v *F W Woolworth and Co Ltd* [1938] 2 All ER 664.

The landlord can require:

1. compensation for damage to or diminution in the value of the property or of any neighbouring property he owns;
2. payment of his legal and other expenses;
3. in the case of an improvement which does not add to the letting value, the tenant to undertake to re-instate the premises at the end of the term.

There is little judicial authority on what will constitute a reasonable or unreasonable withholding of consent. It is thought that similar considerations will be applied as for a qualified covenant against assignment. In particular, the landlord will not be entitled to refuse consent in order to achieve a collateral advantage. The burden is on the tenant to show unreasonableness. However in a recent case (*Iqbal and Others* v *Thakrar and Anor* [2004] All ER (D) 304 (April)) the Court of Appeal has given guidance as to the relevant considerations that a court should consider. Namely:

1. the purpose of consent was to protect the landlord from alterations that would damage his interest;
2. the landlord was not entitled to refuse consent where the ground for this had nothing to do with the property's value;
3. the obligation was on the tenant to prove that the landlord had withheld consent unreasonably and furthermore the tenant was obliged to ensure his proposals were sufficiently clear so that the landlord could make a decision whether to agree to them or not;
4. it was not for the landlord to prove that he had reasonably withheld consent;
5. it might be reasonable for consent to be refused by the landlord for a proposed use even if that use was not expressly prohibited by the lease;
6. a landlord should only be expected to consider his own interests save where it would be disproportionate for him to do so;
7. consent could not be refused on grounds of pecuniary loss alone;
8. it would be a question of fact in each case whether the landlord having regard to the actual reason that caused him to withhold consent had acted reasonably.

In *Iqbal* the court held that it was reasonable to refuse consent because of concerns as to the structural viability of the proposals.

It is also now well established that in considering whether the landlord has acted reasonably, the court will have regard to the reasons that actually led to the landlord's decision. If it transpires that those are not permissible reasons, it is not open to the landlord to show that other reasonable landlords might have withheld consent on other grounds, if those other grounds had not influenced the actual landlord in making its decision: *Redevco Properties* v *Mount Cook Land Ltd* [2002] All ER (D (26 December)).

The Landlord and Tenant Act 1988 does not apply and so the landlord has no duty to give reasons – but if no reason is given a previous case (contrary to the dicta in *Iqbal* above) held that the burden of showing reasonableness is on the landlord: *F W Woolworth and Co Ltd* v *Lambert* [1937] Ch 37; *Lambert* v *F W Woolworth and Co Ltd* (above).

Clearly the tenant must seek prior consent and provide sufficient information about what is proposed if he is to demonstrate that the landlord is acting unreasonably. If the landlord imposes conditions on his consent it will be necessary to consider whether they are reasonable. Section 19(2) sets out three conditions that will be reasonable (see above). A refusal of consent for aesthetic, historic or even sentimental reasons may be reasonable (see *Lambert* above). The landlord may also refuse consent if the alterations proposed would have constituted a tort, such as nuisance or trespass: *Haines v Florensa* [1990] 9 EG 70.

The landlord may take account of good estate management: *Luzatto v Danzig* [2002] All ER (D) 124 (Jun). He may also rely on perceived damage to trading interests or neighborung property: *Sargeant v Macepark (Whittlebury) Ltd* [2004] EWHC 1333 (Ch) - applying the *Iqbal* approach.

An aggrieved tenant can apply to the court for a declaration that the landlord is unreasonably withholding his consent (s 53(1)(b) Landlord and Tenant Act 1954) or carry out the works and wait to see if the landlord takes any action.

Where the landlord or his agents enter into correspondence with the tenant regarding proposed works and consent for them, care should be taken to ensure that this is written without prejudice. A letter may be sufficient "written consent" even if stated to be subject to further legal formalities: *Prudential Assurance Co Limited v Mount Eden Land Limited* [1997] 14 EG 130.

ABSOLUTE COVENANTS

Section 19 does not apply. However the tenant may apply to the court under section 3 of the Landlord and Tenant Act 1927 for leave to carry out a proposed improvement if:

1. it will add to the letting value of the holding at the end of the tenancy; and
2. it is reasonable and suitable to the character of the property; and
3. it will not diminish the value of any other property belonging to the same landlord or any superior landlord.

The right to apply to the court for leave to carry out alterations under section 3 also applies to qualified covenants.

The alterations involved may be substantial. The Act specifically envisages that the alterations might include the complete destruction of the premises and subsequent rebuilding of them: *National Electric v Hudgell* [1939] Ch 353.

Use of the powers in the 1927 Act, section 3 are however subject to the tenant serving prior notice on the landlord who has three months to respond if he wishes to object or do the work himself in return for an increased rent. However, if a tenant serves a section 3 notice but then decides not to proceed, the landlord cannot insist on doing the works himself to obtain the higher rent: *Norfolk Capital Group Ltd* v *Cadogan Estates Ltd* [2004] All ER (D) 203 (Jan).

LAW OF PROPERTY ACT 1925, s 84

If the lease is for a term in excess of 40 years and 25 years have expired, the tenant may apply to the Lands Tribunal under section 84 of the Law of Property Act 1925 to modify or discharge a restriction upon the alteration of buildings.

OTHER STATUTES

Certain specific works to the demised premises may also be authorised by statute, notwithstanding an express covenant against alterations in the lease.

Section 96 of the Telecommunications Act 1984 may permit alterations affecting a telecommunications system in a lease for a term of one year or more. Consent given by the landlord to alterations enabling the installation of telecommunication equipment may also grant rights under the Telecommunication Code to the operator of that equipment which can out last the lease (e.g. rights to enter, maintain and keep the equipment on the land).

Section 169 of the Factories Act 1961 permits an application to the court to obtain consent to do works required by the Act to a factory which are otherwise prevented by a lease.

Section 73 of the Offices, Shops and Railway Premises Act 1963 provides a similar procedure for premises covered by that Act.

Section 28 of the Fire Precautions Act 1971 gives the court power to set aside or modify restrictions in a lease that prevent works required by a fire authority for a fire certificate.

The Disability Discrimination Act 1995 requires employers to make reasonable adjustments to the working environment where this currently places a disabled employee or job applicant at a substantial disadvantage. The Act also requires those who provide goods or services (e.g. a hotel or shop) not to discriminate against disabled persons and to remove or alter any physical barrier that makes it unreasonably difficult for a disabled person to use the service. The service providers include landlord and tenants. For example a landlord of a shopping centre will probably be a service provider in respect of the car parks and common parts. Retail tenants, banks and building societies will be service providers too. Landlords will often be service providers in respect of multi-let buildings.

Premises leased for such uses may therefore require alteration to comply with the Act to which the landlord cannot reasonably withhold his consent. The Act will override any contrary provisions in a lease with regard to alterations to a property. This is, however, subject to obtaining all other necessary consents such as planning permission, listed building consent and mortgagee's consent. Furthermore, as many leases contain a covenant to comply with all statutory obligations, this will include compliance with the Disability Discrimination Act.

REMEDIES

1.   FORFEITURE

Before seeking to forfeit, the landlord must serve notice under section 146 of the Law of Property Act 1925. A breach of covenant prohibiting alterations has been held to be incapable of remedy, and accordingly the Section 146 Notice need not require the breach to be remedied: *Gunter Trustees* v *Residential Apartments Ltd* [1990] NPC 10. However, the landlord should still wait a short period after service of the notice (say fourteen days) before proceeding with forfeiture, to enable the tenant to consider his position. Where a landlord proceeded after only five days this has been held to be too soon: *Courtney Lodge Management Ltd* v *Blake* [2004] All ER (D) 30 July.

Further, the Court of Appeal has held that any covenant-(other than a covenant not to assign without consent) is capable of remedy: *Savva* v *Houssein* (1996) *The Times* May 6. The safe course is therefore both to include in the Section 146 Notice an express requirement to remedy the breach, and to wait a short period to enable the tenant to do so before forfeiting.

The breach of covenant is a once-and-for-all breach, and in order to maintain the landlord's right to forfeit care must be taken not to waive the breach: *Iperion Investments Corporation* v *Broadwalk House Residents Ltd* [1992] 2 EGLR 235.

The tenant, sub-tenant or any mortgagee may seek relief from forfeiture. The tenant is likely to obtain relief if the landlord could not reasonably have withheld consent to the proposed alterations if the tenant had applied for consent and this had been refused. Otherwise, the breach must usually be remedied as a condition precedent to the grant of relief. Tenants may often (but not always) obtain extensions of time to comply with such conditions: *Crawford* v *Clarke* (CA) 3 March 2000.

The tenant may apply for relief either after service of the Section 146 Notice or after peaceable re-entry, by commencing proceedings. Alternatively, he may apply by counterclaim in the landlord's forfeiture proceedings.

2.   INJUNCTION/DAMAGES

The landlord may obtain an injunction to prevent proposed alterations, or to rectify or make good alterations which have been completed. Damages can be claimed where the alterations have been carried out.

CHAPTER 11
UNAUTHORISED USE

CHAPTER 11
UNAUTHORISED USE

Unless the lease restricts the use of the premises to a specific use or uses, or prohibits certain uses, at common law the tenant can use the premises for any purpose that is lawful and does not cause a nuisance.

Invariably the lease will specify the permitted uses. But the user covenant may also stipulate that the tenant must not cause a nuisance to the landlord or to any adjoining owners. The covenant may say that the tenant must not use the premises, or permit or suffer the premises to be used, otherwise than for certain purposes, so that if the premises are sublet and the sub-tenant uses the premises in breach of that covenant, the tenant may be liable if he gave licence or consent for that use or failed to take reasonable steps to prevent it.

Even if the sub-lease user covenant does not mirror the user covenant in the head lease, the covenant in the head lease will bind the sub-tenant: *Hill* v *Harris* [1965] 2 QB 601.

Section 3(5) of the Landlord and Tenant (Covenants) Act 1995 makes it plain that any user covenant restricting the use of land is enforceable against an assignee and any other person using or occupying any premises by the lease in question: *Oceanic Village Ltd* v *United Attractions Ltd* [1999] EGCS 152.

A user covenant may be either absolute, *e.g.* prohibiting the use of the premises except as offices, or qualified, *e.g.* "not without the lessor's consent to use the premises except as offices". User covenants are often framed as negative covenants, but the covenant may also be a positive one (to use the premises as offices).

Failure to use the premises at all will probably not constitute a breach of a positive covenant unless it is expressly stated that the tenant must use the premises for a particular purpose during specified hours, for example to use the premises as a supermarket between the hours of 9am and 5pm. Failure to use the premises in accordance with this covenant whilst, for example, works of improvement are being carried out or the tenant is seeking to re-let the premises ought not to constitute a breach.

The courts are loath to grant injunctions to compel a tenant to comply with a covenant to keep a property open during specified hours: *F W Woolworth plc v Charilwood Alliance Properties Ltd* [1987] 1 EGLR 53. The court does have power to grant a mandatory injunction but this should be exercised only in exceptional circumstances and where the wording of the covenant was clear: *Co-Operative Insurance Society Ltd v Argyll Stores (Holdings) Ltd* (1997) *The Times*, 26 May. If the tenant is in breach of such a covenant the court may award damages: *Costain Property Developments Ltd v Finlay & Co Ltd* [1989] 1 EGIR 237; *Transworld Land Co Ltd v Sainsbury plc* [1990] EGCS 49.

If the user covenant prohibits use of the premises for a particular purpose then no use of that nature is permitted even if the premises are also used for another purpose.

ABSOLUTE COVENANTS

If the tenant applies to alter the use of the premises there is no implied term or statutory restriction on the landlord's response to the tenant's request. The landlord can agree to or refuse the proposal as he sees fit.

QUALIFIED COVENANTS

Section 19(3) of the Landlord and Tenant Act 1927 will apply. Accordingly, if there is no structural alteration proposed, the landlord cannot require payment of a fine or premium (other than his legal or other costs) as a condition of the granting of consent. Any consideration may be a fine (such as a condition that the tenant accept a landlord's break clause): *Barclays Bank plc v Daejan Investments (Grove Hall) Ltd* [1995] EG 15 April, p. 198. He can, however, require payment of a reasonable sum in respect of any damage to, or diminution in the value of, the premises or the landlord's neighbouring premises.

Unlike a qualified covenant against assignment/sub-letting, there is no statutory implication that a qualified user covenant is subject to the proviso that consent must not be unreasonably withheld. Accordingly, unless the lease stipulates to the contrary, the landlord has an unfettered discretion, even where the covenant is qualified, as to whether to give consent.

The covenant may be fully qualified and expressly provide that the landlord's consent is not to be unreasonably withheld. There is less authority on what will constitute reasonable or unreasonable withholding of consent in respect of the user covenant than there is with regard to alienation. However, but it is submitted that similar considerations will be applied as for a qualified covenant against assignment. In particular, it is likely to be unreasonable for the landlord to withhold consent in order to gain a collateral advantage. The Landlord and Tenant Act 1988 does not apply.

Where the courts have had to consider the reasonableness of a landlord's refusal of consent, this has often been in the context of an application for consent to assign, where the assignee proposes to use the premises contrary to the terms of the lease. There is a sequence of case authority in such circumstances, but the House of Lords has now clarified that it would usually be reasonable for a landlord to withhold consent where an assignee proposed to use the premises in breach of the terms of the lease, although there could be circumstances where reliance on this alone would be unreasonable: *Ashworth Frazer Ltd* v *Gloucester City Council (No2)* [2001] UKHL 59; [2002] 05 EG 133.

Consent may be reasonable refused if this would conflict with the landlord's estate management policy: *Crown Estate Commissioners* v *Signet Group plc* [1998] 2 EGLR 200.

A refusal of consent to change from office to educational use on the basis that this would adversely impact on the marketing and thus value of other neighbouring units was held to unreasonable where this could not actually be demonstrated: *London & Argyll Developments Ltd* v *Mount Cook Land Ltd* [2003] All ER (D) 104.

REMEDIES

1.   FORFEITURE

Notice under section 146 of the Law of Property Act 1925 must first be served. Breach of the user covenant often involves a breach of another covenant (for example sub-letting or a covenant prohibiting alterations) and the Section 146 Notice should cover all the breaches alleged.

Some breaches of the user covenant have been held to be irremediable, such as a covenant not to use the premises for any illegal or immoral purpose: *Rugby School* v *Tannahill* [1935] I KB 87. Accordingly, the landlord does not have to give the tenant time to remedy the breach after service of the Section 146 Notice before proceeding to forfeit. He should nevertheless wait, say, 14 days before proceeding, to enable the tenant to consider his position: *Scala House & District Property Co Ltd* v *Forbes* [1974] QB 575

Other breaches are likely to be remediable, and so the landlord must give the tenant a reasonable time to remedy the breach before proceeding to forfeit. The reasonableness of the time for compliance with the Section 146 Notice should be based on the terms agreed between the landlord and the tenant, and not upon any terms that the tenant may have agreed with any third party: *Albany Holdings Ltd v Crown Estate Commissioners* [2003] All ER (D) 18 June. In that case the court held that one month was sufficient time for the tenant to have dealt with a breach of the user covenant by subletting for a prohibited use. In contrast, five days was held to be too short a time: *Courtney Lodge Management Ltd v Blake* [2004] All ER (D) 30 July.

However, a subsequent case has challenged the traditional view of remediable/unremediable breaches. In *Savva v Houssein* (1996) *The Times*, May 6, the Court of Appeal held that all breaches other than a covenant not to assign without consent were remediable. It is therefore sensible always to give the tenant time to remedy the breach after service if the Section 146 Notice before proceeding to forfeit the lease.

A breach of the user restriction is usually a continuing breach, so the landlord can continue to demand and accept rent until be forfeits by commencement of court proceedings or peaceable re-entry, *e.g.* taking in a lodger in breach of a covenant permitting one family use only: *Segal Securities Ltd v Thoseby* [1963] 1 QB 887.

But a breach of the user covenant may also involve other breaches which are once-and-for-all, *e.g.* some illegal uses or subletting, and a rent demand will waive such a breach: *Van Haarlam v Kasner* [1992] 36 EG 135. It is therefore safer not to allow any act of waiver once the landlord has knowledge of any suspected breach of the user covenant.

The tenant, a sub-tenant or mortgagee may apply for relief from forfeiture once the Section 146 Notice has been served or after peaceable re-entry, by the commencement of separate proceedings seeking relief, or alternatively by way of counterclaim in the landlord's proceedings.

The court will usually grant relief if the breach has been remedied or will make the remedying of the breach a condition precedent to relief being granted: *Rose v Hyman* [1912] AC 623. It has been said that the court should not grant relief where the breach of covenant is wilful: *Shiloh Spinners v Harding* [1973] AC 691. However, in practice, relief may still be granted even if the breach is deliberate: *Southern Depot Co Ltd v British Railways Board* [1990] 33 EG 45.

Where the breach is the immoral or illegal use of the premises thereby causing a stigma to attach to them, relief is less certain. Whether it will be granted will depend on the facts of the case, but it is more likely to be refused: *BP Pension Trust Ltd* v *Behrendt* (1986)52 P&CR 117.

2.   INJUNCTION

The landlord may seek an injunction to prevent or restrain a breach of the user covenant. He must not delay in applying to the court, or acquiesce in the breach - for example, by continuing to demand rent.

3.   DAMAGES

The landlord may seek damages for breach of the user covenant.

4.   SPECIFIC PERFORMANCE

The court will, but only very exceptionally, make an order for specific performance of a "keep open" covenant in a lease: *Co-Operative Insurance Society Ltd* v *Argyll Stores (Holdings) Ltd* (1997) *The Times*, 26 May; [1997] 1 EGLR 52.

5.   ENFORCEMENT BY OTHER TENANTS

It is usual in commercial developments for leases to contain standard form or interrelated covenants to restrict usage of each unit. It is not usually possible for one tenant to enforce lease covenants against another because one is not a party to the other's contract. There are two main exceptions to this rule: restrictive convenants and the Contracts (Rights of Third Parties) Act 1999. The Act will in theory allow other tenants to have the benefit of the tenant's covenants in a lease (where this was granted after 11 May 2000) but in practice the Act is usually excluded. Accordingly mutual enforceability is only likely to be possible where a scheme of development (otherwise called a letting scheme) can be demonstrated: see *Williams* v *Kiley* [2002] EWCA Civ 1645; [2002] 49 EG 122.

MODIFICATION OR VARIATION OF USER COVENANTS

A covenant may be modified, varied or released by:

1. a formal deed varying the lease;
2. a licence consenting to a new use;
3. long acquiescence with knowledge of the breach: *Re Summerson* [1900] 1 Ch 112.

LANDS TRIBUNAL

If the user covenant contains an obsolete restriction or if it restricts the reasonable use of the land, an application may be made to the Lands Tribunal, provided the lease is for a term in excess of 40 years and 2.5 years have expired, for an order modifying or discharging the covenant: Law of Property Act 1925, section 84(12), as amended.

LANDLORD AND TENANT ACT 1954, S 53(1)(C)

Where, in the case of a fully qualified covenant (i.e. the landlord's consent is not to be unreasonably withheld), a landlord withholds his licence or consent to a change of user, the tenant can apply to the court for a declaration that, contrary to the terms of the lease, the landlord is acting unreasonably.

This is not, however, possible where the covenant is absolute.

CHAPTER 12

A PRACTICAL APPROACH TO BREACHES OF COVENANT

CHAPTER 12
A PRACTICAL APPROACH TO BREACHES OF COVENANT

This chapter deals with the practical approach to be adopted by the landlord and his advisers and the considerations they should take into account.

NON-PAYMENT OF RENT/SERVICE CHARGE RECOVERABLE AS RENT

This is, of course, by far the most common breach of covenant. The key question is whether the landlord should go for possession (see below). If the decision is made to proceed only for recovery of the money then, other things being equal, distraining for the rent is, by far the most effective means of enforcing payment of the debt. Levying distress does, however, operate as a waiver of breaches of covenant. Alternative remedies would be the service of a statutory demand, utilisation of any rent deposit, negotiating a surrender, or commencing Court action for a money judgment if the tenant is not in occupation or is withholding rent because of a dispute about another matter. Where there are sub-tenants, notice could be served on them to pay their rent direct to the superior landlord under s.6 of the Law of Distress (Amendment) Act.

OTHER BREACH OF COVENANT SUSPECTED-INITIAL STEPS

As soon as the landlord has reason to suspect a breach of covenant (however slight that reason may he) he must take care not to waive the breach. The level of knowledge required is not high and knowledge of the relevant facts by the landlord's agent or employee is likely to be sufficient to impute knowledge to the landlord.

An immediate stop on rent must be imposed and further rent, service charge or other payments due under the lease should not be demanded or accepted. The landlord must ensure that nothing is done which, even arguably, would suggest a continuation of the relationship of landlord and tenant. In particular no notices (such as rent review notices or notices under the Landlord and Tenant Act 1954 section 25) should be served. Service of a Section 146 Notice does not constitute waiver: *Church Commissioners for England* v *Nodjoumi* (1985) 51 P & CR 155.

The landlord should then investigate the situation. Depending upon the nature of the breach, the landlord may make enquiry of the tenant direct. Clearly this would not be appropriate for some breaches (such as use of the premises for an immoral or illegal purpose) as the tenant is unlikely to admit what is suspected. Other breaches, such as unauthorised alterations, are more difficult (if not impossible) to deny and a direct approach to the tenant is most likely to establish the true position quickly.

If a direct approach is unlikely to be successful, the landlord should consider instructing enquiry agents to investigate. This may be particularly appropriate in cases of a suspected breach of the user or alienation covenants. The enquiry agents may be able to keep watch on the premises and obtain information from adjoining owners.

In all cases, the landlord should take steps to obtain as much information and evidence about the suspected breach as soon as possible. Photographs should be taken, for example, to show works being carried out, a new name plate at the premises, any alterations that have been carried out or any other visual evidence then existing in case this is subsequently changed and denied by the tenant. If the landlord provides a receptionist or porter, statements should be obtained and they should be alerted to the suspected breach and asked to keep a careful watch on the premises. This will be particularly important if there is a suspected breach of the alienation covenant and it would be prudent for the receptionist/porter to keep a log of those attending at the premises. This may provide important evidence in due course.

LANDLORD'S AIMS

There are as many different attitudes to tenant default as there are different landlords. Some take a very hard line with the miscreant. Others are quite laid back and take a relaxed view. Most fall somewhere in between. The question the landlord needs to put to his advisers goes something like this: "Can you assure me that, at the end of the day, it is likely that the action you are advocating will prove to have been a worthwhile and cost-effective exercise for me?"

Once the breach has been investigated so far as possible, the landlord must consider what he has discovered, in the light of the specific covenants in the lease, to ascertain whether there is, in fact, a breach. If there is, the landlord must decide what he wants to achieve: is it more important to retain the tenant, an income flow from the premises and the benefit of a tenant's covenants, or is the breach such that the landlord feels he must forfeit the lease? Forfeiture will obviously be appropriate to remove the existing tenant, to enable the landlord to seek to renegotiate a specific provision in the lease, to re-let at a higher rent, or because it is only by action of this nature that the landlord will ensure the breach is remedied. The landlord will obviously consider the effect of the breach on the premises and the value of his reversion. The landlord will also no doubt weigh up the breach against the loss of income flow from the premises if he cannot immediately achieve a new letting to a new tenant and other costs that he may incur e.g. rates, service charges. However he should also consider the effect of the breach on the value of his adjoining premises. For example, immoral use of a building may depress the rental value of other premises in the locality.

POSSESSION OR NOT?

The first question the landlord must ask himself is whether to go for possession of the premises. The threat of possession puts real pressure on the tenant. If the tenant/sub-tenants apply for and obtain relief from forfeiture, the landlord will still get all the arrears of rent etc. paid and relief would probably be conditional on any other breaches of covenant being remedied. Moreover, the terms of relief will almost certainly include a provision for the landlord's costs to be paid.

If, on the other hand, the landlord obtains an order for, and is actually able to obtain, possession he will often be in line for something approaching a windfall. He will get possession (against a business tenant) without having to pay any statutory rateable value compensation under the Landlord and Tenant Act 1954 Part 2, and can re-let the premises possibly at an increased rent. He will, effectively, be getting an early rent review with potentially first class covenant(s).

The landlord's nightmare scenario is that he will end up with an empty property, which he cannot let but in respect of which he may have an ongoing liability for business rates.

Once the tenant is served with the court proceedings claiming possession, two things immediately occur. First the landlord is considered to have thereby effected a forfeiture of the lease and so there is nothing to stop the tenant walking out of the premises and handing the keys back to the landlord or his agents. At the same time the liability of the original tenant and, depending on the wording of their covenants, any sureties will also come to an end.

Of course, the tenant may decide to fight the claim and apply for relief. The landlord will have claimed mesne profits but if the previous contractual rent is higher than the present letting market value of the premises, he may find that when the claim comes to be assessed he ends up with significantly less than the old rent. This possibility was recognised by Lloyd LJ, in *Ministry of Defence* v *Ashman* [1993] 40 EG 144 at p.148.

The proceedings may be drawn-out with the landlord having difficulty proving a breach. Even if, at the end of the day, the landlord is successful in establishing his claim, the tenant and any sub-tenants may obtain relief from forfeiture without, now, having to pay full indemnity costs to the landlord: *Billson* v *Residential Apartments Ltd* [1992] 1 All ER 141.

The second consequence of serving the court proceedings claiming forfeiture is that the tenant's covenants go: *Associated Deliveries Ltd.* v *Harrison* (1984) 272 EG 321, and per Stephenson LJ in *Peninsular Maritime Ltd* v *Padseal Ltd.*:

> "a landlord who has unequivocally elected to determine a lease by serving a writ and forfeiting it can not himself rely on any covenants of the lease in any shape or form but the tenant who has not elected to determine the lease can do so".

Accordingly, there can be no question of the landlord being able to serve a rent review notice during the course of what may prove to be long, drawn-out proceedings. He can, however, serve a Section 25 Notice if the tenant applies for relief: *Meadows* v *Clerical Medical and General Life Assurance Society* [1981] 1 Ch 70.

In summary, therefore, the landlord may find himself asking this question:

> "If the breach(es) of covenant are such that my premises and my adjoining premises are not at risk and, if I have reasonable covenants in the shape of the tenant, original tenant and sureties, what is the point of embarking upon a forfeiture action, the outcome of which is, at best, an imponderable and which, at worst, could be financially disastrous?"

The landlord may take the view that although there has, technically, been a breach of the lease, it will not have any adverse affect on the premises and he will, therefore, be prepared to give retrospective consent. In some cases the landlord may wish to make consent conditional upon the breach being remedied at the end of the term, for example in the case of unauthorised alterations where the landlord may require the premises to be reinstated at the end of the lease.

The landlord may be asked to authorise a change of user which has been carried on in breach of covenant. His response may well be to give consent subject to the tenant paying an increased rent. Under Landlord and Tenant Act 1927, section 19(3) if the proposed change of use does not involve structural alteration, the landlord is not entitled to charge money for granting consent where there is a qualified covenant, except that the court will allow him a reasonable sum in respect of any damage to or diminution in the value of the premises or his neighbouring premises.

Two points are especially relevant here:

- In the first place, the lease should be checked to see whether the change requires the landlord's consent in writing or whether any licence to change the user has to be by deed. If it is merely for the landlord to consent in writing, there is the danger that if the landlord or his agent writes a letter giving consent subject to the increased rent (and even though the letter contemplates the matter being formally recorded in a deed) the letter will constitute consent in writing but the increased rent will fall foul of section 19(3) of the 1927 Act.
- The second point is that arguably all the Act does is prohibit any form of agreement to pay money. It does not give a right to the repayment of monies already paid, nor does it invalidate a covenant to pay money under a deed which has been executed. There is nothing illegal in a landlord attempting to extract more rent for a change of user, but if the arrangement founders because the tenant reneges the landlord cannot enforce the unexecuted contract.

Once the tenant has given the covenant the landlord is home and dry, although there is an anxious period between agreement being reached and the deed being executed. In the interval the tenant, if he is so minded, could refuse to proceed. He would have the landlord's consent in writing in the letter and may be able to avoid paying any increased rent if, by virtue of section 19(3), it was considered to be untoward.

SECTION 146 NOTICE

If the landlord decides, for what ever reason, that forfeiture or the threat of forfeiture is the way forward he must first serve a Section 146 Notice. Even if the landlord does not propose to forfeit the lease at the end of the day, service of a Section 146 Notice will demonstrate that the landlord takes a serious view of the matter and this will strengthen his negotiating position in any discussions he has with the tenant with a view to resolving the situation so that forfeiture does not become necessary.

Service of the Section 146 Notice by affixing it to the exterior of the premises and putting another copy through the letterbox is the most effective manner of service. Furthermore, the fact of having a notice affixed to the premises will, of itself, demonstrate to the tenant the seriousness of the issue. For a precedent letter of instruction to agents to serve a Section 146 Notice, see Precedent 13.

TENANT'S RESPONSE

Upon receipt of an initial letter from the landlord detailing a suspected breach of covenant or following service of a Section 146 Notice, the landlord will expect to receive some explanation or justification of the matters about which he has complained. The landlord's suspicions may be misplaced because the tenant can show that a breach of covenant has not, in fact, occurred. The landlord will obviously consider the explanation or any offer that is made to remedy a breach which has taken place. The breach may be irremediable so that no explanation will satisfy the landlord.

FURTHER ACTION

The landlord must then decide whether he accepts the tenant's explanation or whether he is satisfied that there has been a breach upon which he wishes to take action. In many cases the landlord and tenant may be involved in a game of cat-and-mouse and bluff and counter-bluff if it is not entirely clear whether the acts complained of constitute a breach of covenant. In order to increase the strength of his negotiating position, the landlord may elect to take action to forfeit the lease, although clearly he should be advised as to the costs that may he incurred by the commencement of court proceedings, particularly as the Civil Procedure Rules front-load the costs of litigation. It will also be important to be seen to have acted reasonably in view of the weight the Courts will now place on pre-litigation behaviour when issues of costs arise.

If forfeiture is the landlord's preferred option, he may wish to achieve this by the most direct route, peaceable re-entry. Alternatively, if peaceable re-entry is not available, or if the commencement of proceedings is in part an attempt to put pressure on the tenant to remedy the breach, the landlord may commence court proceedings seeking an order for forfeiture. Clearly he will have to consider the likely outcome of those proceedings, in particular, whether the tenant is likely to he granted relief and, if relief is granted, the conditions that are likely to be imposed. The commencement of proceedings to put pressure on the tenant should not be undertaken lightly unless the landlord is willing to see the tenant take no steps in the proceedings, accept the termination of the lease by forfeiture, and walk away from the lease and the liabilities pursuant to it.

NOTIFYING THE MORTGAGEE

Another, and inexpensive, way of putting pressure on the tenant to remedy a breach is to notify the tenant's mortgagee of the matters about which the landlord complains. Most mortgages require the mortgagor (i.e. the tenant) to comply with the terms of the lease, and a mortgagee will be concerned to ensure that breaches are avoided so far as possible in order to reduce the risk of his security (the lease) being forfeited by the landlord. The mortgagee may, of course, himself apply for relief from forfeiture but this will incur costs. The mortgagee can, therefore, be expected to prevail upon the tenant to remedy the breach.

COMMENCEMENT OF COURT PROCEEDINGS

If the landlord starts forfeiture proceedings in either the High Court or the County Court and these are contested by the tenant, he can apply for Summary Judgment under CPR Part 24, if the tenant's Defence has no real prospect of success and there is no other reason for the matter to go to trial (Rule 24.2). Although the rules prohibit summary judgment against a residential tenant (Rule 24.3), this does not apply to possession of commercial premises.

In any possession proceedings in which the tenant contests the claim, the landlord should seek an interim payment order under CPR Part 25, at the earliest possible date. To avoid waiving the breach the landlord will have had a rent stop in place from the time the breach first came to his attention and the issue of proceedings will permit an application to be made for an interim payment order which will re-establish an income flow from the premises. The order will usually provide for a lump sum payment to cover the accrued "arrears", together with quarterly payments thereafter (see Precedent 8).

CHAPTER 13

STATUTORY DEMANDS

CHAPTER 13
STATUTORY DEMANDS

PRELIMINARY CONSIDERATIONS

The landlord will often obtain judgment against the tenant for the sums due under the lease, be they rent, service charge, or other payments such as insurance premiums.

But it is not necessary to obtain a court order to take action against the tenant under the Insolvency Act 1986 – a winding-up order in respect of a company tenant or a bankruptcy order in the case of an individual tenant can be obtained without any prior court order.

TO SUE OR NOT TO SUE?

Whether the landlord should first obtain a court order will depend on the circumstances of the particular case, the landlord's aims, and the perceived financial status of the tenant. Some preliminary considerations are set out below.

The threat or issue of court proceedings may itself prompt payment. Furthermore, (unless there are other proceedings under way) the tenant will only have to deal with one creditor rather than all creditors as is the case in insolvency proceedings. Court proceedings may therefore improve the landlord's prospects of obtaining payment, particularly if judgment is obtained followed by a charging order which secures the judgment, and raises the landlord to the status of a secured creditor.

But court action is not an end in itself. The landlord may still have to go through the insolvency process to get paid. If this becomes necessary the landlord will have incurred legal costs by pursuing court action which could have been avoided if insolvency proceedings had been commenced immediately. Obtaining judgment and then seeking to enforce it may take considerably longer than if insolvency proceedings had been commenced immediately, and landlords want to know sooner rather than Later whether they are going to obtain payment or whether the sums due from the tenant will have to be written off.

Insolvency proceedings, may, therefore, be both faster and more direct. The landlord is likely to find out at an earlier stage whether he will be paid. Indeed, the threat of insolvency may prompt the tenant to pay more quickly than if court proceedings are threatened, particularly if the tenant is an experienced debtor who knows how to exploit the delays inherent in the litigation process.

If a winding-up or bankruptcy order is made, the liquidator or trustee in bankruptcy will have wide powers to investigate the tenant's previous dealings and may be able to set aside previous dispositions of assets, thereby increasing the sums due to the creditors. This may appear to commend insolvency proceedings if the tenant's ability to pay from current assets is in doubt. But unless a charging order has been made following a judgment, the landlord will be an unsecured creditor and will have to share the available assets with the other creditors. Clearly therefore payment in full is unlikely.

Insolvency may result in the lease being terminated, either by virtue of a provision in the lease giving a right to forfeit, or by the liquidator or trustee in bankruptcy disclaiming the lease.

COMPANY TENANTS

The most common ground for ordering the winding-up of a company is that it is unable to pay its debts. The Insolvency Act 1986 sets out the circumstances in which a company is deemed unable to pay its debts (s 123). But a winding-up petition may be granted even though one of the deemed circumstances in section 123 does not apply, if evidence is adduced that the company is in fact unable to pay its debts: *Taylor's Industrial Flooring Ltd v M & H Plant Hire (Manchester) Ltd* [1990] BCC 44.

A company tenant who fails to pay the rent or other sums due to the landlord is, therefore, susceptible to compulsory liquidation on the basis that it is unable to pay its debts.

The court will deem a company unable to pay its debts if a statutory demand is served on the company in respect of an amount over £750, requiring the company to pay the debt or secure or compound for it to the reasonable satisfaction of the creditor, and the company fails to do so within 21 clear days, i.e. excluding the day of service of the demand and the date of presentation of a winding-up petition. The court may extend the time for compliance (Insolvency Rules 1986, Rule 4.3).

The demand must be in writing, dated and signed by the creditor or his authorised agent, and must be in the form prescribed in rule 4 of the Insolvency Rules 1986. It must be served at the registered office of the company. A precedent endorsement for a demand is at Precedent 20.

The amount demanded must be a liquidated sum payable immediately. The demand must state how the debt arises and the sum due at the date of the demand. In the case of monies due under a lease this will be by reference to the lease, identifying how the sums arose. Interest or other charges due must be separately identified. The sum claimed has to be accurate, although there is some authority to support the view that an overstatement of the sums due will not invalidate the demand provided some monies were properly due: *Re Pardoo Nominees Pty Ltd* (1987) 5 ACLC 496 (Supreme Court of Tasmania).

1. SERVICE

The Insolvency Act 1986 requires the demand to be left at the registered office of the company. It was thought that this prevented service by post, and there is authority to this effect: *Re a Company* [1985] BCLC 37. More recently it has been held that service by post is permissible: *Re a Company* [1991] BCLC 561. If there is no registered office the demand may be served at the principal or usual place of business.

2. CHALLENGING A DEMAND

The tenant may challenge the demand by applying to the court for an injunction to restrain the presentation of a winding-up petition or, if a petition has been presented, to restrain advertisement of and further proceeding with it. Application is to the Companies Court. The tenant must show some prospect of defeating the claim, and that it is solvent. If it can, the court will usually order the landlord to pay the costs of the injunction proceedings on an indemnity basis.

A winding-up petition may not be presented on the basis that a company has "neglected" to comply with a statutory demand within the 21-day period if that neglect is because the debt is disputed: *Re Lymphe Investments* [1972] 2 All ER 385. If only part of the debt is disputed, the court will not restrain the landlord from proceeding unless the undisputed part has been paid: *Re Trinity Insurance Ltd* [1990] BCC 235.

The landlord may not proceed with presentation of a winding-up petition if he rejects a reasonable offer from the tenant to compound or secure the debt. However, the court will hold the landlord's actions to be unreasonable in refusing an offer only if it could be said that no reasonable hypothetical creditor would have refused the offer in the circumstances. The fact that another creditor might respond differently was irrelevant: it had to be the case that the landlord's refusal was outside the range of what was reasonable: *Re a Debtor* (No 32 of 1993) [1994] 1 WLR 899.

The court has stated many times that it is a court of insolvency and not of debt collection. Use of the insolvency procedure to extract payment where there is a disputed debt has been strongly disapproved of by the courts, and a landlord who opposes an application to restrain the presentation of a winding-up petition where there is a dispute over the debt should be advised of the high risk of indemnity costs being awarded against him: *Re a Company* (No. 003079 of 1990) [1991] BCC 683. Where the landlord is proceeding only for rent which has not been paid this is unlikely, but other sums due under the lease may be more susceptible to dispute. In those circumstances the advice must be to start ordinary court proceedings unless the dispute is a sham in which case the insolvency proceedings may continue: *Re a Company* (No. 00 6685 of 1996) [1997] BCC 830. The court will look to see if there is a genuine dispute or not: *London & Global Ltd* v *Sahara Petroleum Ltd* (1998) *The Times*, December 3.

INDIVIDUAL TENANTS

A bankruptcy order may be sought.

Under section 267(2)(c) of the Insolvency Act 1986 a creditor may present a bankruptcy petition in respect of a debt which the debtor appears either to be unable to pay or to have no reasonable prospect of being able to pay. Section 268 of the Act defines "inability to pay" and provides that a debtor will be deemed unable to pay a debt if the debt is payable immediately, and the creditor to whom the debt is owed has served on the debtor a demand requiring him to pay the debt, and the demand has not been complied with nor set aside. The demand must be in writing and in the form prescribed by Rule 6.1 of the Insolvency Rules 1986. The debt must be a liquidated sum of at least £750 and unsecured (Insolvency Act 1986, s 267). A secured creditor may petition for a bankruptcy order if he (a) relinquishes his security, or (b) values the security and seeks to petition only in respect of the unsecured balance: *Re a Debtor* (No 64 of 1992) [1994] 2 All ER 177. Even if the debtor disputes the value placed on the security by the creditor, this will not of itself provide grounds to challenge the validity of the statutory demand.

If the demand is not complied with, within 21 clear days of service, the creditor may present a bankruptcy petition.

The demand may include interest at the rate specified in section 17 of the Judgments Act 1838 if the debt is due by virtue of a written instrument (as will obviously be the case under a lease) and is payable at a certain time. Interest may be claimed for the period from that time to the date of the bankruptcy order (Insolvency Rules 1986, Rule 6.113).

Overstatement of the sum due will not invalidate the statutory demand unless the amount actually due has been paid: *Re a Debtor* (No 490 of 1991) [1992] 2 All ER 664. Nor will it necessarily be invalid if there are formal deficiencies in the demand which would make it technically defective: *Re a Debtor* (No 1 of 1987) [1989] 2 All ER 46. Demands should, nevertheless, be carefully drafted.

1. SERVICE

The creditor must:

> "do all that is reasonable to bring the statutory demand to the debtor's attention and, if practicable, to cause personal service to be effected": Practice Note (No 4 of 1986} [1987] 1 All ER 604.

Ordinarily the demand will be served personally on the tenant. If this is not possible or the tenant is evading service there can be no application for an order for substituted service (now known under the CPR as Service by an Alternative Method: see CPR Part 6 Rule 8) as a statutory demand is not court process. In those circumstances the landlord should follow the guidelines for an attempt to serve a petition prior to an application for an order for service by an alternative method in respect of the petition. These are set out in Practice Note (No 4 of 1986) [1987] 1 All ER 604 (see below). An affidavit of service setting out the steps taken must then be lodged at court when seeking to issue the bankruptcy petition. If the court considers that appropriate steps have been taken it will allow a petition to be issued on that basis. It is important to follow closely the steps set out in the Practice Note.

2. ADVERTISEMENT

A statutory demand may be served by advertisement only if it is based on a prior judgment and the debtor has absconded or is avoiding service and execution is not possible.

3. SERVICE OUT OF THE JURISDICTION

A bankruptcy petition can be presented only against a debtor who is domiciled or physically present in England and Wales. But there will be occasions when it is necessary to serve a statutory demand outside the jurisdiction. The demand is not court process and so permission to serve out of the jurisdiction is not required. Service must be effected in accordance with the Practice Note issued by the Chief Bankruptcy Registrar on 26 February 1988. A creditor wishing to serve a statutory demand in a foreign country with which a civil procedure convention has been made may adopt the procedure prescribed (and must adopt this procedure if the assistance of a British Consul is required). If there is no such convention, service of the demand must be effected by private arrangement in accordance with the Insolvency Rules 1986, r 6.3, and local foreign law.

4.   ALTERNATIVE METHODS OF SERVICE

If it is not possible to serve the statutory demand personally, the landlord should adopt the procedure set out in the 18 December 1986 *Practice Note* (No 4 of 1986) [1987] 1 All ER 604 for the service of bankruptcy petitions, suitably amended for the service of a statutory demand.

The landlord or his process server should make one personal call at the residence and place of business of the tenant if both are known, or at whichever address is known.

If it is not possible to effect personal service, a first class pre-paid letter should be written to the tenant or left for him explaining the purpose of the visit and fixing another date for service of the demand. At least two business days' notice should be given. The letter has to state that if the appointment is not convenient the tenant must stipulate another time and place reasonably convenient, and that if the tenant fails to keep the appointment the landlord proposes to serve the demand by whatever substituted method is intended e.g. post, insertion through a letter-box, or as the case may be. See Precedent 11 for a specimen letter.

When attending the appointment fixed by the letter, the landlord or his process server should enquire whether the debtor has received letters left for him. If the tenant is not there, enquiries should be made as to whether letters are being forwarded to an address within the jurisdiction or elsewhere.

If the tenant is represented by solicitors, the landlord should attempt to effect service by arranging an appointment for personal service through them. A solicitor may accept service of a statutory demand for his client (but not a petition).

5. CHALLENGING A DEMAND

An application to set aside a statutory demand must be made within eighteen days of service. The grounds upon which the court may set aside a demand are set out in the Insolvency Rules 1986, r 6.5(4), namely:

1. The debtor has a counterclaim, set-off or crossclaim that equals or exceeds the debt specified in the statutory demand.
2. The debt is disputed on substantial grounds.
3. The creditor holds some security in respect of the debt and either

   (a) the demand does not state the nature of the security and value of it, and claims only the balance that is unsecured in accordance with rule 6.1(5);
      or
   (b) the court is satisfied that the value of the security equals or exceeds the full amount of the debt.

4. The court is satisfied on other grounds that the demand should be set aside.

The court will not usually set aside a demand because it overstates the sum due or because part of the debt is disputed, unless the debtor has suffered prejudice or the actual sum due or the undisputed part of the debt is paid: *Re a Debtor* (No 490 of 1991) [1992] 2 All ER 664; or because of technical defects in the demand: *Re a Debtor* (No 1 of 1987) [1989] 2 All ER 46.

If the whole sum claimed is disputed the demand may be set aside. If the debtor's defence seems doubtful this may be on terms – such as the debtor must pay the amount claimed into court: *Re a Debtor* (No 517 of 1991) (1992) *The Times*, 25 November. Such orders are likely to be rare: *Re a Debtor* (No 90 of 1992) (1993) *The Times*, 12 July.

When the debtor claims to have a counter claim which equals or exceeds the amount of the debt in the statutory demand the court will normally set the demand aside if in its opinion there is a genuine triable issue: Practice Note (Bankruptcy: Statutory Demand: Setting aside) [1987] 1 All ER 607; *Re a Debtor* No 544/SD/98 10 June, 1999, *Butterworths All England Reporter*.

Provided there is no application pending to set aside a statutory demand, a bankruptcy petition may be presented. But a bankruptcy order cannot be made if:

1. the debtor is able to pay his debts;
2. the petitioning creditor has unreasonably refused to accept an offer to secure or compound for the debt;
3. there has been a breach of the rules or some other reason.

CHAPTER 14
ENFORCEMENT OF JUDGMENTS

CHAPTER 14
ENFORCEMENT OF JUDGMENTS

A. MONEY JUDGMENTS

A landlord will normally wish to enforce a judgment as soon as possible. Where for some reason this is not possible (for example, the tenant can not currently be traced) the landlord is not restricted by section 24 of the Limitation Act 1980 to taking action within six years. After that time fresh action based on the judgment is excluded but attempts to enforce the judgment itself are not: *Lowsley* v *Forbes* [1998] 3 WLR 501. Therefore, applications for charging or third party debt orders are permitted over six years after the judgment, but a statutory demand is not as this will constitute "fresh action": *In re a Debtor* (No 50A-SD-1995) [1997] 2 WLR 57.

1. "ORAL EXAMINATION" – THE ORDER TO OBTAIN INFORMATION

To decide what is likely to be the most effective method of enforcing a money judgment, a creditor needs to know what assets ate available against which enforcement action can be taken. The creditor may already have adequate information, but if not should consider an oral examination of the individual judgment debtor, or an officer of the tenant company. To do this he needs to seek an order called an order to obtain information.

Procedure

The procedure is set out in CPR Part 71. The judgment creditor files without notice, at the court where the judgment was obtained, an application in form N316 (or form N316A if an officer of a company is to be examined) and the appropriate fee. The application can include specific extra questions that the creditor wants to put and documents he wants produced. The application must provide details of what is remaining due under the judgment.

If the application is properly completed, an order to attend court will be issued by the court. It will require attendance at the county court for the district in which the debtor resides or carries on his business. The order will include a penal notice warning the debtor of the risk of committal if he dails to comply with the order.

The order must be served personally on the debtor not less than 14 days before the hearing (CPR 71.3).

It is no longer necessary to tender conduct money, but the judgment debtor can claim his reasonable expenses of attending court from the creditor. The debtor must ask for these at least seven days before the hearing. The creditor is required to file an affidavit, at least two days before the hearing, to the effect that conduct money has been paid or was not requested and confirming how service of the order was effected (CPR 71.5).

On the date fixed for the oral examination, the debtor is examined under oath by a court officer. The judgment creditor or his solicitor may also attend and put questions. See Precedent 15 for a specimen list of questions.

If the debtor fails to attend, the matter is referred to a judge who will normally make a committal order, suspended provided the debtor attends on the adjourned hearing date.

Maximising the effect of the oral examination

If there are any documents which would assist the conduct of the examination, a list of them should be included in the application for the order, or sent to the debtor prior to the hearing. There is, however, no obligation on the debtor to attend with these documents unless specifically ordered to do so by the court when the order to attend is made.

2.   STATUTORY DEMAND

Following the oral examination or on the basis of information he already has, the judgment creditor may conclude that the debtor has no assets or that he is concealing them, and that it will only be by exerting maximum pressure that payment will be received – either from a supportive third party or because the assets are "hidden". In those circumstances if the debt exceeds £750 he may decide to serve a statutory demand as the precursor to presenting a bankruptcy petition or a petition for the compulsory winding-up of a company. See generally Chapter 13.

But note that if execution or other process issued on a judgment is returned wholly or partially unsatisfied, a winding-up or bankruptcy petition may be issued without the need to serve a statutory demand.

3.   THIRD PARTY DEBT ORDER

A third party debt order (previously called a garnishee order) is an order of the court requiring a third party person who is indebted to the judgment debtor to pay to the judgment creditor the whole of that debt, or whatever part of it is necessary to satisfy the judgment debt plus costs. The third party debt order may be enforced against the third party as if it were a money judgment made against that third party. Debts which may be the subject of a third party order include salary due to the judgment debtor, trade debts, rent due to the judgment debtor, or (the most common) sums standing to his credit at a bank or building society. The debt must be due to the judgment debtor alone and must be currently due – it is not possible to obtain a third party debt order in respect of a joint account. Money in court standing to the credit of the judgment debtor cannot be the subject of such an order although the creditor could apply to the Court under CPR Part 23 for payment out to him.

Procedure

This is set out in CPR Part 72. The procedure is in two stages.

Interim Order

The first stage is to obtain an interim order. Application is made without notice by filing in the court where the judgment was obtained a form N349 verified by a statement of truth. If done correctly, the court will make an interim order.

Where the application is made in respect of a deposit-taking institution (such as a bank or building society) which has more than one place of business, the application must if possible give the name and address of the branch at which the debtor's account is held and the account number. Of course, a prudent landlord will have ensured he has details of the tenant's bank on file, or has photocopied previous rent cheques, to make third party debt order applications as effective as possible.

The Master or district judge (as the case may be) will consider the application filed on behalf of the judgment creditor. If this contains the required information and a case is made out for a third party debt order to be granted, the Master/district judge will make a an interim order. The order will specify the date when the court will consider making a final order.

Final Order

The interim order requires the third party to show why a final order should not be made. It must be served on the third party at least 21 days before the hearing date and on the debtor at least seven days before the hearing date and at least seven days after service on the third party. If the third party is a deposit-taking institution with more than one place of business the order should be served both at the registered office and (if known) the branch at which the debtor's account is held. From the date of service of the order on the third party the debt (or such part as is necessary to pay the judgment debt) will be frozen. The debtor has no access to it.

Service is to be effected in accordance with CPR Part 6. If served by the creditor, a certificate of service must be filed at least two days before the hearing.

On the day fixed for the hearing, the court will consider whether a final order should be made. During the seven days between service of the interim order on the third party and service on the debtor, if the third party is a bank or building society, it must inform the court and the judgment creditor of any amounts held by it and whether the credit balance is sufficient to discharge the sum being claimed (or the amount available, if less). Equally, if there is no account, or the third party cannot comply with the interim order, this must be stated within the same time period.

Other third party debtors served with such an interim order (i.e. those that are not deposit taking institutions) must within the same period inform the judgment creditor and the court if the third party contends that no debt is due, or that the debt is insufficient to discharge the interim order.

If a third party debtor objects to the making of a final third party debt order, or maintains that someone else is entitled to the debt, written evidence must be filed at court setting out the grounds of this opposition and served a least three days before the date fixed for the hearing.

If the judgment creditor seeking the third party debt order wishes to dispute the third party's response, it must likewise serve evidence at least three days before the hearing.

If a judgment debtor is an individual and he can show that because of the interim third party debt order against his bank or building society account, he or his family are suffering hardship in meeting what is termed "ordinary expenses" the debtor may apply to any court for a "hardship payment" (see CPR 72.7). In cases of urgency, such an order may be made *ex parte* (i.e. with only the applicant present at court).

If a final order absolute is made the third party must then pay over the money to the judgment creditor.

4. EXECUTION AGAINST GOODS

If the debtor has goods which, if sold, are likely to raise a sum which will discharge (in part or in full) the judgment debt, the creditor may apply to the court for an order for execution to be levied on the debtor's goods. In the

High Court this is known as a writ of *fieri facias ("fi fa")* and in the county court as a warrant of execution. A writ of *fi fa* is executed by a High Court Enforcement Officer (which replaces the role previously undertaken by the sheriff). A HCEO can enforce in any part of England or Wales. A warrant of execution is executed by the bailiff of the county court in whose area the execution is to take place.

Execution may be levied against any moveable property belonging to the debtor but not goods which are owned by third parties, are subject to hire or hire-purchase agreements, or are protected property within the provisions of section 15 of the Courts and Legal Services Act 1990, namely:

1. such tools, books, vehicles and other items of equipment as are necessary to the defendant for use personally in his job or business;
2. such clothing, bedding, furniture, household equipment and provisions as are necessary for satisfying the basic domestic needs of the defendant and his family.

Guidelines as to whether items fall within these definitions are set out in Appendix 3 to *A Court User Guide*, published by the Lord Chancellor's Department in June 1991. For example, a motor vehicle can only exceptionally be retained by the defendant and a TV, video and stereo will not be "necessary" to satisfy basic domestic needs.

Execution to enforce payment of a sum of £5,000 or more must be effected by the High Court (i.e. by a High Court Enforcement Officer). If the sum due is less than £600 enforcement is available only in the county courts. Enforcement of a sum between £600 and £5,000 may be undertaken in either the county courts or the High Court.

Procedure

Levying execution is relatively straightforward. In the High Court a writ of *fi fa* is obtained by filing a *praecipe* in accordance with RSC Order 46, Rule 6, with a copy of the judgment. Where permission to issue the writ is required (see RSC Order 46, Rule 2) this must be obtained first by application without notice under CPR Part 23, supported by a witness statement or affidavit containing the particulars required by RSC Order 46, Rule 4(2). The order granting permission to issue the writ of *fi fa* (where needed) must be lodged with the *praecipe*. After the writ of *fi fa*, duly sealed, is obtained it is then sent by the landlord's solicitor to any High Court Enforcement Officer.

In the county court, the judgment creditor sends to the court a request under CCR Ord. 26, r. 1, including a certificate that the judgment is in arrears and setting out the outstanding balance. Details of interest claimed must also be provided. A fee is payable. The court will allocate a warrant number to the application and will forward it to the bailiff in whose area the warrant is to be executed.

High Court judgments may be enforced by execution in the county court by sending an office copy of the judgment to the county court office with the prescribed request form and a certificate verifying the amount owing. It is, however very unusual to transfer a High Court judgment to the county court for execution.

Similarly, a county court judgment for over £600 may be enforced by a writ of *fi fa* in the High Court. This is much more common because the High Court Enforcement Officers are perceived to be more effective in levying execution or obtaining payment than the county court bailiff. The procedure is governed by CCR, Ord 25, r 13. The creditor requests from the county court in which the judgment was obtained by completing form N293A a certificate of judgment pursuant to CCR, Ord 22, r 8(1) which has the effect of transferring the judgment. When applying for the certificate, a judgment creditor is required to state that enforcement by way of execution against goods is proposed.

Once a certificate of judgment has been obtained, the creditor must present to the judgment clerk at the High Court the certificate of judgment plus a copy. The clerk will allocate a reference number, keep one and return the other certificate to the creditor, who may then treat that certificate for enforcement purposes as a High Court judgment.

Execution by the High Court Enforcement Officer or bailiff is effected by attending at the premises where the goods are located and taking walking possession. If payment is not received within a specified period the High Court Enforcement Officer or bailiff will remove the goods, sell them at auction, deduct the costs of sale and pay the balance to the creditor. If the sums realised exceed the sums due to the creditor the balance will be paid to the debtor.

5.   CHARGING ORDER

A judgment creditor may obtain an order pursuant to the Charging Orders Act 1979 imposing a charge on the debtor's beneficial interest in property of the type specified in section 2 of the Act. This will make him a secured creditor in respect of the charged property and he may also be able to obtain an order for sale. A charging order may be obtained in respect of the debtor's beneficial interest in land (including jointly-held land), shares and funds in court.

The procedure is in two stages. The first stage is to obtain an interim charging order. The procedure is set out in CPR Part 73.

Interim Order

Charging orders are usually made in the county court. The High Court has exclusive jurisdiction to make a charging order only if the property to be charged is a fund in court which is lodged in the High Court. In all other cases the county court has concurrent jurisdiction. The county court has exclusive jurisdiction in respect of county court judgments.

There are no monetary limits. The application for the interim order must be made to the county court where the fund is lodged or, if the property against which a charging order is sought is not a fund in court, the court in which the judgment was obtained.

Application is made under CPR Part 73 without notice supported by filing form N379 in respect of land or form N380 for securities at the county court containing the information prescribed by the form and on payment of the appropriate fee.

The district judge will consider the application and if an interim charging order is granted a date will be fixed consider whether an final order should be made. A copy of the order, together with a copy of the supporting application must be served, not less than 28 days before the return day on the debtor, such other person as the court directs and any other relevant persons under CPR Part 73.5. This is done by ordinary service under CPR Part 6.

Final Order

The power to grant a charging order is discretionary.

On the hearing, the court will consider whether to make a final order . It will take account of the personal circumstances of the debtor and whether any other creditor is likely to be unduly prejudiced. The principles to be considered were set out in *Roberts Petroleum Ltd v Bernard Kenny Ltd* [1982] 1 WLR 301:

1. The burden of showing why a final order should not be made is on the debtor.
2. In exercising its discretion, the court can take account of all the circumstances of the case.
3. The court should exercise its discretion to do equity, as far as possible, between all the parties involved.

If the final order is made it must be served on all parties served with the interim order. To be most effective further steps are often required. A charging order obtained in respect of registered land should be protected by way of a notice on the title (either an agreed notice using form AN1 or a unilateral notice using form UN1), or by registration as a Land Charge if the title is unregistered. A charging order obtained in respect of shares will usually contain a stop notice which prevents the registration of a transfer of the shares until 14 days after notice has been sent to the creditor. Notice of this must be given to the company.

To prevent the debtor disposing of the property before the hearing of the application for the final charging order, the interim order should also be registered as a notice on the title of registered land or as a pending land action in respect of unregistered land. If there is a risk the debtor may try to dispose of the property, an injunction may be sought to restrain him from dealing with it before the hearing.

A charging order may be enforced by application for an order for sale: CPR Part 73.10. Such an application would require fresh proceedings under CPR Part 8. Even if the charging order is only in respect of the debtor's beneficial interest in jointly-owned land, an order for sale may be sought as the creditor is a person interested within section 30 of the Law of Property Act 1925: *Midland Bank Ltd v Chart* [1988] 2 All ER 4.34.

6.   ATTACHMENT OF EARNINGS ORDER

If the debtor is employed, the creditor may apply for an attachment of earnings order under which the debtor's employer must deduct a specified amount from the debtor's wages or salary and pay it into the court, who will then account to the creditor. Application must be made in the county court and the procedure is set out in CCR, Ord 27. It is unusual for a money judgment obtained in respect of a commercial lease to be enforced in this manner as the tenant is unlikely to be an employee. On the other hand, a surety may be an employed person.

B.   ENFORCEMENT OF ORDERS FOR POSSESSION

1.   COUNTY COURT

Enforcement of a county court order for possession is by warrant of possession pursuant to CCR, Ord 26, r 17 (which is retained in force as a Schedule to the CPR). That rule provides that an order for the recovery of land *shall* be enforceable by warrant of possession. It has been held that this prevents self-help and requires the issue of a warrant as the only manner to enforce an order in respect of *residential* premises: *Haniff* v *Robinson* [1993] 1 All ER 185. This does not apply to premises which are exclusively commercial.

The landlord files at court a request in the prescribed form, which may also combine a request for a warrant of execution if a money judgment remains unpaid. No permission is required. The application for the warrant can be made on the day after the date the possession order is to take effect. If an order for possession was made suspended upon payment or other terms, the suspension ends immediately the tenant defaults and so the landlord may apply immediately for a warrant of possession without further notice to the tenant or application to the court (other than the request for issue of the warrant), unless the order for possession specifically requires a further application to be made or if six years or more have elapsed since the original order: CCR, Ord 26, r 5 and *Hackney London Borough Council* v *White* (1995), *The Times*, 17 May.

A fee is payable for the issue of the warrant of possession. If execution of a money judgment is also requested the fee is calculated by reference to the amount for which the warrant is issued.

Once the warrant has been issued it will be passed to the bailiff. The landlord will be notified of a date when the bailiff will attend to execute the warrant. The landlord or his agent should meet the bailiff at the premises with a locksmith. In contrast to the execution of a writ of possession in the High Court, it is not necessary in the county court for all goods to be removed from the premises in order to effect execution of the warrant of possession: County Courts Act 1984, section 111(1). The judgment is *in rem* and so the bailiff can evict anyone he finds on the premises, even if they were not a party to the proceedings: *R* v *Wandsworth County Court, ex parte London Borough of Wandsworth* [1975] 3 All ER 390. Once the warrant has been executed the bailiff will ask the landlord or his agent to sign a receipt on the warrant to acknowledge that possession has been given to them.

If the tenant unlawfully re-enters the premises after the warrant has been executed, the landlord can apply for a warrant of restitution: CCR, Ord 26, r 17(4). Permission of the court is required to issue such a warrant. Application for permission is made without notice, with evidence setting out the derails of wrongful re-entry into possession. The warrant of restitution may be used to evict anyone on the land even if they were not parties to the original proceedings, provided their trespass is properly to be regarded as essentially one transaction with the original trespass of which complaint had previously been made. If not, fresh proceedings may be required.

If the tenant wishes to appeal the order for possession, he may apply for a stay of execution of the order (CCR Ord. 25, r. 8) pending the hearing of the appeal. However, the warrant cannot be set aside once it has been executed, unless the order for possession is also set aside: *Peabody Donation Fund Governors v Hay* [1986] 19 HLR 145.

Application may be made by the tenant pursuant to CCR, Ord 37 to set aside the possession order. Such an application may be made if the order was obtained against a party in his absence.

Re-hearing

Order 37 also gives the county court power to order a re-hearing. Any application for a re-hearing must be made on notice stating the grounds of the application. The notice of application must be served on the opposite party not more than 14 days after the date of trial and not less than seven days before the date fixed for the hearing of the application.

The notes to CCR, Ord 37, r 1 as originally published before the CPR suggest that the following matters will be taken into account:

1. default or misconduct by an officer of the court;
2. absence of a party;
3. default or misconduct by the opposite party;
4. fresh evidence;
5. perjury or mistake of a witness;
6. surprise;
7. mistake by counsel.

It is somewhat difficult to envisage circumstances in which a new trial will be ordered on the basis of either of the last two grounds.

2.   HIGH COURT

The defendant must first be served with a copy of the judgment. This applies to both proceedings to enforce a money judgment (see above) and a judgment for possession.

Any other persons in occupation of the premises should also be served with a copy of the judgment, even if they were not parties to the proceedings. They must be given a reasonable opportunity to apply for relief: RSC, Ord 45, r 3(3)(a).

If the tenant fails to give up possession on the date specified in the judgment, the landlord may enforce the order by obtaining a writ of possession (RSC, Order 45, r3(2)). Permission of the court is required to issue a writ of possession. The application for permission is made without notice supported by a witness statement or affidavit to the Master. For a specimen affidavit see Precedent 14.

The affidavit should be lodged with the Masters' Secretaries. After about one week it can be collected with the Master's order. Generally speaking permission will be given only if the court is satisfied that all persons in occupation have received notice of the proceedings and have thus been able to apply for relief from forfeiture.

If the possession order was suspended, the court will not grant permission without the tenant having first had the opportunity to be heard. In those circumstances the application for permission should be made on notice.

Once permission has been obtained, the landlord can obtain the writ of possession by filing at court a *praecipe* together with a completed writ of possession. A fee is payable. The judgment must be produced to the court. The court will seal the writ of possession and return it to the landlord's solicitor, who will forward it to a High Court Enforcement Officer ("HCEO"). The writ of possession may be joined with a writ of *fi fa* if a money judgment is unsatisfied.

Having received the writ the HCEO will notify the landlord's solicitors of a date when the writ win be executed. Notice of that appointment will also be sent to the premises. On the appointed date the landlord or his agent should attend at the premises with a locksmith. The HCEO will clear the premises of all persons and goods. Strictly speaking, the execution of the writ of possession will not be completed until all goods have been removed.

If the HCEO is unable to execute the writ and the tenant refuses to leave, application may be made for an order for committal for contempt.

If the tenant unlawfully re-enters after the writ has been executed, the landlord can apply for a writ of restitution. Application is made without notice to the Master supported by affidavit.

3. ENFORCEMENT OF POSSESSION ORDER BY LANDLORD PERSONALLY

If the landlord has obtained a court order for possession, he can enter without waiting for a formal warrant or writ of possession unless there is a residential element (e.g. a shop with flat above). Where there is a residential element the landlord should proceed only under a warrant or writ of possession – the tenant will still be entitled to the protection of section 3 of the Protection from Eviction Act 1977: *Haniff* v *Robinson* [1993] 1 All ER 185.

If the landlord decides to execute the possession order himself, he must use no more force than is necessary: *Aglionby* v *Cohen* [1955] 1 QB 558. Moreover the provisions of section 6 of the Criminal Law Act 1977 will also apply, whereby the use or threat of force can be a criminal offence. Enforcing a right of re-entry consequent upon an order for possession requires actual eviction of the tenant. In some cases this may require the attendance of several persons, which could constitute an offence under section 6 or a riot. Accordingly, where the premises are occupied, the attendance of a High Court Enforcement Officer or county court bailiff is more likely to achieve re-entry without the risk of allegations of breaches of section 6, riot or damage to/ loss of the tenant's goods.

If the tenant gives up possession voluntarily in accordance with the court order, the attendance of the bailiff or High Court Enforcement officer is, obviously, not required and the landlord can resume possession. If there is any doubt as to whether the tenant has departed (for example, if goods have been left), a formal eviction will provide the necessary certainty.

4.   GOODS REMAINING ON THE PREMISES

If the landlord has an outstanding money judgment he can apply for a writ of *fi fa* or warrant of execution so that execution can be levied on any goods found on the premises by the High Court Enforcement Officer/bailiff when the possession order is enforced. However, if this is not done – if, say, the value of the goods exceeds the amount of the judgment, or there is no money judgment outstanding – the landlord will be faced with the problem of what to do with goods left at the premises following enforcement of the possession order. In the nature of things this is not a situation that arises very often, but it can create difficulties for the landlord.

Strictly the goods could be regarded as trespassing on the premises (*James* v *Gospel & White* [1998] NPC 108) and arguably it would be open to the landlord to move them onto the street and forget about them. In practice, however, there may be items of some value and the landlord will feel obliged to do something to protect the goods. But as soon as he takes some action in relation to looking after them, he will acquire the common law duties as bailee to take reasonable care of the goods and not convert them. The prudent landlord will ensure that an inventory is taken (possibly also photographs) and that the goods are securely stored and insured. The landlord cannot convert the goods and so cannot sell or destroy them. On the other hand he can, of course, dispose of anything which is obviously junk or rubbish. If there is any doubt about this it is probably safer to keep the goods rather than dispose of them.

The tenant will be entitled to the return of the goods. If the landlord refuses to hand them back, the tenant may have a right of action under the Torts (Interference With Goods) Act 1977 for wrongful interference with goods. Alternatively, if the tenant does not take the goods back or cannot be found, the landlord, as a bailee, may apply to the court under sections 12 and 13 of the same Act for an order of sale.

Section 12 gives a bailee a power of sale of uncollected goods. The section applies if the bailor is in breach of an obligation to take delivery of the goods, or if the circumstances are such that the bailee can reasonably be expected to be relieved of a duty to safeguard the goods but he is unable to trace or communicate with the bailor. If the facts fall within these provisions, the landlord may sell the goods under the statutory power of sale contained in section 12(3). After deducting the costs of sale, the balance must be paid to the bailor.

Section 13 of the Act makes provision for the sale of goods in circumstances covered by section 12 by order of the court and payment into court of the proceeds of sale. This procedure will give the landlord the maximum protection against any allegation that he has dealt unlawfully with the goods, and is therefore to be preferred.

It may be thought that the landlord's predicament derives from his decision to protect the goods rather than put them into the street. In so doing the landlord could be regarded as making a rod for his own back, and an alternative procedure might be to try to hand the goods in at the police station – assuming, of course, that the police can be persuaded to take them, which is unlikely.

Sections 12 and 13 do not apply to goods that do not belong to the tenant (such as goods under a hire agreement), and so the landlord has no right to sell such goods.

CHAPTER 15

EFFECT OF INSOLVENCY ON ENFORCEMENT OF JUDGMENTS

CHAPTER 15

EFFECT OF INSOLVENCY ON ENFORCEMENT OF JUDGMENTS

Many landlords who are not immediately seeking possession of the premises, but only payment of the rent and other sums due under the lease, will often go direct to the remedy of distress wherever possible. Landlords do, nevertheless, sometimes prefer to issue proceedings for payment of the monies due to them, and the question considered here is to what extent, in an insolvency situation, they can enforce any judgment which has been obtained. It should also be remembered that once judgment for arrears of rent has been obtained, that judgment can be enforced only by execution. It is not then possible to distrain for the arrears of rent covered by the judgment.

LIQUIDATION

1. AFTER PETITION PRESENTED

Enforcement proceedings cannot be commenced afrer a petition for the compulsory winding-up of a company has been presented. Any attempted execution is void: Insolvency Act 1986, section 128. The position is less clear in the case of a voluntary winding-up, but it is likely that any enforcement action would be restrained if an application for a stay was made under section 112 of the 1986 Act by the liquidator or any contributory or creditor and the court took the view that the execution would confer an unfair preference.

2. BEFORE WINDING-UP

If enforcement procedures have been completed before the commencement of a winding-up, the judgment creditor can retain the benefit of the execution. In the case of procedures such as third party debt or charging orders, he will have to have obtained a final order, not just an interim order.

If a creditor has begun enforcement procedures but failed to complete them before the commencement of liquidation (for example, if only an interim order has been obtained), he will not be entitled to retain the benefit. An application for a charging or third party debt order will be dismissed, and if the bailiff or High Court Enforcement Officer ("HCEO") has seized goods but has not completed the execution before the commencement of the winding up, he will have to withdraw from the goods.

Even if execution is completed before the commencement of the winding-up, the judgment creditor is not entirely in the clear until 14 days have elapsed following the sale of the goods or payment to the bailiff or HCEO. If within that time the bailiff or HCEO receives notice that a petition for winding-up has been presented, or that a meeting has been called at which a resolution for voluntary winding-up is to be proposed, the judgment creditor will only be able to retain the prescribed amount change, to. The bailiff or HCEO will have to pay the balance over the prescribed amount after deducting his costs, to the liquidator: s.346 Insolvency Act 1986.

3.   COURT'S DISCRETION

The court has a discretion to permit a creditor to retain the proceeds of execution, but this is rarely exercised. Compelling reasons would be required to displace the general rule that all unsecured creditors should rank equally in the liquidation.

ADMINISTRATION ORDER

Leave, or the consent of the administrator. is also required after an administration order has been sought or made: Insolvency Act 1986, section 43 and 44 of Schedule B1.

RECEIVERSHIP

Execution procedures cannot be pursued against goods in respect of which a receiver is appointed once the charge has crystallised. Note also that from 15 September 2003 a floating charge may usually be enforced by the appointment of an administrator which will have the effect referred to above.

BANKRUPTCY

The position is similar to liquidation.

Once a bankruptcy petition has been presented the court may stay any execution: Insolvency Act 1986, section 285(1).

Once a bankruptcy order has been made, execution cannot be levied without the court's consent: section 285(3).

If enforcement procedures have not been completed before the commencement of bankruptcy proceedings, the creditor cannot retain the benefit of the incomplete execution. If a bailiff or High Court Enforcement Officer has completed execution for a sum over £500 and then, within 14 days of completion of the execution, he receives notification that a bankruptcy petition has been presented, he must pay over to the trustee in bankruptcy the excess over £500 less his expenses: section 346.

OBTAINING PAYMENT FROM A THIRD PARTY JUDGMENT CREDITOR

Although not a method of enforcement of a judgment obtained by the landlord, it is convenient to deal here with the landlord's right to require payment of arrears from a judgment creditor who is levying execution against the tenant's goods.

1.   HIGH COURT

The landlord can serve notice under section 1 of the Landlord and Tenant Act 1709 claiming payment of not more than one year's rent. In the case of a weekly tenancy the landlord is restricted to a claim for four weeks' arrears. For other lettings of less than a year the maximum sum the landlord can claim is four periods of rent, whatever that may be – four months if payable monthly.

The judgment creditor instructs the High Court Enforcement Office ("HCEO") to levy execution, but the HCEO has no duty to ask the landlord whether there are any outstanding arrears. It is up to the landlord to notify the HCEO and to serve the requisite notice, which can be done at any time until the HCEO parts with the proceeds of sale.

2.   COUNTY COURT: COUNTY COURTS ACT 1984, s 102

The landlord's claim to require payment of the arrears must be made within five days of seizure of the goods, or before they are removed from the tenant's premises. The claim must be in writing, signed by the landlord or his agent, and must state the amount due and the period to which it relates. The bailiff will apply the proceeds of sale to pay first the costs of sale, and thereafter the landlord's claim up to a maximum of four weeks' rent if the tenant has a weekly tenancy, two rent periods if the tenancy is for less than a year, or one year's rent in any other case. Any remaining balance will then be paid to the execution creditor.

3.   INSOLVENCY OF TENANT

If the tenant becomes bankrupt or goes into liquidation before the landlord gives notice to the HCEO/bailiff, the landlord will only be entitled to up to six months' rent and will not be entitled to claim rent in respect of any period subsequent to the date of his notice: Insolvency Act 1986, section 347(6).

LIABILITY OF DIRECTORS

If there is little or no prospect of the landlord recovering against the tenant company, the original tenant, the assignee(s) or surety(ies), there is the outside possibility of a claim against the directors of the tenant company for fraudulent or wrongful trading under the Insolvency Act 1986. This is obviously very much a "long shot" in respect of which it would be necessary to consult the standard texts on company law and take advice on the facts of the particular situation that has arisen. Action, though rare, would be taken by the liquidator, and whatever is recovered is held as part of the general assets of the company for distribution amongst all the creditors.

CHAPTER 16

DISCLAIMER

CHAPTER 16
DISCLAIMER

GENERALLY

The Insolvency Act 1986 enables a liquidator and a trustee in bankruptcy to disclaim leasehold property.

To keep matters simple, references in this chapter will be to disclaimer by a liquidator. The rules governing disclaimer by a trustee in bankruptcy are more or less the same. It should also be noted that whatever may be the strict legal position, there will often be many opportunities throughout the disclaimer process for the parties to come to some compromise rather than try to struggle through what is a somewhat complex area of the law.

WHY DISCLAIMER?

A company in liquidation remains liable to pay the rent and perform the lease covenants. Disclaimer enables the liquidator to terminate this liability and wind up the affairs of the company.

WHO CAN DISCLAIM?

- A liquidator.
- A trustee in bankruptcy.
- The Crown in relation to dissolved companies: Companies Act 1985, section 656.

Receivers, administrative receivers and administrators have no power to disclaim.

PROCEDURE

The liquidator will consider the lease and, if it has no value, proceed to disclaim it. An agreement for a lease may also be disclaimed: *Re Maughan* v *P. Monkhouse* (1885) 14 QB 956.

Leave to disclaim is not now required, except by a trustee in a few cases: Insolvency Act 1986, section 315(4).

The liquidator will sign notice of disclaimer and file it in court. The court endorses the notice with the date of filing. The date of endorsement is the date of prescribed notice of disclaimer.

Notice of disclaimer is then given by the liquidator within seven days to all who claim an interest in the property, e.g. the landlord, original lessee and any guarantor(s). If the liquidator subsequently becomes aware of others with an interest in the premises he must give notice to them too.

Underlessees and mortgagees of whom the liquidator is aware must also be served with the notice. The disclaimer does not take effect until 14 days after service of the last notice and provided no application for a vesting order is made within that time.

If an application is made it is still open to the court to direct that the disclaimer shall take effect.

The disclaimer operates from the date of the court endorsement of the prescribed notice: Insolvency Rules 1986, r 4.187(4).

In a case where the bankrupt was the assignee of a lease and his trustee disclaimed his interests in the licence to assign, the Court of Appeal held that this must mean that the lease itself was being disclaimed: *MEPC* v *Scottish Amicable Life Assurance Society* [1993] 36 EG 133.

"PRODDING" PROVISIONS

Insolvency Act 1986, s 178(5)

Any person interested in the property (usually the landlord) can give notice to the liquidator requiring him to decide whether to disclaim. The liquidator then has 28 days to disclaim, but the court can allow extra time (sections 178 (5) (b) and 376).

If the liquidator does not disclaim within the time allowed he is deemed to have adopted the lease and the landlord will be able to claim the rent as a liquidation expense to be paid before the other unsecured creditors. This is likely to be a major incentive for a liquidator to decide quickly. Whether the rent will be a liquidation expense is no longer a matter for the court's discretion but is clearly recoverable as an expense: *Re Toshoku Finance plc (in liquidation)* [2002] 1 WLR 671.

EFFECT OF DISCLAIMER

1.   INSOLVENCY ACT 1986, SS 178(4) AND 315(3)

The disclaimer determines the rights, interests and liabilities of the company. It does not affect the rights or liabilities of any other person except so far as is necessary to release the company from liability: *Hindcastle Limited* v *Barbara Attenborough Associates Limited* [1996] 1 EGLR 94.

2.   LEASE STILL VESTED IN ORIGINAL TENANT

The tenant is discharged from liability. The landlord proves in the liquidation for his losses arising from the disclaimer. Rent arrears to the date of disclaimer can be proved for in full, but a claim for loss of future rent will be discounted to reflect accelerated receipt – *In re Park Air Services plc* (1999) *The Times* February 5; and see the detailed valuation decision in *Christopher Moran Holdings Ltd* v *Bairstow* [1996] 40 EG 136.

The *Park Air* decision gives tenants of commercial premises a powerful weapon to use against landlords. It will enable tenants of over-rented premises to avoid the full liability for rent under the lease by disclaimer in liquidation. Landlords may accordingly have to consider more carefully offers to surrender.

The question arises whether the disclaimer terminates the lease in this situation. According to *Hindcastle* (see above) it does have that effect unless other persons have an interest in the property (e.g. sureties, mortgagees, subtenants). Where there are such interests the lease continues. In practice, in most cases because of the landlord's wish to preserve his income stream, the lease will only come to an end where the disclaimed lease was vested in the original tenant and there is no surety or sub-tenant.

3. LEASE HAS BEEN ASSIGNED

The present tenant is discharged from further liability and the landlord proves in the liquidation.

Subject to the Landlord and Tenant (Covenants) Act 1995 (see chapter 7), former tenants who gave the landlord a direct covenant including, of course, the original tenant, remain liable in contract: *W H Smith Ltd* v *Wyndham Investments Ltd* (1994) *The Times*, 26 May; [1994] EGGS 94; *Hindcastle Ltd* v *Barbara Attenborough Associates Ltd* (see above). In spite of the disclaimer, the lease still exists.

EFFECT OF DISCLAIMER ON GUARANTORS WHO STOOD AS SURETY FOR:

1. FORMER TENANTS (INCLUDING ORIGINAL TENANT) HAVING PRIVITY OF CONTRACT WITH LANDLORD

The liability of former tenants is not affected by disclaimer and therefore the liability of their guarantors is similarly unaffected: *Hindcastle Ltd* v *Barbara Attenborough Associates Ltd* (see above).

2. CURRENT TENANT

Although the liability of the current tenant ends on disclaimer, the liability of his guarantor remains unaffected: *Hindcastle Ltd* v *Barbara Attenbrough Associates Ltd* (see above). The House of Lords made it clear in *Hindcastle* that disclaimer of a lease terminates only the liability of the insolvent company, not its guarantors or any other interest persons.

In any event, most guarantee clauses require the surety to take up a new lease after disclaimer. Delay does not prevent a landlord relying on this right and it is not subject to the usual technicalities of options: *Active Estates Ltd* v *Parness* [2002] 36 EG 147.

When considering the liability of guarantors, it will always be important as a matter of construction to consider the precise obligation undertaken under the lease. The Courts will not impose liability unless it is clear on the words used that the liability exists: *Estates Gazette Limited* v *Benjamin Restaurants* [1995] 1 All ER129.

THE "AGGRIEVED" APPLICANT

Before the Insolvency Act 1986, the trustee in bankruptcy and liquidator needed leave of the court in order to disclaim, and the courts would sometimes refuse leave where the interests of a third party would be affected – where, for example, disclaimer would release a surety.

Under the new law leave is not now required except that a trustee in bankruptcy needs leave in the case of certain tenancies (mostly residential) which vest in him not upon his appointment, but only after he serves notice on the bankrupt requiring them to vest.

Even though leave is not now generally required, section 168(5) of the Insolvency Act 1986 enables somebody who is aggrieved by an act or decision of a liquidator to apply to the court to have the disclaimer set aside, and it had been thought that the court might grant such an order in situations in which, under the old law, an interested party might have been able to show that he was prejudiced by the disclaimer.

In *Re Hans Place Ltd* [1992] 44 EG 143 the court refused to make such an order. A tenant of business premises had sub-let them at a rent which far exceeded the rent it had to pay under its own headlease, and there were also two guarantors in respect of the subtenancy. The sub-tenant went into liquidation and the liquidator disclaimed the sub-lease which, being still vested in the original subtenant, had the effect of releasing the guarantors. Although that undoubtedly prejudiced the landlord of the sub-tenant, the court refused to grant an order setting aside the disclaimer because there was no bad faith on the part of the liquidator in disclaiming the sub-tenancy.

Re Hans Place Ltd was however decided before *Hindcastle Ltd* v *Barbara Attenbrough Associates Ltd* (see above) which overruled *Stacey* v *Hill* and held that disclaimers did not release a guaranter. The prejudice perceived in *Re Hans Place Ltd* would therefore no longer arise and it is difficult to envisage many occasions when applications under section 168(5) will be needed.

POSITION WITH REGARD TO UNDERLESSEES AND MORTGAGES

What is the effect of disclaimer so far as under-tenants are concerned and for mortgagees who, by virtue of section 87 of the Law of Property Act 1925, are put in exactly the same position as under-tenants?

In order to free the tenant from liability, it is necessary to extinguish the landlord's rights against the tenant and also the sub-tenant's rights against the tenant. The tenant's interest in the premises is determined by the disclaimer but this does not affect the interest of the sub-tenant. It is not necessary to determine the sub-tenant's interest in the premises in order to free the tenant company from liability. Therefore the sub-tenant's interest continues. It is unaffected by the determination of the tenant's interest in the premises. The subtenant continues to hold the premises on the same terms and subject to the same rights and obligations as would be applicable if the tenant's interest had continued. The sub-tenant does not continue to occupy the premises upon the terms of his sub-tenancy, rather he must now comply with the terms of the disclaimed lease. The position is as if the tenant's interest had continued but with the subtenant complying with the Head Lease in order to preserve that lease: *Hindcastle Limited* v *Barbara Attenborough Associates Ltd* (see above).

If the sub-tenant is an occupying business tenant, he will be entitled to claim the protection of the Landlord & Tenant Act 1954 Part II. Nothing will have happened to determine the tenancy under that Act – section 24 of which provides that the tenancy cannot be determined otherwise than in accordance with the Act. Although not a case on the 1954 Act, it has been held that disclaimer does not result in the termination of a statutory sub-tenancy: *Re Vedmay* [1994] 10 EG 108.

The position of mortgagees of the insolvent company is much the same as that of sub-tenants. As long as the tenant's obligations are complied with, the mortgagee may have the benefit of the demised premises: *Re Wilson* (1871) LR 13 EG 186.

If the landlord proceeds for forfeiture, the sub-tenant will have to apply for and obtain relief, paying any accrued arrears of rent.

THE POWER OF THE COURT TO MAKE A VESTING ORDER

This is found in section 181 of the Insolvency Act 1986; for personal bankruptcy see section 320.

1. PERSONS WHO CAN APPLY FOR A VESTING ORDER

1. Anybody who claims an interest in the disclaimed property – e.g. underlessees, mortgagees and the landlord.
2. Anybody who is liable in respect of the disclaimed property – e.g. former tenants (including the original tenant) and guarantors.

2.   TIME FOR APPLYING

Application must be made within three months of the applicant becoming aware of the disclaimer, or receiving a copy of the liquidator's notice of disclaimer, whichever is the earlier. The time limit may be extended by the court: section 376 and Rule 4.3 Insolvency Rules 1986.

3.   PRIORITY OF CLAIMS

The underlessee or mortgagee has priority.

The court may make, in favour of the underlessee or mortgagee, an order under section 182(l)(a) or (b) of the Act.

Under section 182(l)(a) the underlessee or mortgagee will be liable to perform all the company's obligations under the lease at the commencement of the winding-up.

An order under section 182(1)(b) would mean that after disposing of the lease the underlessee or mortgagee would not be liable for past breaches of covenant or breaches arising after he assigned.

In some cases the court may have to choose between competing applications for a resting order: *Re Ginwell Ltd* [2002] All ER (D) 92 (May).

4.   POSITION WHERE UNDERLESSEE/MORTAGEE IS NOT PREPARED TO ACCEPT THE COURT'S ORDER

They will be excluded from all interest in the property. An underlessee will have to vacate and a mortgagee will lose his security.

The court can vest the property in somebody who is liable to perform the insolvent tenant's covenants. It has a discretion as to the terms of the vesting order *unless* the insolvent tenant is an individual, in which case it must make an order in line with section 182(l)(a) or (b) above.

5.   EFFECT OF VESTING ORDER

There is no need for a conveyance, assignment or transfer. The vesting order is taken into account in assessing the claim in the liquidation by the person who has obtained an order.

A sub-tenant of part may obtain a vesting order of part of the premises: Insolvency Act 1986, section 182(2).

ALTERNATIVE APPROACHES

This is an area where it is likely that agreements will be reached. The landlord may take a surrender from the liquidator (thereby preserving a sublease) the original tenant might take an assignment from the liquidator and the landlord might reach some agreement with the sub-tenant.

1.   TWO QUESTIONS THAT ARISE

1. What does the landlord want – possession and rent, or just the rent, or the guarantor to take a new lease?
2, Who are the possible targets – former tenants, guarantors, sub-tenants or mortgagees?

2.   OPTIONS FOR LANDLORD

1. Forfeit for non-payment of rent or insolvency (if permitted by the lease).
2. Take possession and re-let – but that will end the liability of the original and other tenants and guarantors.
3, After disclaimer, take rent from a sub-tenant thereby preserving the disclaimed lease.
4. Force a guarantor to take a new lease – but this ends the liabilities arising under the old lease.
5. Sue the original or other tenants' guarantor(s) for arrears following, where appropriate, the notice procedure laid down in section 17 Landlord and Tenant (Covenants) Act 1995.
6. Bring the underlessee(s), mortgagee(s), original and former tenants and their guarantor(s) before the court to elect whether to take a vesting order.

CHAPTER 17

FORFEITURE AND INSOLVENCY

CHAPTER 17
FORFEITURE AND INSOLVENCY

In most modern commercial leases, the forfeiture clause expressly provides a right for the landlord to forfeit in the case of insolvency. Such a right must be expressly stated as it will not be implied by the common law.

It will be important to consider the precise wording of the clause. There are several types of "insolvency" which may give rise to the right to forfeit – for example, if a tenant enters into a composition or voluntary arrangement with his creditors, if goods are vested in a trustee, if a petition is presented for the winding-up or bankruptcy of the tenant or for the making of an administration order, or the appointment of a receiver. Sometimes the right to forfeit will arise on the commencement of an "act of insolvency" (such as the presentation of a petition) or it may arise only if a bankruptcy or winding-up order is actually made.

The lease may entitle the landlord to forfeit in the case of insolvency of a third party, such as a guarantor but a Section 146 Notice will have to be served: *Halliard Property Co Ltd v Jack Segal* [1978] 1 WLR 377.

On the other hand, the landlord may seek to forfeit for some other breach of covenant unrelated to insolvency. The fact of the tenant's insolvency may affect the landlord's ability to do this (see below and the summary table at the end of this chapter).

The effect of insolvency on peaceable re-entry is dealt with in Chapter 4, on rent deposits in Chapter 2, and on enforcement of judgments in Chapter 15.

LAW OF PROPERTY ACT 1925, s 146

If the landlord wishes to forfeit the lease for insolvency, it may or may not be necessary to serve a Section 146 Notice and relief may or may not be available. Most insolvency-type breaches are probably irremediable but the tenant should be given 14 days to consider his position: *Civil Service Co-operative Society* v *McGrigor's Trustee* [1923] 2 Ch 347. The situation is governed by section 146(9) and (10) of the Law of Property Act 1925. In summary the position is as follows.

1.   SECTION 146(9)

A Section 146 Notice is not required prior to forfeiture for the bankruptcy or liquidation of the tenant and relief is not available if the lease relates to:

(a)   agricultural or pastoral land;
(b)   mines or minerals;
(c)   a public house;
(d)   a dwelling-house let with the use of furniture or other chattels;
(e)   any property where the personal qualifications of the tenant are important to preserve the value or character of the property, or on the ground of neighbourhood to the landlord or any person holding under him. For an examination of this somewhat obscure provision see *Hockley Engineering Co Ltd* v *V & P Midlands Ltd* [1993] 18 EG 129.

2.   SECTION 146(10)

In the case of any other type of lease, the need to serve a Section 146 Notice and the availability of relief will depend upon when the landlord seeks to forfeit:

2.1   Before the lease is sold

Section 146 will not apply if the landlord seeks to forfeit after the first year of the bankruptcy or liquidation. During the first year a Section 146 Notice will have to be served and relief may be available.

2.2   After the lease has been sold

If the landlord seeks to forfeit the lease after the trustee in bankruptcy or liquidator has sold it, whether section 146 applies will again depend upon the timing.

During the first year of the liquidation or bankruptcy, a Section 146 Notice must be served on the assignee who will be able to apply for relief.

After the first year, a Section 146 Notice must be served on, and relief will be available to, the assignee if the trustee or liquidator sold the lease during that first year, but if the lease was not sold until after the first year, section 146 will not apply.

FORFEITURE BY PEACEABLE RE-ENTRY

See Chapter 4. The landlord's right is usually restricted.

FORFEITURE BY COURT ACTION

An "act of insolvency" on the part of the tenant will often affect the landlord's right to forfeit the lease by court action (as opposed to peaceable re-entry) based on that insolvency or for another breach of covenant. The position in each type of "insolvency" is considered below.

COMPULSORY LIQUIDATION

The landlord does not require leave of the court to commence forfeiture proceedings before a winding-up order is made, even if a winding-up petition has been presented. But the company, a creditor or a contributory can apply to court for a stay of proceedings.

Once a winding-up order has been made, the landlord will require leave of the court to commence or continue any court action. Accordingly, if the tenant company is in liquidation the quickest way for the landlord to obtain possession will probably be to issue a summons in the liquidation seeking an order for possession – a "Blue Jeans Order" (*Re Blue Jeans Sales Ltd* [1979] 1 WLR 362).

A sub-tenant or mortgagee may still seek relief in the usual way even if a landlord proceeds in this manner.

VOLUNTARY LIQUIDATION

There is no restriction on the landlord's right to forfeit, but the court can stay the proceedings under sections 112 and 126 of the Insolvency Act 1986.

ADMINISTRATION

A landlord wishing to forfeit a lease once a petition for an administration order has been presented or an administration order made must first obtain the leave of the court or the permission of the administrator. The considerations to which an application for leave will be subject were set

out in *Re Atlantic Computer Systems plc* (No 1) [1992] 1 All ER 476 at
pp. 501–503:

1. It is for the landlord to show that leave should be given.
2. The court should grant leave if it will not impede the purpose of the administration order.
3. In other cases the court will balance the interests of the land lord and the other creditors.
4. In doing so the court must give due weight to the proprietary interest of the landlord.
5. It will usually be sufficient for leave to be granted if the landlord would otherwise suffer significant loss. However this may be outweighed by a greater loss that will be suffered by others, or if that loss is disproportionately greater than the benefit to the landlord of leave being granted.
6. In assessing these losses the court will take account of all matters such as the financial position of the company, its ability to pay rent, the proposals of the administrator, the period of the administration order, the effect on the administration if leave were given and on the landlord if leave were refused, the purpose of the administration, the prospects of it being achieved, and the history of the administration.
7. The court must consider the probability of the suggested consequences.
8. The court will consider the conduct of the parties and any other circumstances.
9. The matters set out above are relevant if the court decides to impose conditions on either the grant or refusal of leave, for example, that the administrator must pay the current rent.

It is not necessary to show any impeachable conduct by the administrator in
order obtain leave (*Royal Trust Bank* v *Buchler* [1989] BCLC 130), but a
court is less likely to grant leave if the landlord has delayed in making an
application for permission to proceed (*Bristol Airport plc* v *Powdrill* [1990]
2 WLR 1362).

In *Re AGB Research* [1994] NPC 56, (see also *Redleaf Investments Ltd* v
Talbot page 63 above) premises were let to AGB but the landlord had retaken
possession of them and granted a new lease to O. On the subsequent appointment of administrators for AGB the landlord argued that he had not
forfeited the lease because this could not be done without leave of the court
under section 11(3) of the Insolvency Act 1986. Vinelott J held that the
landlord could not argue, that as against the administrators, the original
lease still existed because it was forfeited when the landlord granted a new
lease to O.

INDIVIDUAL VOLUNTARY ARRANGEMENTS

Section 252(2) of the Insolvency Act 1986 provided that no proceedings can be issued or continued, without leave of the court, whilst an interim order under section 252 is in force. This did not apparently prevent peaceable re-entry or the landlord's right of forfeiture. In order to promote an "enterprise culture" these loopholes were closed by the Insolvency Act 2000 so that peaceable re-entry and distress are both now prohibited (without the leave of the court) during the 14 day moratorium and since the IVA has been approved by creditors (except for a new, post-IVA debt). It has been held that an IVA cannot, however, affect the liability to pay future rents: *Burford Midland Properties Ltd* v *Marley Extrusions Ltd* [1995] 30 EG 89. However, there is a greater weight of authority (although all at first instance) which goes the other way and had held that future rental payments can be included: *Doorbar* v *Alltime Securities Ltd* [1994] BCC 994 (on IVA); see also *Cazaly Irving Holding Ltd* v *Cancol Ltd* [1995] EGGS 146 (a CVA).

COMPANY VOLUNTARY ARRANGEMENTS

The Insolvency Act 2000 imposes a 28 day moratorium in relation to small companies. This moratorium applies between the presentation of the proposal and the creditors' meetings. It can be extended by application up to a maximum of two months. During this moratorium, landlords (like other creditors) are restricted in the enforcement action they can take and therefore, without the leave of the court, a landlord may not issue proceedings of any type (including possession proceedings). Furthermore, the landlord may not levy distress, peaceably re-enter or take monies from a rent deposit charged by way of security.

A small company for these purposes is defined as one that satisfies at least two of the conditions set out in section 247 Companies Act 1985, namely:

- a turnover of not more than £2.8 million;
- a balance sheet of not more than £1.4 million;
- not more than 50 employees.

In the case of a large company CVA, the landlord will be bound by the terms of the CVA if he consents to it.

BANKRUPTCY

The landlord does not require leave of the court to commence forfeiture proceedings if the tenant is bankrupt.

Section 285 of the Insolvency Act 1986 prevents any person enforcing remedies in respect of unpaid debts once a bankruptcy order has been made, but so long as the landlord does not go for a money judgment he can seek an order for possession simpliciter: *Ezekiel* v *Orakpo* [1977] QB 260. Again, a sub-tenant, mortgagee or the trustee in bankruptcy can apply for relief in the usual way.

RECEIVERSHIP

The appointment of an administrative receiver or LPA receiver has no effect on the landlord's right to forfeit, but any such receiver can apply for relief.

However, since the Enterprise Act 2002 came into force on 15 September 2003, the right to appoint a receive in respect of floating charges has been abolished other than or capital market arrangements (section 72B) and public-private partnership projects (section 72C). From that date secured creditors will therefore be compelled to use the administration process to enforce floating charges. Forfeiture in administration is restricted (see above).

DISSOLUTION

If a company does not appear to be carrying on business or to be in operation, often because it has not complied with the Companies Act paperwork requirements (for example, failing to file annual accounts at Companies House) the company may be struck off the Register of Companies and dissolved pursuant to section 652 of the Companies Act 1985. A company that is struck off and dissolved no longer has any legal existence. Its property vests in the Crown (or the Duchy of Lancaster or the Duke of Cornwall as the case may be) as *bona vacantia* pursuant to section 654 of the Companies Act. Where a tenant company is dissolved the benefit of the lease will therefore vest in the Crown which may then exercise all beneficial interests in respect of it.

If the lease reserves a rack rent it is unlikely that there will be much value in the lease for the Crown particularly if the rent has been recently reviewed. In such circumstances, rather than taking on the onerous obligations under the lease (including the obligation to pay rent and comply with the other covenants) the Crown may prefer to disclaim the lease, exercising the power contained in section 656 of the Companies Act.

There is no machinery by which the Crown receives formal notification of property that has vested in it following the dissolution of a company. It is therefore left to individual landlords to contact the Crown when they become aware of the dissolution of their tenant, to notify them of this fact and to enquire as to whether the Crown will adopt the lease or disclaim it.

A landlord may serve notice on the Crown requiring the Crown to elect within three months of service of the notice whether or not to disclaim. Notice should be served on the Treasury Solicitor at Queen Anne's Chambers, 28 Broadway, London SW1H 9JS (Telephone 020 7210 3000).

If the Crown does not disclaim, it then becomes the direct tenant and subject to the landlord's usual remedies in respect of any breaches of covenant. If the Crown does disclaim the lease, the effect of this will depend upon whether there are any derivative interests or other persons in occupation. If there are, the landlord should put them to their election as to whether or not they will take a Vesting Order in respect of the lease, in default of which possession proceedings would be commenced against them on the basis that any occupier was, in effect, a squatter.

If there are no derivative interests or other persons in occupation, the disclaimer will, in effect, terminate the leasehold title.

If the property was held on trust by the company, on dissolution it does not vest in the Crown and the beneficiary may apply for an order vesting it in the beneficiary – *Re Strathblaine Estates* [1948] Ch 228.

There may, on rare occasions, be a reason to wish to restore the company to the Register. Broadly there are two statutory procedures for this.

Section 651 of the Companies Act permits the court to declare a dissolution void on the application of any person appearing to the court to have an interest. This could include a landlord as creditor. Such an application must be made within two years from the date of the dissolution.

Alternatively, application may be made under section 653. This also requires an application to the court and is available only where the Registrar of Companies has struck the company off the Register because he has reasonable cause to believe the company was not carrying on business or in operation. The time limit for such applications is 20 years from the date of dissolution.

If the company is revived, it enables the board of the company (or the liquidator) to get at its assets. If a landlord has significant sums owed to it, it may be appropriate to consider such an application rather than allowing the company's assets to become *bona vacantia*.

DISSOLUTION: FOREIGN COMPANIES

If a lease is granted to a foreign company that is dissolved, section 656 of the Companies Act clearly does not apply. However, any property that such companies own in England and Wales will still become *bona vacantia* and will vest in the Crown under common law. The common law does not provide a procedure for the Crown to disclaim the lease. However, if the lease is of no value, the landlord may be able to negotiate a surrender of the lease by the Crown. Where there are no derivative interests or other persons in occupation this is an effective method of regularising the position. However, where such interests have been created, they will survive a surrender. The landlord would, therefore, probably be better advised to forfeit the lease, most likely because of arrears of rent, after having had the company restored to the relevant Register.

Remedies Table

Legal Status of Tenant		Remedies	
	Distress		Forfeiture
		Peaceable Re-entry	By Court Action
IVA	NO unless leave	NO unless leave	NO unless leave
Bankruptcy	YES But subject to limits as to amounts. 347 IA 1986	YES *Re A Debtor No 13 A* [1993] 41 EG 142	YES s. 285 IA 1986 & *Ezekiel* v *Orakpol* [1977] QB 260
Administration	NO – unless leave	NO – unless leave or consent	NO – unless leave
Receivership	YES	YES	YES
Compulsory Liquidation	NO – unless leave	NO – unless leave	NO – unless leave, but seek "Blue Jeans Order" for possession
CVA (large companies).	*YES	YES	YES unless aggred

CHAPTER 18

SUB-TENANTS AND MORTGAGEES

CHAPTER 18
SUB-TENANTS AND MORTGAGEES

References are made in the text of this book where appropriate to the is-
sues affecting sub-tenants and mortgagee. This chapter seeks to expand and
consolidate these references.

SUB-TENANTS AND MORTGAGEES GENERALLY

Sub-tenants and mortgagees have no direct contractual relationship with the
landlord. The burden of tenant covenants binds only those who take an assignment of the whole term and so will not bind sub-tenants. Even if the lease
contains a covenant not to sub-let without consent, once the head landlord
has given his consent, the sub-tenant can then sub-underlet freely unless there
is an express prohibition in his sub-lease: *Villiers v Oldcorn* (1903) 20 TLR
11. Landlords commonly attempt to avoid this problem by requiring the sub-
tenant to enter into direct covenants with the landlord.

Both an application for consent to underlet and consent to charge the premises will be subject to the provisions of the Landlord and Tenant Act 1988
(see Chapter 9). Such consent cannot be unreasonably withheld if there is an
express stipulation to that effect in the wording of the covenant or if those
words are implied by section 19(1) of the Landlord and Tenant Act 1927.

The Court's approach to cases where the landlord has given consent to
underletting conditional upon the sub-tenant entering into direct covenants
with him has not been consistent. In *Re Spark's Lease* [1905] 1 Ch 456, it
was held that it was reasonable to require such covenants, but in *Balfour*
v Kensington Gardens Mansions Ltd (1932) 49 TLR 29, the Court decided
that it was unreasonable to impose this condition as it amounted to an attempt by the landlord to obtain a collateral advantage. It is thought that
Balfour is the preferred decision because *Spark's* turned on its particular
facts, including, importantly, the fact that the landlord was himself in occupation of part of the premises.

Any unlawful sub-lease will neverthess vest a sub-tenancy in the sub-tenant (*D'Silva* v *Lister House Development Ltd* [1971] see Chapter 17) who may also obtain rights under the Landlord and Tenant Act 1954, Part II.

An unlawful sub-tenancy will, of course, constitute a breach of the alienation covenant in the headlease. Such a breach is a once-and-for-all breach and the landlord must, therefore, be careful not to waive the breach once he has knowledge of the unlawful sub-letting. Waiver is dealt with above (Chap 3), but it should be noted here that service of a notice under the Law of Distress (Amendment) Act 1908 may constitute waiver.

LEASE TERMINATION: AN OVERVIEW OF THE EFFECT ON SUB-TENANTS AND MORTGAGEES

Leases may come to an end in various ways with differing results for a sub-tenant or mortgagee.

Some situations are more straightforward than others. On the expiry of a fixed term the lease automatically terminates unless there is a statutory right to remain in possession (e.g. a statutory continuation tenancy under the Landlord & Tenant Act 1954 Part II). In such circumstances the rights of a mortgagee and sub-tenant will also come to an end unless the sub-tenant has a statutory right to remain.

On surrender of a head lease, a sub-lease continues in the same form as it was granted. The sub-tenancy effectively becomes a head lease. A mortgagee of a lease is in the same position as a sub-tenant and is unaffected by the surrender *E S Schwab & Co* v *McCarthy* [1995] 31 P&CR 196.

A notice to quit automatically terminates any sub-tenancies carved out of the lease, regardless of whether the notice to quit is served by the landlord on the tenant or vice versa (see *Barrett* v *Morgan* [2000] 1 All ER 481 and *Pennell* v *Payne* [1995] QB 192). The position as compared to a surrender is therefore very different as where there is a surrender any sub-tenancy continues.

Leases may also be subject to determination by a break notice. Such a notice may give either the landlord or the tenant the option to end the lease early. Service of a break notice terminates not only the lease to which it refers but also any sub-tenancies carved out of it – see dicta in *Pennell* and *Barrett* above. Unless excluded, the Landlord & Tenant Act 1954 Part II does, however, continue to apply.

If the head lease is disclaimed any sub-lease will continue: *Hindcastle* v *Barbara Attenborough Associates Ltd* [1997] AC 17.

However the most complex area for tenants and sub-tenants is forfeiture. This will be looked at in detail later in this chapter, however, in summary the position is as follows:

- *Forfeiture by peaceable re-entry*
  The head lease and sub-lease come to an end on re-entry subject to any application for relief by the tenant, sub-tenant or mortgagee.
- *Forfeiture by court proceedings*
  The lease is not terminated until judgment confirming forfeiture is made. That order then relates back to the date of service of the proceedings. However the tenant, sub-tenant or mortgagee may apply for relief.

ARREARS OF RENT OR SERVICE CHARGE

1.   SUB-TENANTS

Unless there is a direct covenant between the sub-tenant and the landlord, there is no obligation on the sub-tenant to pay arrears of rent or service charge to the landlord.

The landlord may create such an obligation by serving a notice under section 6 of the Law of Distress (Amendment) Act 1908. Where rent is in arrear under the headlease the landlord may serve notice on the sub-tenant requiring him to pay the rent due under the sub-lease to the head landlord direct until such time as all arrears under the headlease have been discharged. See Precedent 10 for a specimen notice.

A Section 6 Notice will have priority over the rights of an administrative receiver or an LPA receiver under a fixed charge: *Rhodes* v *Allied Dunbar Pension Services Ltd* [1989] 1 WLR 800.

In the case of liquidation, administration or bankruptcy the position is unclear. A Section 6 Notice is probably not an "action or proceeding" prohibited by the Insolvency Act after the commencement of liquidation, and it may therefore be argued that such a notice can be served notwithstanding the liquidation of the tenant (*cf* the cases on the 1986 Act before the alterations made by the Insolvency Act 2000: in *McMullen & Sons Ltd* v *Cerrone* (1993) 66 P&CR 351 it was held that distress does not constitute "other legal process"). It is also unlikely that service of a Section 6 Notice will constitute the enforcement of security for the purposes of an administration order or the commencement of legal process for the purposes of a bankruptcy order (*cf Re Park Air Services plc* (1999) *The Times*, February 5: exercising a right of re-entry is not enforcement of a security – again a pre-Insolvency Act 2000 case but arguably relevant to this point.) Accordingly, leave of the court for such a notice is unlikely to be required. It has been held that distress levied by a landlord after a bankruptcy petition can continue: *Ex parte Birmingham and Staffordshire Gaslight Co, re Fanshaw* (1871) LR 11 Eq 615. Therefore it may be possible to serve a Section 6 Notice notwithstanding bankruptcy, administration, or liquidation, although the position has not been tested and therefore is not entirely free from doubt.

2. MORTGAGEES

A mortgagee has no direct liability to pay arrears of rent or service charge to the landlord, and there is no mechanism whereby the landlord can create such liability (the section 6 Notice procedure does not apply to mortgagees). The landlord may, nevertheless, wish to write to the mortgagee, inform him of the arrears of rent and ask him to pay. The mortgagee may be prepared to do so in order to avoid forfeiture proceedings (and the consequent risk to his security) and so this may prove to be an effective way of obtaining payment quickly and without cost.

DISTRESS

Distress is dealt with in detail in Chapter 5. It is considered here from the view-point of the sub-tenant or mortgagee.

A landlord may distrain on goods that are on the demised premises whether they belong to the tenant, a sub-tenant, a mortgagee or some other third party. However, a sub-tenant may avoid distress on his goods in one or more of the following ways:

1. The goods can be removed from the premises prior to distress being levied.
2. The sub-tenant can pay the rent to the landlord and thereafter seek an indemnity for the payment from the tenant: *Exall* v *Partridge* (1799) 8 Term Rep 308.
3. If the sub-tenant's goods are distrained upon by the landlord and subsequently sold, the sub-tenant can then seek an indemnity for the value of the goods from the tenant: *Edmunds* v *Wallingford* (1885) 14 QBD 811. In such circumstances the sub-tenant may also be able to rely on the remedies previously available to the landlord, by way of subrogation.
4. The sub-tenant can protect his goods from distress by giving notice to the landlord, pursuant to section 1 of the Law of Distress (Amendment)

Act 1908, that the goods do not belong to the tenant. The notice must be in writing, given to the landlord or his bailiff, and signed by the sub-tenant or his solicitor. It must state that the tenant has no interest in the goods and that they are not goods which are within the exceptions mentioned in the Act. The sub-tenant must set out the amount of the rent he pays under the sub-lease and must undertake to pay this to the landlord until the arrears under the headlease are paid. The notice must specify the goods to which it relates, and should therefore be accompanied by an inventory of the protected goods. The notice may be served at any time before distress is complete, but a new notice must be served for each new distraint.

It is unclear whether a mortgagee can serve such a notice if he has goods on the premises, because the third party protection afforded by the Act will apply only to those who have no beneficial interest in the tenancy or any part of it.

Once a Section 1 Notice has been served the landlord is precluded from proceeding with the distress against the sub-tenant's goods. If the landlord does, nevertheless, proceed, the sub-tenant can recover the goods by an application to a stipendiary magistrate or two justices of the peace.

If the sub-tenant fails to pay the rent due under the sub-lease to the landlord, the landlord can sue him for the sub-rent or distrain against his goods, because service of the Section 1 Notice effects a statutory assignment of the tenant's rights to receive the rent, thereby vesting in the landlord the same remedies that would have been available to the tenant.

The landlord can still enforce his remedies against the tenant even though a Law of Distress (Amendment) Act notice has been served – assuming, of course, that the notice has not resulted in the landlord recovering payment of all the sums due to him.

FORFEITURE

A sub-tenant or mortgagee is vulnerable to action by the landlord to forfeit the headlease. There is no obligation on the landlord to serve the sub-tenant or mortgagee with a copy of any Section 146 Notice (unless there is specific provision to this effect in the lease), although in some cases the landlord may do so to cause the sub-tenant or mortgagee to put pressure on the tenant to remedy the breach, or to get an application for relief under way without delay. Where a landlord serves a notice under section 146 alleging disrepair, a mortgagee (even a mortgagee in possession) is not entitled to serve a counter-notice under the Leasehold Property (Repairs) Act 1938: *Smith* v *Spaul* [2003] 1 All ER 509.

1. PEACEABLE RE-ENTRY

If a copy of the Section 146 Notice is not given to the sub-tenant or mortgagee, and the landlord then proceeds to forfeit by peaceable re-entry, the sub-tenant or mortgagee will have had no prior warning of the risk of forfeiture. Even if they have, they will invariably have no power to remedy the breach themselves, unless the mortgagee seeks to enter into possession because of a breach of the covenants in the mortgage deed. Proceedings seeking relief will therefore have to be commenced.

2. COURT ACTION

If the landlord proceeds to forfeit by court action, a sub-tenant or mortgagee has more protection if he is a party to the proceedings however as a result of a recent Court of Appeal decision and changes to the rules of court procedure mortgages have less protection if a landlord forfeits the lease: *Smith* v *Spaul* [2003] 1 All ER 509. In that case the landlord sought to forfeit the lease for disrepair. The landlord served a Section 146 Notice on the mortgagee which had taken possession of the premises. The mortgagee served a counter notice claiming the benefit of the Leasehold Property (Repairs) Act 1938. This would normally require the landlord to obtain the court's permission before forfeiting the lease. However, the landlord successfully commenced proceedings without seeking permission as the court held that a mortgagee is not entitled to be served with a Section 146 Notice and that a landlord would not be bound by a mortgagee's notice under the 1938 Act.

Accordingly, it is clear that mortgagees of commercial leases have no automatic entitlement to be notified of proceedings commenced by a landlord to forfeit a lease. Nor is there any general duty on a landlord to notify a mortgagee that it intends to take such action. Therefore a mortgagee may know nothing of the forfeiture of a lease until it has occurred.

It is no longer the case that a landlord of commercial premises must name in possession proceedings all parties which may be entitled to relief from forfeiture, although it does remain the case in residential possession proceedings.

In order to preserve its security, a mortgagee would have to apply for relief from forfeiture, normally within a period of six months.

The effect of forfeiture is to determine the lease when the possession order is made with effect from the date of service of the court proceedings, not the date of issue of them: *Canas Property Co Ltd* v *K L Television Services Ltd* [1970] 2 All ER 795. The act of service of the proceedings constitutes an unequivocal election by the landlord to determine the lease in reliance on the breach of covenant: *Ivory Gate Ltd* v *Spetale* [1998] EGCS 69.

As the effect of forfeiture is to determine the lease, all interests created under it including any mortgages and sub-tenancies will also be destroyed. "The branch falls with the tree", subject to any application by the sub-tenant or mortgagee for relief from forfeiture.

Merely allowing the sub-tenant to remain in occupation on the same terms will be insufficient to constitute forfeiture: *Ashton* v *Sobelman* [1987] 1 WLR 177. But if, after forfeiting the lease, the landlord agrees with the sub-tenant that he may have a new lease and it is made clear that this constitutes the grant of such new lease, there will then be an effective forfeiture.

RELIEF FROM FORFEITURE

1.   RELIEF FOR ANY BREACH OF COVENANT

Relief may be granted to a sub-tenant or mortgagee under section 146(4) of the Law of Property Act 1925. Although relief granted to a tenant is retrospective, relief granted to a sub-tenant or mortgagee under this section is not, and operates by vesting a new term in the sub-tenant/mortgagee. Accordingly, the landlord will be entitled to the income from the premises between the date of forfeiture and any vesting order: *Official Custodian for Charities* v *Mackey* [1984] 3 All ER 689.

Sub-tenants

In granting relief the court may impose terms as to payment of any arrears of rent, costs, or the remedying of the breach of covenant. The court also has a discretion as to the term, rent and premises to be comprised in the new lease granted by way of relief under section 146(4), although the lease cannot be for a term longer than the sub-tenant previously had. This restriction will not, however, prevent a sub-tenant obtaining relief where he has rights under the Landlord and Tenant Act 1954, Part II, and the continuation tenancy has already commenced: *Cadogan* v *Dimovic* [1984] 1 WLR 609.

The terms of the new lease will generally be the same as under the head-lease – the basic principle is to put the landlord back into the position he was in before the forfeiture: *Chatham Empire Theatre (1955) Ltd* v *Ultrans Ltd* [1961] 1 WLR 817. If the sub-tenant had a lease of part only, he will usually only obtain and be forced to take a lease of part (see *Chatham Empire*

Theatre above). However, the sub-tenant may have to undertake obligations previously contained in the headlease which are more onerous than in his sub-lease: *Hill* v *Griffin* [1987] 1 EGLR 81.

Relief is usually given on condition that the accrued arrears of rent are paid. If the sub-tenant had a sub-lease of part, in order to obtain relief he will usually have to pay all the arrears accrued under the headlease, not just the part of the arrears that relate to the property comprised in his sub-tenancy: *London Bridge Buildings Co* v *Thomson* (1903) 89 LT 50. However, when fixing the future rent to be paid under the new lease, the sub-tenant will normally have to pay only a proportionate part of the rent relative to the premises over which relief is given, albeit at the rate comprised in the headlease (see *London Bridge Buildings Co* v *Thomson* above).

The court's approach is perhaps best expressed by Farwell J in *Re Lord De Clifford's Estate* [1900] 2 Ch 707:

> "[a right of forfeiture . . . [is] intended to secure money or the performance of a contract. Equity gave no relief unless it could secure the payment of the money or the performance of the contract in favour of the person entitled to enforce forfeiture, and it granted relief on the ground that it thereby gave effect to the . . . contract between the parties."

However, on occasion the court's discretion will only be used sparingly (*Creery* v *Summersall* [1949] Ch 751), particularly where the sublet property is not capable of convenient occupation separate from the rest of the demised premises: *Fivecourts Ltd* v *Leisure Development Co Ltd* QBD 18 August 2000. In considering relief the court will take account of the fact that the subtenant has been "thrust" on the landlord.

Neverthess, relief may on occasion even be granted to an unlawful sub-tenant: *Duarte* v *Mount Cook Land Ltd* [2001] 33 EGCS 87.

Relief may be under section 146(4), although the court also has an inherent jurisdiction to grant relief. However, where there is a statutory power, it will normally be exceptional for any relief to be on the basis of the court's inherent jurisdiction: *Duarte* v *Mount Cook* (above).

Mortgagees

Section 146(4) also permits a mortgagee to obtain relief. This is clear from the wording of the section where the mortgage is granted by sublease. Modern mortgages are invariably legal charges. But a mortgage by legal charge will still give rise to the right to apply for relief, as section 87 of the Law of Property Act 1925 provides that a charge by legal mortgage will be subject to the same rights as if it were by sub-lease.

A person with a charging order absolute under the Charging Orders Act 1979 or an equitable charge may also apply for relief: *Ladup Ltd* v *Williams and Glyn's Bank plc* [1985] 1 WLR 851. See also *Croydon (Unique) Ltd* v *Wright* Butterworths Case reports 29.7.99 and *Bland* v *Ingram's Estates Ltd* [2001] 24 EG 163. Where others have been in occupation, see *Bland* v *Ingram's Estates Ltd (No2)* [2001] 50 EG 92 for details of how to take account of the benefit of occupation on granting relief.

Relief granted to a mortgagee will also be by way of vesting order and the grant of a new lease. The new lease will take effect as a substitute security, not as an assignment of the old lease: *Chelsea Estates Investment Trust Co Ltd* v *Marche* [1955] Ch 328. Accordingly, the tenant's equity of redemption will continue and if he pays off the sums due to the mortgagee them, notwithstanding the previous forfeiture, he may achieve the somewhat anomalous position of being able to regain the premises.

A mortgagee who has obtained relief will almost certainly seek to sell the lease as soon as possible to realise the asset. Until he does, he will be liable to comply with all the covenants in the lease including, of course, payment of rent.

Application for relief

Where the landlord knows of the mortgagee, he is obliged to state this in the particulars of claims which will be sent to the mortgagee. The mortgagee can then pay any arrears up to the date of possession ordered by the court and will obtain automatic relief under section 138 of the County Courts Act, or section 210 of the Common Law Procedure Act (see below). Where, however, there is a dispute or forfeiture is for a reason other than arrears, an application for formal relief is required. The application will normally join in the tenant. The application should be by counterclaim or by Notice of Application (CPR, Part 23) in the landlord's action or, if the landlord has proceeded by peaceable re-entry so that there are no existing proceedings, by originating proceedings.

Section 146(4) states that the application for relief may be made whilst the landlord "is proceeding". Until *Billson* v *Residential Apartments Ltd* [1992] All ER 141 (see Chap 4 above) it was thought that once the landlord had effected forfeiture by peaceable re-entry he was no longer "proceeding" and an application for relief could not be brought. However it was made clear in *Billson* that this was not the case. An application for relief can be brought under section 146(4) by a sub-tenant or mortgagee after the landlord has effected physical re-entry within a reasonable time of that forfeiture. No precise time limit is laid down, but the six-month period laid down in the Common Law Procedure Act 1852 may, by analogy, be held to apply.

The grant by the landlord of a new lease before the application for relief is made is not an absolute bar to relief: *Bank of Ireland House Mortgages v South Lodge Developments* [1996] 14 EG 92. The mortgagee will usually in such circumstances obtain a reversionary lease and the premium received by the landlord for the new lease.

If the landlord forfeits by court action for a breach other than non-payment of rent and has executed a possession order, the right to apply for relief is lost: *Rogers v Rice* [1892] 2 Ch 170. But the sub-tenant or mortgagee should have had ample opportunity to apply for relief, as a copy of the particulars of claim should have been sent to him (CPR, Sched. 2 CCR, Ord 6, r 3).

If the possession order is set aside or appealed successfully, notwithstanding that the landlord had enforced the order, an application for relief can still be made: *Rexhaven v Nurse* (1996) 28 HLR 24. Accordingly, if the sub-tenant does not know of the possession proceedings until after the possession order has been enforced, he might apply to the court to set aside the judgment, be joined as a party and apply for relief.

An unlawful sub-tenant can also apply for relief: *Factors (Sundries) Ltd v Miller* [1952] 2 All ER 630, and *Duarte v Mount Cook Ltd* [2001] (see above), as can a judgment creditor with a charging order over the leasehold property: *Bland v Ingram's Estates Ltd* [2000] All ER (D) 2441.

2.   RELIEF FROM FORFEITURE FOR NON-PAYMENT OF RENT

In addition to the right to apply for relief under section 146(4) of the Law of Property Act 1925, a sub-tenant or mortgagee may obtain relief from forfeiture under the statutory provisions which provide for the grant of relief following non-payment of rent.

High Court

Where six months' rent or more is in arrear, relief can be sought under section 38 of the Supreme Court Act 1981 and section 210 of the Common Law Procedure Act 1852 (see Chapter 3, above). The application can be made after the landlord has executed the possession order, but it must be made within six months of that execution. The six months rule will be strictly applied to mortgagees: *United Dominions Trust v Shellpoint Trustees* [1993] EGCS 57.

If less than six months' rent is in arrear, section 210 of the Common Law Procedure Act will not apply and relief can only be obtained under the court's inherent jurisdiction.

The landlord is not obliged to join any sub-tenant or mortgagee in the proceedings, but the particulars of claim must name any sub-tenant or mortgagee of whom the landlord is aware: CPR, Part 16, Practice Direction 6 (8). Paradoxically, the CPR, unlike the old court rules, do not seem to require the proceedings to be sent to any such party (as RSC, Ord. 6, r 2, has not been retained) but good practice would suggest this is sensible to ensure any application for relief that is going to be made is made as soon as possible. The application for relief should, be by counterclaim or application under CPR, Part 23 in the landlord's action.

If the sub-tenant or mortgagee has not received notice of the landlord's proceedings (presumably because the landlord was not aware of their existence), the application for relief may be made either by Part 7 claim form or, if the facts are not in issue, by originating proceedings under CPR Part 8.

County Court

Section 138 of the County Courts Act 1984 provides a procedure similar to section 210 of the Common Law Procedure Act. The entitlement to relief is automatic if all arrears of rent are paid into court five days before the hearing: section 138(2); *Escalus Properties Ltd* v *Robinson* [1995] 31 EG 71. Under section 138(9C) an application for relief can be made at any time within six months from the date on which the landlord recovers possession under a court order, by any person who has an interest derived from the tenant's interest. This will permit a sub-tenant or mortgagee to apply for relief within the six months' time limit and on such application the court may make an order, subject to such terms and conditions as it thinks fit, to vest the land in the sub-tenant or mortgagee for the remainder of the term of the lease, or for a shorter term.

The application for relief should be made by way of counterclaim or application in the landlords proceedings. If the subtenant or mortgagee has not had notice of these proceedings, the application may be made by fresh proceedings under CPR, Part 7, or if the facts are unlikely to be in issue CPR Part 8 may be used.

If the application for relief is not made within six months, section 138(7) of the County Courts Act 1984 provides that the tenant shall be barred from all relief. Section 138(9c) provides that the application by a mortgagee or sub-tenant for relief may be made as if he were the tenant. Consequently the six months' time limit is final and any mortgagee or sub-tenant who does not apply within this period will be "barred from all relief": *United Dominions Trust* v *Shellpoint Trustees* [1993] ECGS 57.

Costs

As one time the court would usually order the person obtaining relief to indemnify the landlord in respect of his costs as a condition of relief. However, following the dicta of Lord Templeman in *Billson* v *Residential Apartments Ltd* [1992] 1 All ER 141 (see Chap 4 above) this has been disapproved of as an invariable rule and it is more likely that, although the landlord will still obtain an order for payment of his costs, this will be on the standard basis only.

Even if the tenant covenants in the lease to pay the landlord's costs, the court will probably not order an indemnity unless the covenant expressly provides for an indemnity payment: *Primeridge Ltd* v *Jean Muir Ltd* [1992] 1 EGLR 273.

However, where it does so provide, the court will normally order payment of indemnity costs unless there is a good reason not to: *Church Commissioners for England* v *Ibrahim* [1997] 3 EG 136.

INSOLVENCY

If the tenant becomes insolvent, the lease may well be disclaimed by the liquidator/trustee in bankruptcy as onerous property. The effect on a sub-tenant is that the sub-tenant may remain in occupation for so long as the terms of the headlease are observed. This will include payment of the rent and compliance with the other covenants.

If the sub-lease was protected by the Landlord and Tenant Act 1954, Part II, the effect of disclaimer of the headlease is probably that the protection continues because section 24 of the 1954 Act expressly provides that such a lease may not be determined otherwise than in accordance with that Act. The provisions relating to disclaimer in the Insolvency Act 1986 make no reference to such a tenancy – see Chapter 16 above.

The effect of a disclaimer on a mortgagee is the same as for a subtenant: *Re Wilson* [1871] LR 13 Eq 186.

Both a sub-tenant and a mortgagee may apply for a vesting order in respect of the disclaimed lease under sections 181 or 320 of the Insolvency Act 1986, depending upon whether the tenant is in liquidation or bankruptcy respectively. Equally the landlord may apply to the court to put the sub-tenant or mortgagee to their election as to whether or not they will take a vesting order, and upon their failure to do so to exclude them from all interest in the premises: Insolvency Act 1986, ss 182(4) and 321(4). The effect of such an exclusion order on a sub-tenancy protected by the Landlord and Tenant Act 1954 is unclear.

The application for a vesting order must be made within three months of the date the applicant became aware of the disclaimer: Insolvency Rules 1986, r 4.194/6.186. This time limit may however be extended: Insolvency Rules 1986, r 4.3, and Insolvency Act 1986, section 376.

A detailed discussion of the procedure, terms and effect of a vesting order are set out in Chapter 16.

A sub-tenant or, if appropriate, a mortgagee may obtain a vesting order of part only of the premises comprised in the headlease (Insolvency Act 1986, ss 182(2) and 321(2)), although this will be subject to the same obligations to which the tenant was subject in respect of the whole of the demised premises. Unfortunately the Act does not deal with the other terms that may be required if such a vesting order is granted, such as the requirement for a service charge where the premises are in multiple occupation, rights over the common parts and apportionment of rent.

The insolvency of the tenant may itself give the landlord the right to forfeit the lease (see Chap 17). This must, however, be expressly stated in the proviso for forfeiture and will not be implied by law. A mortgagee (or undeed a sub-tenant) may seek relief from forfeiture where the landlord forfeits for insolvency and is not required to obtain a vesting order: *Barclays Bank plc v Prudential Assurance Company Ltd* [1997] 10 EG 159.

CHAPTER 19
RECOVERY OF COSTS

CHAPTER 19
RECOVERY OF COSTS

As pleased as the landlord will no doubt be to receive payment of the outstanding arrears of rent/service charges or to be told that the tenant has remedied the breach of covenant(s), his satisfaction will be somewhat short-lived if he then receives a substantial account for professional fees from his solicitors and/or surveyors. The question is to what extent the landlord can recover his costs from the tenant or others?

It is necessary to consider the position both before and after proceedings have been issued, at common law and under any express terms of the lease. It is also necessary to consider the impact of the Landlord and Tenant (Covenants) Act 1995 – see below.

BEFORE PROCEEDINGS ARE ISSUED

The landlord is in some difficulty. So far as legal costs are concerned, Principle 17.05 of *The Guide to the Professional Conduct of Solicitors* (8th ed), provides that:

> "When writing a letter before action (now a letter of claim) solicitor must not demand anything other than that recoverable under the due process of law.
>
> Commentary
>
> 1. For example, where a solicitor is retained to collect a simple debt, he or she must not demand from the debtor the cost of the letter before action, since it cannot be said at the stage when the first letter is written, that such costs are legally recoverable."

This provision effectively prevents a solicitor from writing to the tenant demanding payment of rent arrears/service charges and also the costs to his landlord client of instructing the solicitor to write the letter – at this stage the costs cannot be said to be legally recoverable.

1. BREACHES OR COVENANT OTHER THAN NON-PAYMENT OR RENT

Section 146(1) Law of Property Act 1925 entitles a landlord to compensation for the breach of covenant mentioned in the Section 146 Notice but, according to *Skinners' Company* v *Knight* [1891] QB 542, this does not include the cost of the preparation of the notice.

Whether costs other than the cost of preparing the notice (such as the costs of discovering and investigating the breach) are recoverable is a matter to be argued.

If the landlord serves a Section 146 Notice and the breach of covenant is remedied by the tenant before proceedings are issued, the landlord cannot, unless there is specific provision in the lease to the contrary, recover his costs in relation to the preparation and service of the Section 146 Notice: *Nind* v *Nineteenth Century Building Society* [1894] 2 QB 226. Where a right of re-entry or forfeiture is waived by the landlord at the request of the tenant, or where relief under Section 146 of the Law of Property Act 1925, is granted the landlord is entitled to his costs: Section 146 (3). In a case to which the Leasehold Property (Repairs) Act 1938 applies, if the tenant claims the benefit of the Act, the landlord can recover costs under section 146(3) only with leave of the court (1938 Act, s 2).

2. DEBT OR DAMAGES?

It may be open to a landlord to claim his legal fees prior to litigation if his claim is for an unliquidated sum, *i.e. not for arrears but for damages*. As a matter of general law, where a creditor claims from a debtor a liquidated sum, *e.g.* rent, he cannot claim, in addition, his legal costs incurred in recovery of the debt unless there is some contractual provision in the lease enabling him to do this, or he issues proceedings. If the tenant discharges the debt, the landlord cannot then issue proceedings merely because the tenant refuses to pay legal costs. If the landlord were to issue proceedings, the tenant would have a complete defence – either that he had paid the rent or, if the landlord refused payment, that he had tendered it.

However, where the landlord's claim is for unliquidated damages, *e.g.* for interim dilapidations during the term of the lease, there is an argument for saying that he can, in addition to his claim for damages, also claim the costs he has incurred in preparing and pursuing the claim prior to the issue of proceedings. The reason is that the courts will not allow a defendant to rely on the defence of tender in the case of unliquidated claims: *John Laing Construction Ltd* v *Dastur* [1987] 1 WLR 686; *Smith* v *Springer* [1987] 1 WLR 1720.

In a buoyant market a landlord faced with a breach of covenant, other than non-payment of rent, would normally have threatened and instituted forfeiture proceedings and clear provision is usually made in the lease for recovery of the costs relating to the Section 146 Notice. In a weaker market, landlords are considering other means of dealing with tenant default and an action for damages rather than forfeiture may then be the landlord's preference.

AFTER PROCEEDINGS HAVE BEEN ISSUED

In the ordinary way, if the landlord is successful in his claim against the tenant, he will be awarded his costs of the proceedings on the standard basis. It used to be thought that where a tenant claimed relief from forfeiture the court would order him to pay the landlord's solicitors' costs on a solicitor and own client, full indemnity basis. But in *Billson* v *Residential Apartments Ltd* [1992] 1 All ER 141 Lord Templeman disapproved of that practice. It would seem, therefore, that in future landlords can only expect to recover their standard basis costs in litigation.

Following the introduction of the Civil Procedure Rules, it will also be important for a landlord to act reasonably, both before and after proceedings are issues, and to bear in mind the need to follow the spirit of the pre-action protocols and the fact that the courts will view all litigation in accordance with the principle of proportionality (see Chapter 2). Failure to take account of this may put at risk the landlord's ability to recover all his costs.

CPR RESTRICTIONS ON COSTS RECOVERY

There are already restrictions on the legal costs that can be recovered where proceedings are commenced for a money judgment (*i.e.* seeking payment of a debt such as rent arrears without a claim for possession). Most claims for outstanding arrears will fall within the small claims jurisdiction of the county court where costs are restricted.

As from 25 March 2002 changes to the costs recoverable in possession actions have been introduced.

In possession claims issued on or after the 25 March 2002, where one of the grounds for possession is arrears of rent (whether or nor the order for possession is suspended on terms) and the Defendant has neither delivered a defence, admission or counterclaim nor otherwise denied liability, then the costs on giving judgment on the return date are fixed – unless the court orders to the contrary – at £57.25. The total of the costs (court fee and solicitors charges) which are likely to be ordered when the court makes the possession order in a contested case (whether outright or suspended) will be £246.75.

However, it will be important to continue to serve a statement of costs for assessment, based on a reasonable charge.

If the courts apply the new rules rigidly there will be a substantial shortfall in the costs recovered by landlords, unless the courts accept valid reasons why the fixed costs should be increased. It will be important to ensure that evidence is available at all possession hearings to show *actual* costs, in order to invite the court to exercise its discretion.

If there is a contractual right in the lease to recover costs, then it may still be possible to recover any shortfall through the service charge.

EXPRESS PROVISION IN THE LEASE

A lease may seek to make a tenant liable for the landlord's legal costs, and any other costs, incurred as a result of the tenant's breach or, indeed, incurred for any stipulated reason. Usually the lease will provide for the tenant to pay the landlord's costs incidental to the preparation and service of statutory notices, *e.g.* Section 146 and Section 147 Notices, and it is common practice to include a claim for these costs in the notice itself. Equally, it is likely that there will be provision for the tenant to pay costs where a landlord reserves the right to enter for the purpose of carrying out repairs. The lease may specifically provide for the tenant to pay the landlord's costs on the indemnity basis. If indemnity costs are provided for, the landlord is entitled to them even in a straightforward case unless there is a very good reason for the court to make a different order: *Church Commissioners for England* v *Ibrahim* [1997] 3 EG 136.

It is unusual, however, for a landlord to reserve the right to claim costs incidental to the recovery of damages for any other breaches of covenant. The penalty for late payment of rent is usually dealt with by way of a stipulation for interest, and landlords are usually content to leave it at that. If no express provision is made in the lease the landlord cannot expect his solicitor to recover costs in addition to the debt/damages, except through the issue of proceedings.

1.   SERVICE CHARGE

Apart from the express covenants referred to above, the service charge provisions may well include an obligation on the part of the tenant to pay the land-lord's costs – legal, surveying and accounting – arising from the administration and management of the property. Again, it is a matter of drafting, but the courts have made it clear that where a landlord seeks to recover his legal or other fees by way of the service charge, clear and unambiguous words must be used. The courts will almost certainly not imply an obligation on the tenant to pay legal fees by way of "management costs" if there is no express provision for payment of legal fees. Accordingly, the service charge provision must state in terms that the landlord's legal fees incurred in collecting rent and service charge, whether or not proceedings are issued, are to form part of the service charge: *Sella House Ltd* v *Mears* [1989] 1 EGLR 65.

Generally the courts show considerable resistance to allowing landlords to recover their costs of litigation through the service charge. This is especially so where, in litigation relating to service charges, the landlord has been ordered to pay the tenant's costs, and even though the service charge clauses specifically entitle the landlord to recover legal costs in obtaining contributions from tenants. At the end of the day, costs are always in the discretion of the court – see *Morgan* v *Stainer* [1993] 33 EG 87, and *Holding & Management Ltd* v *Property Holdings & Investment Trust plc* [1989] 1 WLR 1313 in which it was said that a landlord should not seek "through the back door what had been refused at the front".

In *Morgan* v *Stainer* [1993] 33 EG 87 the landlord and a number of his tenants had compromised proceedings started by the tenants and the landlord agreed *inter alia* to pay the costs of the claimant tenants. He then tried to recover those costs and his own legal costs through the service charge provision, whereby the tenants covenanted to pay all legal and other costs incurred by the landlord in obtaining maintenance contributions from any tenant in the building. The landlord's claim failed. It was held that the costs were not incurred in obtaining maintenance contributions and were not, therefore, within the service charge clause. It was inherent in the agreement reached between the parties to the litigation that not only would the landlord pay the tenants' costs but that also that he would pay his own costs and would not claim any of the costs through the service charge provision. Even if the costs had fallen within that provision, there was to be implied into it a term that costs had to have been reasonably and properly incurred in order to be recoverable and the landlord had not put before the court evidence such as to establish that the costs which he had agreed to pay to the tenants and which he had borne himself had been reasonably and properly incurred or were a fair and reasonable item to be included in the service charge.

In *Iperion Investments Corporation* v *Broadwalk House Residents Ltd* [1995] 46 EG 188 it was said that where a landlord has been unsuccessful in litigation against a tenant it would ordinarily be appropriate to make an order that the costs incurred by the landlord in that abortive litigation should be excluded from the service charge that would otherwise be payable by the tenant.

2.   LANDLORD AND TENANT (COVENANTS) ACT 1995

Section 17 of the Act provides an additional safeguard for former tenants and their guarantors so far as recovering any fixed charged is concerned. Unless the landlord complies with the notice procedure laid down in the section, he will be unable to recover any rent, service charge or other liquidated sum from a former tenant or his guarantor. See page 105 above.

3.   SURETY COVENANT

Where there is a surety it is common to provide for him to pay and make good to the landlord on demand all losses, damages, costs and expenses incurred by the landlord as a result of the tenant's default. Again, it is a matter of drafting, but the surety covenant is often drawn very widely, imposing on the surety what is, in fact, a more onerous obligation in respect of costs than is imposed on the tenant. In such circumstances, a landlord may be able to recover the arrears from the tenant and then look to the surety for payment of additional costs not recoverable from the tenant. It must be said, however, that the courts have tended to construe these covenants strictly against the landlord and it would be open to the surety to argue that unless the term "all legal and surveyors' fees" actually appeared in the clause it should not be implied. But the courts do not always take such a strict view (see Chapter 6).

CHAPTER 20
INSTALMENT ARRANGEMENTS

At some stage during the debt-recovery process there is always the possibility of the tenant approaching the landlord with an offer to pay off his indebtedness by instalments.

Of course, the landlord is under no obligation to entertain or agree to such a proposal. His decision will, presumably, be based on purely economic considerations and, in particular, how long it will take the tenant to discharge his liabilities.

Let us suppose the landlord is minded to accept such an arrangement. What is the legal position?

In strict legal terms and unless, improbably, the agreement is drawn up in a deed, the tenant will not have provided any consideration for the landlord agreeing to accept payment by instalments. But by a combination of the equitable doctrine of Promissory Estoppel and the common law doctrine of Waiver, the agreement will have a limited legal effect and will be binding upon the landlord unless and until he gives reasonable notice to bring the arrangements to an end: *Charles Richards Ltd* v *Oppenhaim* [1950] 1 KB 616.

What, then, are the matters the landlord must bear in mind before committing himself to an instalment package?

1. The landlord's letter proposing the arrangement must be clearly and boldly headed "WITHOUT PREJUDICE".
2. The letter must state that, in the event of default by the tenant, all the monies then outstanding (including any accrued interest), and not just the instalment(s) in arrear, will immediately become due and payable.
3. The landlord may stipulate, as part of the deal, that *all* his legal and other costs must be paid by the tenant. A specific sum should prefereably be stated.
4. The landlord may wish to require the tenant to pay interest on the monies outstanding. This may not be necessary if, as is usually the

case, the lease itself contains provision for the payment of interest on late payments.

5. The agreement might provide for the arrangement to be reviewed after, say, three months and for the landlord to have the right, following such review, to give one month's notice to determine the arrangement. Alternatively, the arrangement may be determinable on notice at any time.

6. Payment of the instalments by standing order or direct debit is much to be preferred to the tenant being left to send in a cheque each month. At the very least the landlord should require to be given a series of post-dated cheques.

7. If there is no surety under the lease, the tenant's request to be allowed to pay by instalments may well afford the landlord the opportunity of agreeing to such a proposal conditionally on the tenant providing a surety, both in respect of the tenant's liabilities under the lease and with regard to the payment of the instalments.

When considering instalment arrangements, care should be taken to bear in mind the provisions of the Landlord & Tenant (Covenants) Act 1995 and in particular the need to serve a Section 17 Notice on any former tenant or guarantor within six months of the charge becoming due in order to retain the right to pursue recovery of it. If a landlord agrees an instalment programme without serving the notices required by section 17 and the tenant then defaults, the landlord may find that he is now out of time to pursue any former tenant or guarantors for some of the unpaid monies.

Generally, reference should be made to Precedent 18. To avoid future arguments or uncertainty, recording any instalment arrangement in writing, preferably signed by both parties (or their representatives) is essential.

PRECEDENTS

PRECEDENT 1
PARTICULARS OF CLAIM – ARREARS OF RENT

IN THE STARBRIDGE COUNTY COURT Claim No. [ ]
BETWEEN:

ALEXANDER PROPERTIES LIMITED Claimant
and
DE VOLT LIMITED Defendant

PARTICULARS OF CLAIM

1. The Claimant is the freehold owner of business premises known as Commercial House, 1 London Road, Starbridge ("the Premises"). A copy of the proprietorship register at H.M. Land Registry which proves the Claimant's ownership is attached as Annex 1.
2. By a lease dated [ ] the Premises were demised to the Defendant for a term of [ ] years commencing on [ ]. A copy of the lease is attached to these particulars of claim as Annex 2.
3. The said lease reserves and the Defendant covenanted to pay a rent of £18,000 per annum payable by equal quarterly payments in advance on the usual quarter days. The said rent is £9,000 in arrears.

PARTICULARS

Quarter's rent due [date]	£4,500
Quarter's rent due [date]	£4,500
TOTAL	£9,000

4. The Claimant is entitled to and claims interest on the said arrears of rent at the rate of 8% per annum pursuant to section 69 County Courts Act 1984 in the total sum of [ ] calculated from the relevant due dates to the date hereof.

PARTICULARS

Interest on the sum of £4,500 from [   ] to [   ] amounting to £[   ].

Interest on the sum of £9,000 from [   ] to the date hereof amounting to £[   ].

TOTAL: £[   ]

5. The Claimant is also entitled to and claims interest under the said Act on the total outstanding sum of £9,000 from the date hereof until judgment or sooner payment at the said rate of 8% per annum. The daily rate of such interest is £[   ].
6. The value of the Claimants' claim excluding interest and costs is £9,000.

AND THE CLAIMANT CLAIMS:

1. Arrears of rent of £9,000 under paragraph 3 hereof;
2. Interest of £[   ] under paragraph 4 hereof;
3. Further interest at the daily rate of £[   ] from the date hereof until judgment or sooner payment under paragraph 5 hereof;
4. Costs.

Signed ....
Dated 2005

Statement of Truth
I believe/the claimant believes that the facts stated in these particulars of claim are true.

Full Name ....
Signed ....

PRECEDENT 2

PARTICULARS OF CLAIM – ARREARS OF RENT AND POSSESSION

PARTICULARS OF CLAIM

1. The claimant is the freehold owner and entitled to possession of the business premises known as Commercial House, 1 London Road, Starbridge ("the Premises"). A copy of the proprietorship register at H.M. Land Registry which proves the Claimants ownership is attached to these particulars of claim as Annex 1.
2. By a lease dated [ ] ("the Lease") the Premises were demised to the Defendant for a term of 20 years from [ ] at an annual rent of £3,500, subject to review. A copy of the lease is attached to these particulars of claim as Annex 2.
3. The Defendant covenanted to pay the rent by equal quarterly payments in advance on the usual quarter days.
4. The said rent is £1,750 in arrear.

PARTICULARS

One quarter's rent due [date]	£875
One quarter's rent due [date]	£875
TOTAL	£1,750

5. The Lease contains a proviso for forfeiture and re-entry if, amongst other matters, the whole or any part of the rent is unpaid for 21 days after becoming due whether formally demanded or not.
6. The Claimant will refer to the counterpart of the Lease at trial for its full terms and effect.
7. By reason of the said non-payment of rent the Lease has become and is hereby forfeit to the Claimant.
8. The Claimant is entitled to and claims interest on the said arrears of rent at the rate of 8% per annum, pursuant to section 69 County Courts Act 1984 in the total sum of £[] calculated to the date hereof.

PARTICULARS

Interest on the sum of £875 from [   ] to [   ] amounting to £ [   ].

Interest on the sum of £1,750 from [   ] to the date hereof amounting to £[   ]

TOTAL: £[ ]

9. The Claimant is also entitled to and claims under the said Act interest on the total outstanding sum of £1,750 claimed under paragraph 4 above from the date hereof until judgment or sooner payment at the said rate of 8% per annum. The daily race of such interest is £[   ].
10. The Claim for possession of the Premises does not relate to residential premises.
11. The Claimant is not aware of any sub-tenanty or mortgage. The person in possession of the premises is [   ].
12. The value of the claimant's claim excluding interest and, costs is £1750.

AND THE CLAIMANT CLAIMS:

1. Possession of the Premises;
2. Arrears of rent of £1,750 under paragraph 4 hereof (daily rate £9.59);
3. Interest of £[ ] under paragraph 8 hereof;
4. Further interest at the daily rate of £[ ] from the date hereof until judgment or sooner payment under paragraph 9 hereof;
5. Mesne profits from [ ] at the rate of £3,500 per annum (daily rate £9.59) until possession;
6. Costs.

Signed ....
Dated 2005

Statement of Truth
I believe/the claimant believes that the facts stated in these particulars of claim are true.

Full Name ....
Signed ....

PRECEDENT 3

PARTICULARS OF CLAIM – FORFEITURE FOR BREACH OF COVENANT

PARTICULARS OF CLAIM

1. The Claimant is the freehold owner and entitled to possession of the business premises known as Commercial House, 1 London Road, Starbridge ("the Premises"). A copy of the proprietership register at H.M. Land Registry which proves the claimant's ownership is attached to these particulars of claim as Annex 1.
2. The Claimant demised the Premises to the First Defendant by a lease dated [ ] ("the Lease") for a term of 25 years from the 29th September [ ] at a rent of £18,000 per annum payable quarterly in advance on the usual quarter days. A copy of the Lease is attached to these particulars of claim as Annex 2.
3. By the Lease the First Defendant covenanted, amongst other matters, as follows: [Here set out (i) the alienation and (ii) Section 146 Notice costs covenants].
4. The Lease contained a proviso for forfeiture and re-entry in the event, amongst other matters, of any breach of the tenant's covenants. The Claimant will refer to the counterpart of the Lease at trial for its full terms and effect.
5. In breach of the covenant referred to in paragraph 3(i) hereof the First Defendant has allowed the Second Defendant into occupation of the Premises.
6. By a Notice dated [ ] and served on both Defendants pursuant to the provisions of Section 146 Law of Property Act 1925 the Claimant specified the said breaches of covenant and required the same to be remedied in so far as they may be capable of remedy and required compensation to be paid for the breaches. A copy of the said notice is at Annex 3 endorsed by thc process server who served it with details of the manner of service.
7. The said breaches or some of them are incapable of remedy and the Lease has become and is now forfeit to the Claimant Compensation has not been paid for the breaches.

8. Without prejudice to the Claimant's claims to forfeit the Lease, there is due to the Claimant from the First Defendant the sum of £[   ] by way of rent and/or mesne profits.

PARTICULARS

Rent due [	]	£[ ]
Rent due [	]	£[_____]
TOTAL		£[_____]

9. The Claimant is entitled to and claims interest on the sum of £[   ] pursuant to section s 69 County Courts Act 1984 at the rate of 8% per annum from each relevant quarter day to the date hereof such interest amounting to £[   ]. The daily rate is £[   ]. The Claimant will claim interest continuing from the date hereof until judgment or sooner payment.

PARTICULARS

Interest on the sum of £[   ] from [   ]
to the date hereof (([   ] days) (daily rate £[   ]) £[   ]

Interest on the sum of £[   ] from [   ]
to the date hereof (([   ] days) (daily rate £[   ]) £[   ]

TOTAL   £[   ]

10. The First Defendant no longer occupies the Premises.
11. The Second Defendant continues to occupy the Premises in breach of covenant.
12. The annual value of the Premises is now £25,000.00
13. The Claimant has incurred expenses in the sum of £250 in respect of the preparation and service of the Notice referred to in paragraph 6 hereof.
14. The claim for possession of the Premises does not relate to residential premises.
15. The Claimant is not aware of any sub-tenancy or mortgage. The person in occupation of the premises is [   ].
16. The value of the Claimant's claim excluding interest and costs is £[   ].

AND THE CLAIMANT CLAIMS:

(1)   As against the First Defendant:

    (i)   £[   ] under paragraph 8 (daily rate £[ ];

    (ii) Mesne profits at the rate of £25,000.00 per annum from the [   ] until possession;

    (iii) £[   ] interest under paragraph 9 continuing until judgment or sooner payment (daily rate £[ ]);

    (iv) Interest at 8% per annum on the mesne profits referred to in (ii) hereof;

    (v)   £250 under paragraph 13.

(2)   As against the Second Defendant: mesne profits at the rate of £25,000 per annum from the date hereof until possession together with interesr as aforesaid at 8% per annum from the date hereof until possession.

(3)   As against both defendants, possession of the Premises and costs.

Signed ....

Dated 2005

Statement of Truth

I believe/the claimant believes that the facts stated in these particulars of claim are true.

Full Name ....

Signed ....

PRECEDENT 4

SECTION 146 NOTICE – BREACH OF USER COVENANTS

NOTICE – SECTION 146 LAW OF PROPERTY ACT 1925

TO: De Volt Limited or the lessee of Commercial House, 1 London Road, Starbridge ("the Offices") comprised in a lense dated the [ ] ("the Lease") and made between Alexander Properties Limited of the one part as "Lessors" and De Volt Limited of the other part as "Lessee"

AND TO ALL OTHERS WHOM IT MAY CONCERN

WE, [name] of [address], Solicitors and Agents for Alexander Properties Limited hereby give you Notice as follows:

1. The Lease contains covenants in relation to the use of the offices as follows:
   [Here set out the user covcnant(s)].
2. The above mentioned covenants have been broken and the particular breaches which are complained of are: (Here set out the unlawful use of which complaint is made].
3. We require you to remedy all the aforesaid breaches in so far as the same are capable of remedy and to make compensation in money to the Lessors for such breaches.
4. (a) By the Lease you further covenanted [Here set out the Section 146 Notice costs covenant].
   (b) By reason of the matters referred to above in this Notice Alexander Properties Limited have incurred not less than £350 costs in respect of the preparation and service of this Notice and you are hereby required to pay the said sum to them.
5. NOW TAKE NOTICE that on your failure to comply with this Notice within a reasonable time it is the intention of Alexander Properties Limited aforesaid to re-enter the Offices by action or otherwise and to forfeit the Lease and to claim damages for the said breaches of covenant.

Dated this day of   2005

(Signed) ....
[*Name*]
[*Address*]
Solicitors and Agents for the said Alexander
Properties Limited

PRECEDENT 5

SECTION 146 NOTICE – BREACH OF REPAIR COVENANTS

NOTICE UNDER SECTION 146 LAW OF PROPERTY ACT 1925 AND UNDER SECTION 1 LEASEHOLD PROPERTY (REPAIRS) ACT 1938

TO: De Volt Limited or the lessee of Commercial House, 1 London Road, Starbridge comprised in a lease dated the [ ] and made between Alexander Properties Limited as Lessor and De Volt Limited as Lessee ("the Lease")

AND TO ALL OTHERS WHOM IT MAY CONCERN

WE, [name] of [address] Solicitors and Agents for Alexander Properties Limited hereby give you Notice as follows:

1. The Lease contains covenants by you the said De Volt Limited in relation to the premises demised thereby as follows: [Here set out all the repairing covenants].
2. In breach of the said covenants the dilapidations in the schedule annexed hereto have been allowed to accrue.
3. We require you to remedy the said breaches in so far as the same are capable of remedy and to make compensation in money to the said Alexander Properties Limited for such breaches.
4. (a) By the Lease you further covenanted as follows: [Here set out the lessee's covenant to pay the lessor's costs in proceedings under s 146 LPA 1925].
   (b) By reason of the matters referred to above in this Notice Alexander Properties Limited have incurred not less than £350 costs in respect of the preparation and service of this Notice and you are hereby required to pay the said sum to them.
5. If you fail to comply with this Notice within a reasonable time it is the intention of the said Alexander Properties Limited to re enter upon the premises and forfeit the Lease and to claim damages for the said breaches of covenant.
6. YOU ARE ENTITLED UNDER THE LEASEHOLD PROPERTY (REPAIRS) ACT 1938 TO SERVE UPON THE SAID ALEXANDER

PROPERTIES LIMITED A COUNTER-NOTICE CLAIMING THE
BENEFIT OF THE SAID ACT.
7. SUCH COUNTERNOTICE MUST BE SERVED WITHIN TWENTY-
EIGHT DAYS FROM THE DATE OF THE SERVICE OF THIS
NOTICE UPON YOU.
8. SUCH COUNTERNOTICE MUST BE IN WRITTNG AND MAY BE
SERVED UPON THE SAID ALEXANDER PROPERTIES LIMITED
BY DELIVERING THE SAME TO OUR OFFICE DURING NOR-
MAL OFFICE HOURS. SUCH COUNTERNOTICE SHALL ALSO
BE SUFFICIENTLY SERVED IF IT IS SENT BY POST IN A REGIS-
TERED LETTER ADDRESSED TO US AT OUR OFFICE AND IF
THAT LETTER IS NOT RETURNED THROUGH THE POST
UNDELIVERED; AND THAT SERVICE SHALL BE DEEMED TO
BE MADE AT THE TIME AT WHICH THE REGISTERED LETTER
WOULD IN THE ORDINARY COURSE OF POSTAGE BE
DELIVERED.

Dated this day of   2005

(Signed) ....

[Name]

[Address]

Solicitous and Agents for the said Alexander Properties
Limited

[Annex schedule of dilapidations]

PRECEDENT 6
NOTICE OF FORFEITURE

TO ALL WHOM IT MAY CONCERN

TAKE NOTICE that these premises, Commercial House, 1 London Road, Starbridge have been repossessed today by the landlord, Alexander Properties Limited of 1 Porchester Street, London, SW1, following forfeiture of the lease by peaceable re-entry.

AND FURTHER TAKE NOTICE that following the repossession the locks to the premises have been changed. Any attempt to enter the premises is prohibited without the written permission of the landlord or its solicitors or agents.

Any queries regarding this Notice should be addressed in writing to Messrs Smith and Co of [address].

Dated this day of   2005

....

Smith and Co
Agents for Alexander Properties Limited

PRECEDENT 7

LETTER BEFORE ACTION – RENT ARREARS

The Secretary
De Volt Limited
[*Ref*]
[*Date*]

Dear Sir,
Commercial House, 1 London Road, Starbridge

We act for your Landlord, Alexander Properties Limited of 1 Porchester Street, London, SW1.

We understand from our client's Managing Agents, Messrs Smith & Co, that rent of £[ ] due from you has not been received despite request for payment. A copy of the rent demand is attached.

In these circumstances our client has had no alternative but to instruct us to issue proceedings against you, without further notice or delay, for possession of the above premises and payment of all monies owing, interest and costs if payment of the sum of £[ ] is not received at our office within 7 days of the date of this letter.

If you have made payment in full in the last day or so please disregard this letter, but if you are in any doubt about this, or if you have any other related query, please contact Messrs Smith & Co immediately at [*address*] (telephone number: [   ]).

Yours faithfully

PRECEDENT 8
INTERIM PAYMENT APPLICATION

IN THE STARBRIDGE COUNTY COURT
BETWEEN:

Claim No. [ ]

ALEXANDER PROPERTIES LIMITED Claimant
and
DE VOLT LIMITED (1)
XYZ LIMITED (2) Defendants

Part A

We [name of firm] solicitors on behalf of the Claimant intend to apply for
an Order (a draft of which is attached) that:

(i) the Defendants make an Interim Payment to the Claimant forthwith of
£[   ] and periodic payments on each successive quarter day commencing [   ] 2005 of £[   ] or such other sum as the Court thinks
just pursuant to CPR, Part 25.6
(ii) the costs of this application be paid by the Defendants to the Claimant
in any event because the First Defendant has breached the alienation
covenants in the lease of premises at Commercial House, 1 London
Road, Starbridge and allowed the Second Defendant into occupation.
Both Defendants will be liable to pay the Claimants for use and occupation of the premises during the claim.

Part B

We wish to rely on the attached witness statement.

[*To be endorsed on Application Notice Form N244*]

PRECEDENT 9

WITNESS STATEMENT IN SUPPORT OF INTERIM PAYMENT APPLICATION

Filed on behalf of the Claimant
Deponent:
Statement No.1
Made this [   ] day of [   ]   2005
Exhibits: A1

IN THE STARBRIDGE COUNTY COURT Claim No.[   ]

BETWEEN:

ALEXANDER PROPERTIES LIMITED Claimant
and
DE VOLT LIMITED First Defendant
and
XYZ LIMITED Second Defendant

WITNESS STATEMEMT
in support of Interim Payment Application

1, [*name*] of [*address*] say as follows:

1. I am a solicitor in the employ of [name of firm] of [address of firm] aforesaid, solicitors for the above-named Claimant and am duly authorised by the Claimant to make this Statement on its behalf. The information in this statement has been provided to me by the Claimant.
2. The Claimant is the owner of the premises known as Commercial House, 1 London Road, Starbridge ("the Premises") which were demised to the First Defendant by a lease dated [   ] ("the Lease") for a term of [   ] years from [   ] at a rent of £[   ] per annum such rent being payable by equal quarterly payments in advance on the usual quarter days. A true copy of the counterpart of the Lease is now produced and shown to me marked ["Al"].

3. The Claimant says that in breach of the covenants contained in the Lease the First Defendant has underlet and/or parted with possession of the Premises. The Claimant also says that the First Defendant has used the Premises in breach of the user covenant contained in the Lease. Because of these breaches the Claimant has refused to accept payment of rent from the First Defendant and has commenced proceedings for possession of the Premises. The particulars of the Claimant's claim appear in the Particulars of Claim herein and I verify the material facts of this application.

4. Further, the Claimant says that the Second Defendant is not the tenant of the Premises and is in occupation of the Premises in breach of covenant and without the Claimant's consent.

5. If final judgment or Order was made or given in favour of the Claimant, the Defendants would in my belief be held to pay in respect of the use and occupation of the Premises during the pendency of this action the sum of £[   ] to [   ] 2005 and thereafter quarterly payments at the rate of £[   ]. This liability arises out of the Lease.

6. Even if final judgment or Order were given or made in favour of the Defendants they would still be under an obligation to pay the Claimant for the use and occupation of the Premises during the pendency of this action.

7. The sum of £[ ] specified in paragraph 5 hereof is calculated as follows:

PARTICULARS

[Set out [quarters] rent due to date that remain unpaid]

8. The Claimant therefore claims a lump sum payment from the Defendants jointly of £[   ] and thereafter claims periodic payments from the Defendants of £[   ] per quarter on the usual quarter days from [ ] 2005

9. I believe that the facts stated in this witness statement are true.
    Signed................................
    Name................................
    Date................................2005

PRECEDENT 10
LAW OF DISTRESS (AMENDMENT) ACT NOTICE

NOTICE – SECTION 6 LAW OF DISTRESS (AMENDMENT)
ACT 1908

TO: [*Name of sub-tenant*]
OF: [*Address*]

Alexander Properties Ltd of 1 Porchester Street, London SW 1, here-by GIVES YOU NOTICE that:

1. Your landlord De Volt Ltd owes your superior landlord Alexander Properties Ltd £18,000 (Eighteen Thousand Pounds) arrears of rent in respect of De Volt Ltd's tenancy of [*address of demised premises*].
2. As sub-tenant of the premises or some part of them you are required to make future payments of rent (whether now accrued due or to accrue due in the future) not to De Volt Ltd but to Alexander Properties Ltd until such arrears have been duly paid. The said payments are to be made direct to Alexander Properties Ltd c/o [*name and address of solicitor*] quoting reference [*ref*].

Dated [   ]   2005

Signed...........................
[*Firm name*]
[*Address*]
Solicitors and Agents for Alexander Properties Ltd

PRECEDENT 11

LETTER SEEKING APPOINTMENT TO SERVE STATUTORY DEMAND

[Date]

Dear Sir,

Commercial House, 1 London Road, Starbridge

We act for Alexander Properties Limited.

Process Servers instructed by this firm called today at [address] to effect service upon you of a Statutory Demand pursuant to the Insolvency Act 1986. As you were not available when they called it was not possible to effect service. Accordingly, the Process Servers, Messrs Jones & Associates, will make a further call at [address] in order to serve the Statutory Demand on the [   ] day of [   ] 2004 at [   ] hours.

In the event that the time and place referred to in the preceding paragraph are not convenient, you should indicate some other time and place reasonably convenient for the purpose and telephone Messrs Jones & Associates (telephone number: [   ]) to notify them of this.

If you fail to keep the appointment with our Process Servers our clients propose to serve the Demand by insertion through the letter-box of [address], In the event of a Bankruptcy Petition being presented, the Court will be asked to treat such service as service of the Demand upon you.

Yours faithfully,

PRECEDENT 12

NOTICE TO LIQUIDATOR TO ELECT WHETHER TO DISCLAIM LEASE

NOTICE TO ELECT

IN THE MATTER OF De Volt Limited
and
IN THE MATTER OF The Insolvency Act 1986, s 178(5)

We, Alexander Properties limited of 1 Porchester Street, London, SW1 freehold owners and landlords of Commercial House, 1 London Road, Starbridge which is demised to De Volt Limited under the terms of a lease particulars of which are set out in the Schedule hereto, require the liquidator to decide within 28 days of receiving this notice whether he will disclaim the above property or not and to notify us of his decision.

DATED the day of   2005

(Signed) ....
[Name]
and [Address]
Solicitors and authorised
agents on behalf of
Alexander Properties
Limited.

To the liquidator of the above-named company
[Address]

[Attach schedule giving date of and parties to lease]

[Note: Notice to be sent by recorded delivery]

PRECEDENT 13

LETTER OF INSTRUCTIONS FOR SERVICE OF SECTION 146 NOTICE

[*Date*]

Dear Sirs,

Commercial House, 1 London Road, Starbridge

We act for Alexander Properties Limited, landlords of the above premises.

We enclose four identical Notices under Section 146 Law of Property Act 1925 in respect of the premises.

We would be grateful for your assistance in serving this Notice which should be effected in the following manner:

1. Please put the first copy of the Notice through the letter-box of the premises without an envelope or covering letter.
2. The second copy of the Notice should be affixed securely to the front door or some other conspicuous part of the premises.
3. Please then immediately endorse the third copy with the time, date and manner of service of the first two and by whom this was effected. This should, please, be done by the process-server who should then sign the third copy, giving also the date and time of his endorsement. Please then return this third copy to us.
4. The fourth copy is for your file.

Thank you for your assistance.

Yours faithfully,

PRECEDENT 14

AFFIDAVIT SEEKING PERMISSION TO ISSUE HIGH COURT WRIT OF POSSESSION (CPR SCHED 1, RSC ORD. 45, R 3)

Filed on behalf if the Claimant
Deponent:
Affidavit No. 1
Sworn this [ ] day of [ ] 2005
Exhibits: A1

[TITLE OF ACTION]

AFFIDAVIT IN SUPPORT OF APPLICATION FOR PERMISSION
TO ISSUE WRIT OF POSSESSION

I, [name] of [address], Solicitor of the Supreme Court, hereby MAKE OATH and say as follows:

1. I am a partner in the firm of [name] of [address] aforesaid, solicitors for the Claimant. I am duly authorised to swear this affidavit on the Claimant's behalf.
2. The claim form in this action was served on the Defendant on [   ] 2005
3. On [   ] 2005 Judgment was obtained for possession of Commercial House, 1 London Road, Starbridge ("the Premises").
4. On [   ] 2005 I sent a copy of the said Judgment by pre-paid first class post to the Defendant and to Mr XYZ who is also in occupation of the Premises together with a letter giving details of the Judgment and asking them to vacate the Premises forthwith in the letter I stated that if they failed to vacate the Premises or apply to the Court for relief or otherwise within 14 days the Claimant would proceed to recover possession under the Judgment without further notice. A true copy of the said letter is now produced and shown to me marked "Al". I have received no reply or response to the letter.

5. I am informed by Mr Smith, Managing Director of the Claimant Company, and believe that save for the Defendant and Mr XYZ there is no other person in actual occupation of the whole or any part of the Premises.

6. I believe that the Defendant has received sufficient notice of these proceedings to enable him to apply to the Court for relief and, since the date of the Judgment, both the Defendant and Mr XYZ have had time to do so. Accordingly, I respectfully request permission on behalf of the Claimant to issue a Writ of Possession of the Premises [and for payment of the amount set out in the Judgment in this action dated [   ] 2005]*

SWORN at [   ]

this [   ] day of [   ] 2005

Before me, [   ]
a Solicitor empowered
to Administer Oaths

*This part to be included only if a Writ of Fi Fa and Possession is sought.

Note: Alternatively, the evidence supporting the application for permission to issue the writ can be contained in a witness statement.

PRECEDENT 15
QUESTIONS FOR ORAL EXAMINATION

Pursuant to an order to obtain Information

IN THE STARBRIDGE COUNTY COURT   Claim No. [   ]

Claimant:

Defendant:

Oral Examination this [   ] day of [   ] 2005

Time commenced

QUESTIONS: ANSWERS:

1.   What is your full name?
2.   What is your present residential address?
3.   What is your present occupation?
4.   What is the name of your employer?
5.   What is the address of your place of work?
6.   What is the address of your employer's Head Office?
7.   What is your Works No./Pay Ref.?
8.   What is your take home pay?
9.   What is your gross pay?
10. What are your weekly overtime earnings?
11. Do you receive a bonus/commission? If so, how much?
12. Do you receive a pension or any other income? If so, state
     amount and source.
13. Are you single/married/widowed/divorced?
14. What are the names and ages of any children or other per-
     sons dependent on you?
15. Does your wife or anyone else contribute to the family in-
     come? If so, how much?
16. Are you a tenant, or do you own the premises in which you
     live?

QUESTIONS: ANSWERS:

17. What is your rent, mortgage instalment? To whom do you pay? Are you in arrears – details please.
18. When were the premises purchased?
19. If premises mortgaged, name of mortgagor?
20. What was the purchase price and amount of original loan?
21. Do you sub-let any part of your premises? If so, at what rental?
22. What rates are payable?
23. What is the name and address of your bank?
24. What is your present bank balance?
25. Do you have a Post Office, building society or other savings account – details please?
26. What is the present balance in such accounts?
27. Do you own any property or investments? If so, what?
28. Does anyone owe you money? If so, who and what amount?
29. What vehicle do you drive? Give model and registration number.
29. What vehicle do you drive? Give model and registration number.
30. Have you paid for it?
31. What hire purchase instalments, clubs, etc., do you pay?
32. What other regular payments do you make?
33. What Court Orders (including Maintenance) are there against you?
34. What arrears (if any) are there?

I [*name of debtor*] having been duly sworn, state that the answers I have given to the question herein are true.

(Signed)..

Signed and sworn by the above-named Judgment Debtor on the [   ] day of [   ] 2005

BEFORE ME................
Officer of the Starbridge
County Court.

PRECEDENT 16
WITNESS STATEMENT SUPPORTING APPLICATION TO SERVE PROCEEDINGS OUTSIDE THE JURISDICTION

I, [name] of [address] solicitor of the Supreme Court will say as follows:

1. In the proposed proceedings herein the proposed Claimants seek possession of premises known as 50 Alice House, Porchester Street, London SW1 of which they are the freehold owners and which were let to the proposed Defendants [   ] and [   ] for a term of 99 years from 25 December 1986 to 24 December 2085.

2. The proposed First Defendant, is resident at [*insert foreign address abroad*]. The proposed Second Defendant, is resident in the United Kingdom.

3. The premises, the subject of this action, 50 Alice House aforesaid, are premises which are unoccupied and I am advised by the proposed Second Defendant that correspondence sent to this address will not come to the attention of the proposed First Defendant as he lives abroad and no facility has been put in place for correspondence sent there to be forwarded to him.

4. I respectfully apply for an Order that the Claim Form, Particulars of Claim and all subsequent Court documents may be served out of the jurisdiction upon the proposed First Defendant on the grounds that the premises which are the subject matter of the action is situate within the jurisdiction of this County Court.

5. I also respectfully apply for leave to serve the above documents and any subsequent Court documents in the English language as opposed to the language spoken in [*insert foreign address*]. I make this additional application on the basis of saving costs and on the basis that the proposed First Defendant is fluent in the English language, as is his partner, the proposed Second Defendant. I attach to this application emails and correspondence received from the proposed. First Defendant from which his knowledge of the English language can be seen.

[*Note: This can be most suitably endorsed in Part C of the Application Form N244 seeking permission to serve outside the jurisdiction.*]

PRECEDENT 17

UNDERTAKING

To: [Name of Landlord] of [address]

50 Alice House, Porchester Street, London SW1

We refer to the lease dated 21 Februar y 1996 ("the Lease") granted by you for a term of 99 years from 25 December 1986 expiring on 24 December 2085 in respect of the above property ("the Prem ises").

We hereby undertake that we shall at no time act in breach of any covenant therein and in particular we shall nor charge, underlet, licence or part with or share possession or occupation of the whole or any part of the Premises or assign part only of the Premises or suffer or permit the same, nor shall we assign the Premises without complying with the conditions in the Lease, in particular in respect of the requirement to obtain the freeholder's consent in respect of the matters specified.

We also undertake that we will also use our best endeavours to ensure that any sub-lessees do not in turn sublet the Premises other than in accordance with the Lease.

Signed ....

Tenant

Dated ....

PRECEDENT 18

LANDLORD'S LETTER PROPOSING INSTALMENT ARRANGEMENT

WITHOUT PREJUDICE

Dear Sir,

Commercial House, 1 London Road, Starbridge

As you know, we act for your landlord, Alexander Properties Limited.

Our client has passed to us a copy of your letter setting out your proposals to settle the outstanding sums due to our client.

Our client has considered your proposals but they are unacceptable. However we are instructed that our client would be prepared to accept payment of the outstanding sums by instalments.

The total sum due is as follows:

1. Rent due [date]: £[   ].
2. Interest on the rent under Clause [   ] of the lease at the rate of [   ] % per annum: £[   ].
3. Insurance premium due [date]: £[   ].
4. Total £[   ].

We are instructed that our client will accept payment of the sum of £[   ] on the basis of and subject to the following terms and conditions:

1. Payment of an initial sum of £[   ] to be made by 5 p.m. on Friday [   ] 2004 at the offices of our client's Managing Agents,
2. The remaining balance of £[   ] to be paid in the following manner:

(a) payment of the sum of £[   ] to be made to the office of Messrs Smith & Co by instalments of £[   ] per week. The first instalment of £ [   ] is to be paid by [   ] 2004 and thereafter payment of a further

sum of £[   ] is to be made weekly on every subsequent Friday of
each successive week until the said sum of £[   ] has been discharged,
time to be of the essence.

(b) If any instalment or any part thereof is not met on the due date the
entire balance then outstanding, and not just the instalment in arrear,
shall immediately become due and payable. Our client reserves the right
to take enforcement proceedings, or such other action as it deems fit,
immediately and without further notice.

(c) Our client can accept any payment which is made late, but any such
acceptance of late payment cannot be taken as a waiver of our client's
rights and in particular of the fact that time remains of the essence as
regards each and every subsequent weekly payment.

(d) In the event that our client disposes of the freehold of the premises at
a future date, the entire balance then outstanding will immediately fall
due.

Our client will review these arrangements in three months' time but reserves
the right to revoke them at any time and for whatever reason.

The above re-payment schedule is, of course, in addition to payment of the
current rent and other sums due to our client under the lease as these fall
due – they are purposely not set out above.

Kindly sign and send back to us, by fax today, the enclosed copy of this letter
to signify your agreement to the terms set out above.

Yours faithfully,

PRECEDENT 19
LETTER REFUSING CONSENT TO ASSIGN

Dear Sir,

Commercial House, 1 London Road, Starbridge

As you know, we act for your landlord, Alexander Properties Limited.

We refer to your clients' application to our clients for consent to assign their lease of the above premises made by letter dated [*date*] together with the initial enclosures comprising:

  (i)   Solicitors' reference
  (ii) Trading reference
  (iii) Landlord's reference
  (iv) Financial statements of the proposed assignee
  (v)   Promotional brochure of the proposed assignee
        and completed by the further letter dated [*date*] with further enclosures comprising the following additional documents:
  (vi) Bank reference
  (vii) Accountant's reference
  (viii) A further trading reference.

This is our clients' formal response to that application for the purposes of the Landlord and Tenant Act 1988.

Our clients have, together with their advisers, given careful consideration to this application and its supporting material. They have also inspected the premises operated by the proposed assignee at 369 Snosrap House, Norwich.

The following points are pertinent by way of background.

  (a) The subject premises form part of our clients' estate comprising substantial holdings in and around Starbridge. Our clients' policy is, naturally, to manage their estate so as to maximise its value as they see best and to scrutinise and control the tenant mix in the interests of good estate management.

(b) Our clients' policy is to seek to improve the quality of the estate in the long term by encouraging the use of premises for good quality occupations and with good quality tenants whose businesses are of a broad appeal to a wide cross section of the public.

(c) The proposed assignee is an entity which carries on a business as a chain of sex shops.

(d) Our clients are aware that your clients have parted with possession of the premises to a company who are using them to sell low grade goods of poor quality. This follows a previous breach of the alienation covenants by your client.

Taking account of all the circumstances of this matter our clients are not prepared to give their consent to this application to assign for each of the following reasons.

1. Our clients refuse consent on the grounds of good estate management. Our clients do not consider that the business of the proposed assignee fits their estate management policy and aspirations for the future of their estate. Our clients consider that to permit the assignment to this proposed assignee would have an adverse effect on our clients' ability to maintain and improve the quality and strength of occupiers and therefore the value of their estate. Additionally, sex shops do not have a broad appeal to a wide cross section of the public and for this reason such a use is also contrary to our clients' estate management policy.

2. Our clients have a specific policy that they do not wish to have sex shops in their premises. They have no other tenants who operate the business of a sex shop.

3. The lease of the premises confines the use to "the sale of high class goods". Our clients consider that the use of the premises by the proposed assignee would be a breach of this clause. Our clients require the user covenant to be observed.

    There is a further point which arises from this objection. It is plain that neither your clients nor the proposed assignee accept our clients' interpretation of the lease since otherwise the application for consent to assign would not be made. It follows that if the assignment takes place our clients would have a prospect of an argument with the assignee over the meaning of the lease and its precise operation and enforcement of it. Our clients are, reasonably in our view, nor prepared to expose themselves to this prospect.

4. Your clients are already in breach of the alienation covenants.

5. Whilst financial references have been supplied for the proposed assignee, our clients have considered this information with their advisers. Having considered this our clients do not consider that the financial position of the proposed assignee demonstrates the financial

strength necessary to have confidence in their ability to support the rent and service charge. The proposed assignee's net declared profit does not even equal the annual rent and service charge. Consent is therefore withheld on the grounds of the inadequacy of the proposed assignee's financial status.

Yours faithfully

from the date hereof until judgment or sooner payment at the said rate of 8% per annum. The daily rate of such interest is £[   ].

10. The Claim for possession of the Premises does not relate to residential premises.

11. The Claimant is not aware of any sub-tenancy or mortgage. The person in possession of the Premises is [   ].

12. The value of the claimant's claim excluding interest and costs is £1750.

13. The Claimant believes that the facts set out in these Particulars of Claim are true.

AND THE CLAIMANT CLAIMS:

1. Possession of the Premises;
2. Arrears of rent of £1,750 under paragraph 4 hereof (daily rate £9.59);
3. Interest of £[   ] under paragraph 8 hereof;
4. Further interest at the daily rate of £[   ] from the date hereof until judgment or sooner payment under paragraph 9 hereof;
5. Mesne profits from [   ] at the rate of £3,500 per annum {daily rate £9.59} until possession;
6. Costs.

Dated:

Statement of Truth

I believe [or the Claimant believes] that the facts contained in these Particulars of Claim are true.

Full Name: ....

Signed: ....

PRECEDENT 20
ENDORSEMENT FOR STATUTORY DEMAND

1. The Creditor is the freehold owner of premises situated at 50 Alice House, Porchester Street, London SW1 ("the Premises").
2. The Debtor occupies the Premises pursuant to a Lease ("the Lease") dated [   ] 2004 and made between (1) the Creditor and (2) the Debtor for a term of 59 years and 279 days. The Lease expires on [   ] 2063.
3. Pursuant to clause 3(1) (a) of the Lease the Debtor convenanted to pay both rent and additional rent as defined by the Lease to the Creditor. At clause 3 (1) (c), the Lease provides that if any rent remains unpaid for more than 21 days after becoming due the Debtor must pay interest on the sum due as from the date on which the same became due until the date of actual payment at a rate of 3% per annum above the lowest of the bank base rates of the members of the Committee of London Clearing Bankers prevailing at the time.
4. The Debtor is in arrears of rent and additional rent under the Lease in accordance with the attached Schedule totalling £[   ]. The Creditor is also entitled to interest on the amount of the arrears as shown in the attached Schedule and this is included in the sum due as set out in the Schedule.
5. The Debtor has failed to secure or compound for the debt.
6. The amount due at the date of this demand is £[   ].

INDEX

peaceable re-entry, 220
relief, 221-226
user, and, 152-153
Forfeiture for non-payment of rent
costs, 58-59
demand for payment, 39-40
introduction, 38-39
procedure
amendment, 45
commencement, 41
default judgment, 45
directions, 45
interim payments, 45
introduction, 40-41
particulars of claim, 41-44
service, 44
summary judgment, 45
relief
county court, 45-46
High Court, 46
procedure, 46-47
Forfeiture for other breaches
court proceedings
costs, 58-59
interim payments, 57
introduction, 55-56
relief, 57-58
s.146 notice
contents, 47-48
effect, 54-55
introduction, 47
service, 49-50
waiver, 50-54
Forfeiture, proceedings for
costs, 58-59
non-payment of rent, for
and see Forfeiture for non-
payment of rent
demand for payment, 39-40
introduction, 38-39
procedure, 40-47
other breaches
and see Forfeiture for other
breaches
court proceedings, 55-58
s.146 notice, 47-55

Garnishee order
introduction, 178-179
order absolute, 179-180
order to show cause, 179
Guarantees
enforcement
generally, 89
purchaser of reversion, 89-90
insolvency, and
surety, 90
tenant, 90
introduction, 84
liability period, 87-88
limitation, 88
original tenant, and liability of,
95-96
principles, 85-86
rent review, and, 88
types, 84-85
variation
common law, 86-87
statute, 87

Indemnities
enforcement
generally, 89
purchaser of reversion, 89-90
insolvency, and
surety, 90
tenant, 90
introduction, 84
liability period, 87-88
limitation, 88
principles, 85-86
rent review, and, 88
types, 84-85
variation
common law, 86-87
statute, 87
Injunction
alterations, and, 148
assignment, and, 142
dilapidations, and, 119-120
user, and, 153
Insolvency
administration order

Printed in the United Kingdom
by Lightning Source UK Ltd.
129426UK00001B/49-57/A